AN IMPERIAL WORLD
Empires and Colonies Since 1750

Douglas Northrop
University of Michigan

D1531484

PEARSON

Boston   Columbus   Indianapolis   New York   San Francisco   Upper Saddle River
Amsterdam   Cape Town   Dubai   London   Madrid   Milan   Munich   Paris   Montréal   Toronto
Delhi   Mexico City   São Paulo   Sydney   Hong Kong   Seoul   Singapore   Taipei   Tokyo

Editorial Director: Craig Campanella
Editor in Chief: Dickson Musslewhite
Executive Acquisitions Editor: Jeff Lasser
Editorial Assistant: Marielle K. Guiney
Senior Marketing Manager: Maureen Prado Roberts
Marketing Assistant: Cristina Liva
Production Manager: Meghan DeMaio

Creative Director: Jayne Conte
Cover Designer: Suzanne Duda
Cover Image: © Prokudin-Gorskii/Library of Congress
Editorial Production and Composition Service: Anand Natarajan/Integra Software Services
Printer/Binder/Cover Printer: Courier Companies

On the cover: A *zindan* (prison) in colonial Central Asia. This photograph, taken sometime between 1905 and 1915 by the Russian photographer Sergei Prokudin-Gorskii, represents technological wizardry for its day. Prokudin-Gorskii produced stunning full-color images by combining separate exposures taken with blue, green, and red filters. A Russian photographer with his new-fangled cameras would not have been out of place in Muslim Central Asia around 1910: parts of the region had recently been incorporated into the tsarist Russian Empire, while others became semi-sovereign "protectorates." Here a Central Asian guard poses while carrying a Russian-made rifle, and (unlike his prisoners) wearing a Russian-style uniform and boots. The paradox of colonized men or women administering justice on behalf of faraway empires—while wearing imperial clothes, and using imperial technology—can be witnessed in colonial systems around the world.

Credits: Preface: p. ix, Photo by Alfred J. Andrea, 2012. All rights reserved. **Introduction: p. 3,** The Granger Collection, NYC. **Chapter 1: p. 35,** Snark/Art Resource, NY; **p. 40,** Classic Image/Alamy; **p. 52,** HIP/Art Resource, NY; **p. 53,** Private Collection/The Stapleton Collection/The Bridgeman Art Library. **Chapter 2: p. 86,** General Research and Reference Division, Schomburg Center for Research in Black Culture, The New York Public Library, Astor, Lenox and Tilden Foundations; **p. 88,** Presbyterian Historical Society, Presbyterian Church (U.S.A.) (Philadelphia, PA). **Chapter 3: p. 132,** Advertising Archives. **Chapter 4: p. 162,** Douglas Northrop; **p. 177,** akg/Imagno. **Chapter 5: p. 212,** REUTERS/David Gray.

Library of Congress Cataloging-in-Publication Data
Northrop, Douglas Taylor.
  An imperial world : empires and colonies since 1750 / Douglas Northrop.
    p. cm.
  Includes bibliographical references.
  ISBN-13: 978-0-13-191658-6 (alk. paper)
  ISBN-10: 0-13-191658-0 (alk. paper)
  1. Colonies—History. 2. Imperialism—History. 3. Colonies—History—
  Sources. 4. Imperialism—History—Sources. 5. World history.
  6. World politics. I. Title.
  JV61.N67 2013
  325'.3—dc23

                                                          2012017707

10 9 8 7 6 5 4 3 2 1   13 12

ISBN-10:   0-13-191658-0
ISBN-13: 978-0-13-191658-6

Contents

Foreword

Connections: Key Themes in World History focuses on specific issues of world historical significance from antiquity to the present, employing a combination of elements: an introduction that places the theme into a broad historical context; four case-study chapters that combine to illustrate the dynamics of the theme across a wide range of cultures; four primary sources appended to each chapter that challenge the reader to probe more deeply into the issue at hand; images, maps, and, where appropriate, charts that illuminate each case study; and an epilogue ("Making Connections"), which contains both a summary analysis and, more important, further points for the reader to ponder. All of these features are presented in a reader-friendly manner.

The increasingly rapid pace and specialization of historical inquiry has created an ever-widening gap between professional publications and general surveys, especially surveys of world history. The purpose of *Connections* is to bridge that gap by placing the latest research and debates on selected topics of global historical significance, as well as some of the evidence upon which historians base their insights, into a form and context that is comprehensible to students and general readers alike.

Two pedagogical principles infuse this series. First, students master world history most easily if allowed to focus on specific themes and issues. Such themes, by their very specificity, as well as because of their general application, enable students to perceive and understand the overall patterns and meaning of our shared global past more clearly than is possible through reading, by itself, a massive world history textbook. Second, students learn best when asked to think critically about what they are studying. So far as the study of history is concerned, critical thinking necessarily involves analysis of primary sources.

To that end, we offer a series of brief, tightly focused books that embrace a radical simplicity and a provocative format. Each book goes to the heart of a key theme, phenomenon, or issue in world history—something that has connected humans across cultures, continents, and time spans. By actively engaging with this material, the reader comes to understand in a nuanced and meaningful manner how often distantly located human cultures have been connected to one another as key actors in the epic story of world history.

Alfred J. Andrea
Series Editor

Series Editor's Preface

The 2010 Football World Cup held in South Africa and sponsored by the Fédération Internationale de Football Association (FIFA) has come and gone, having enthralled a global viewing public that is estimated to have been in excess of one billion persons. As 11 July approached, the day on which Spain would meet the Netherlands in the championship match, newspapers were reporting a curious phenomenon: large numbers of black South Africans were cheering for the Netherlands, and Latin American fans appeared to be solidly behind Spain. When Spain prevailed by a score of 1-0, Mexico City and Little Havana in Miami went wild with delirium. Wait a minute! Was not the Netherlands the home country that sent tens of thousands of colonists to South Africa, colonists who became Afrikaners? Had not an Afrikaner minority imposed a state-mandated system of oppressive apartheid on black South Africans for almost a half century from 1948 to 1994? Had not the Afrikaner government also stripped black Africans of their citizenship in 1958? Why cheer for the mother country of oppression? And why were so many Latin Americans fervently hoping for a Spanish victory? Most of mainland Latin America, from Mexico to Cape Horn (the major exception being Brazil), was subject to repressive Spanish colonial rule for roughly three centuries, and independence for most of Latin America was achieved in the early nineteenth century only after several bloody revolutions. Cuba was an even more extreme example of Spanish dominance. Claimed and held by Spain from 1492 to 1898, it finally achieved at least nominal independence in 1898, the result of a Cuban insurrection coupled with armed (and colonial-driven) intervention by the United States that Secretary of State John Hay characterized as "a splendid little war." Why all of the cheering for former colonizers, especially colonizers who had been overthrown in reaction to their oppressive policies?

Douglas Northrop provides an answer in this "splendid little book." As he notes, although many former colonies formed their national identities in the crucible of their fierce anticolonial struggles, once free, many of these former colonies found themselves still tied by history, blood, culture, and language to their former colonizers. This is certainly the case for most of Latin America, where language, religion, and overall culture carry the stamp (or "footprints," to use Northrop's term) of Mother Spain. The colonial past is long past, but these cultural artifacts, which form such an important part of Latin American identity, remain. Hence the cry "¡Vamos España!"

(Go, Spain!) echoed throughout Latin America and in US cities with large Hispanic-American populations.

The South African support of and affection for the Netherlands team also had its ties to the colonial past, strange as it might initially seem. Despite its historic and genetic ties with the Afrikaners, the modern Netherlands had been in the forefront of the global condemnation of apartheid. Beyond that, its team is multiracial, reflecting the Netherlands' long history of colonial activity in Asia and the Caribbean. To name but three, Eljero Elia and Edson Braafheid are both of Surinamese descent, and Giovanni van Bronkhorst has a Moluccan mother.

Indeed, as already suggested, colonialism's vestiges are with us today, even in sport. I am often reminded of that when I see cricket players from India (where it is a national passion and a rite of passage for young men), Pakistan, Africa, the Caribbean, and elsewhere across the globe playing this game that defies my understanding on the verdant pastures of Central Park in Manhattan. And the late-nineteenth and early-twentieth-century US interventions in the Caribbean become all the more real for me when Big Papi, David Ortiz, is at the bat for my beloved Red Sox. Despite all of its negative consequences, the occupation of the Dominican Republic by US Marines from 1916 to 1924 resulted, generations later, in some of the finest baseball players on Earth now playing in the major leagues. And how can we ever forget Roberto Clemente of Puerto Rico?

These references to colonialism in the context of sport might strike many as frivolous, but the point is serious. As Douglas Northrop points out time and again in this book, colonialism defined the modern era and left its imprint on popular culture in ways that are not always obvious. No corner of the globe, no culture, no nation, not even those few that successfully resisted would-be colonizers and did not themselves colonize, was left untouched by it.

A recent visit to Manchuria and Taiwan also helped me become more fully aware of the vastly different memories occasioned by twentieth-century colonialism. In Changchun, Manchuria, the Historical Museum for Japan's Occupation in Northeast China has a multi-storied bronze mural in relief with life-sized, free-standing statues placed before it. As the accompanying photo shows, the message is unambiguous: Japan cruelly exploited and brutalized the inhabitants of Manchuria. Several days later I was in Taipei, Taiwan. On a walk through the campus of Taiwan National University, I chanced upon a building constructed as an agronomic laboratory in 1925 for a Japanese scientist, Dr. Eikichi Iso, "the father of Taiwanese Japonica Rice." The rice strain developed by Dr. Eikichi in that building revolutionized Taiwan's rice production, making it possible for its farmers to grow crops that were not only substantially larger but also of superior quality. In memory of this Japanese colonial agronomist,

Chinese Slave Laborers Suffer and Die under Japanese Military Occupation.

the city's Department of Cultural Affairs designated the structure as a municipal historical site. Yes, colonialism was a many-faced phenomenon and its memories are equally variegated.

Reading the multiple drafts of this book from inception to completion has been a joy. Northrop writes with great authority, clarity, passion, and a touch of poetry, and the primary sources and illustrations he has chosen are telling—often chillingly so. This little book is unassuming in its length but bold in its narrative, conclusions, and supporting evidence because of the solid scholarship that underpins it. As such, it should be required reading for any student who seeks to understand the role that colonialism has played around the world over the past several centuries. More than that, it is provocative. As Northrop points out in his epilogue, not only are the consequences, or footprints, of colonialism still with us today, but forms of neo-colonialism are arguably alive and well.

Alfred J. Andrea
Series Editor
Professor Emeritus,
The University of Vermont

About the Author

Douglas Northrop is an associate professor of history and Near Eastern Studies at the University of Michigan. A specialist in the modern history of Central Asia, Northrop earned his Ph.D. at Stanford and taught Soviet, Islamic, European, colonial, and world/global history at Pitzer College and the University of Georgia before coming to Michigan. His first book, *Veiled Empire*, investigated Bolshevik attempts to remake and modernize Central Asian society by ending the seclusion of local women. This book won both the W. Bruce Lincoln Prize and the Heldt Prize. His current research brings together environmental, colonial, cultural, and urban history in telling the story of the tsarist and Soviet empires through the lens of natural disaster—specifically, a series of major earthquakes that struck cities along the Eurasian frontier during the nineteenth and twentieth centuries.

Acknowledgments

This book, through the simple fact of its existence, bears testimony to many key people who made it possible—my colleagues, editors, students, and family.

All books express an author's intellectual genealogy. My first experience teaching global history came at Pitzer College in Claremont, California, where Prof. Daniel Segal invited me to join and contribute to his extraordinary survey class on the modern world. I am lastingly grateful: in the years since then, world history has pushed my teaching and scholarship in new and fruitful directions. I still teach a version of that course, and elements of it run through *An Imperial World*. Dan also generously read some of these chapters. More fundamentally, he modeled for me how intellectual rigor can (and should) suffuse what we do in the classroom, and how scholarship and pedagogy must be deeply interconnected.

The *Connections* series aims precisely at this model: presenting difficult but crucial issues, accessibly enough for newcomers, yet rigorously and without over-simplification. Readers can judge whether this volume succeeds. If it does, much credit goes to the editors who shepherded it from idea through draft to finished product. First in line for thanks is Prof. Alfred Andrea, the tireless series editor, whose careful eye misses nothing, and whose encyclopedic knowledge rarely fails. Al encouraged me whenever the writing slowed, cheered whenever it accelerated, and turned around my endless chapter drafts with dizzying speed. The staff at Pearson Prentice-Hall also provided support and encouragement at key moments—in particular, the former executive editor for this series, Charles Cavaliere, and his successor Jeff Lasser.

Books also show the impact of a writer's interactions with individual readers. Some assistance is easy to single out—such as that provided by my Georgia colleague, Prof. Reinaldo Román, who read and commented on Chapter 3, or a Michigan colleague, Prof. Derek Peterson, who helped me obtain permission to use an archival source in Chapter 2. I am also grateful to Sarah Hamilton for her willingness to translate—on very short notice—a document in Chapter 3. Other input is harder to quantify, but in this case includes suggestions and support from many colleagues at Michigan, particularly the participants in U-M's "Global Dimensions" seminar and speaker series. Hardest of all to tease out—but important for readers to realize—is the influence of hundreds of students in Claremont, Athens, and Ann Arbor who took my world history courses. They heard these arguments take shape and change, watched primary sources come and go, considered the visual materials, and mulled the methodological questions. Their reactions and suggestions, even if they did not know it, shaped how I conceived and later wrote this book.

This list ends—according to an authorial convention, familiar to anyone who reads history books—with the most personal of debts. My wife, Michelle McClellan, did not write any of the words that follow, but none of them could have appeared without her. (She is also as happy as I am that they are now finished.) Our sons Jeremy and Sawyer have taught me—through their ongoing excitement about learning—how much better it is not to answer students' questions definitively (if that is even possible), but rather to open new paths to explore. I dedicate this book to them, university students of the future. Perhaps they too will explore the history of empires—or other forms of human connection around the world.

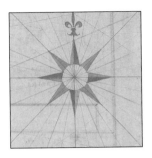

Introduction: Starting Points

Encountering Empires

In May 1876 Britain's Queen Victoria claimed for herself a new title, Empress of India—a position that had never before been held, by a British monarch or anyone else. Her claim, urged in London by her prime minister, Benjamin Disraeli, but not legitimated by a popular vote in India (or for that matter in England), had nevertheless been years in the making. Nearly two decades earlier, in 1857, the British East India Company, a nominally private enterprise that had seized control of much of South Asia, faced an armed rebellion among thousands of local troops, known as sepoys, whom it had hired for defense. The revolt spread quickly, and it took almost two years to defeat this rebellion (or "mutiny," as the British called it). Afterward the government in London decided that it had no choice but to assume direct control of India, seen as the crown jewel in Britain's world-spanning colonial empire. The Crown's presence grew stronger, as many of the most important political decisions affecting millions of South Asians came to be made thousands of miles away, in London, by royal edict or by parliamentary representatives elected by the citizens of Britain, not those of India. Most of India's accumulated wealth, natural resources, human capital, economic output, and military capacity officially served British interests, and on the surface at least, South Asians found themselves subordinated and placed into an almost child-like position relative even to junior colonial officials, soldiers, and businessmen. Not all Britons thought this was a good idea. Victoria's own son, the Prince of Wales, Albert Edward, took a trip to India in 1875–1876. He sickened at seeing how his countrymen treated the "natives," complaining in a letter to his mother about the "rude and rough manner" with which political officers treated even princes, and denounced their use of racial epithets and religious denigration. "It is indeed much to be deplored," he concluded, "and the system is, I am sure, quite wrong."[1]

Yet such criticism did little to halt the growth and assertiveness of British imperial power. So great was the supremacy claimed by London that for several months after Victoria's decision to name herself empress, her government in Delhi, the Indian capital, did not even bother officially to announce the legal change. At last, on New Year's Day, 1877, her most prominent Indian subjects received invitations to a special meeting called for this purpose, the First Imperial Assemblage (or "Durbar"). This Durbar included a curious mixture of Indian and British ceremony designed to mark India's full integration into the British Empire. (See Figure 0.1.)

The Queen's **viceroy** (her chief royal representative and, thus, the main imperial authority in India), Lord Lytton, invited local princes and nobles along with the governors of every province and many British officials. Victoria's assumption of imperial power had to be proclaimed with enormous pomp and circumstance. Hence the pageantry was carefully planned, with nothing left to chance. Although wide swathes of northern and central India lay under the grip of a massive famine at the time, the Durbar had been carefully designed to emphasize both Indian and British ideas of grandeur and political power. One journalist estimated that during the extravaganza, which included a week-long feast for 68,000 Indian officials and notables, approximately 100,000 Indians starved to death elsewhere. But in Delhi, every detail was awe-inspiring and huge in

---

[1]Quoted by Chandrika Kaul, "Monarchical Display and the Politics of Empire," *Twentieth Century British History* 17:4 (2006), 468–469.

THE IMPERIAL DURBAR AT DELHI: PROCLAMATION OF THE QUEEN AS EMPRESS OF INDIA.

FIGURE 0.1   The Imperial Proclamation Durbar, January 1, 1877, Delhi, India.

scale—as measured by both Indian and British eyes. According to Lord Salisbury, the British secretary of state for India, the spectacle had to be "gaudy enough to impress the orientals," in order to hide "the nakedness of the sword on which we really rely."[2] With this dramatic, almost theatrical purpose in mind, when the local princes had gathered, Lord and Lady Lytton mounted an elephant to form a procession that was, in the judgment of another British observer who was a senior military officer,

> about the most gorgeous and picturesque which has ever been seen even in the East.... Delhi must have witnessed many splendid pageants, when the Rajput, the Moghul, and the Mahratta dynasties, each in its turn, was at the height of its glory; but never before had Princes and Chiefs of every race and creed come from all parts of Hindustan, vying with each other as to the magnificence of their entourage, and met together with the same object—that of acknowledging and doing homage to one supreme Ruler.[3]

[2]Quoted by Mike Davis, *Late Victorian Holocausts* (London, 2001), 28.
[3]Frederick Roberts, *Forty-one Years in India* (New York, 1901), 332.

Although Queen Victoria herself did not come to India for the ceremony, her portrait hung in a place of honor, and she sent a message assuring her new subjects that their "happiness, prosperity, and welfare" was her highest priority.[4] The prominent guests in attendance filled several enormous tents, nearly a thousand feet long, redolent with banners and satin decorations. A military honor guard stood by the entrances. When the appointed hour arrived, an army band announced the viceroy's arrival with a triumphant trumpet blast. Wearing the ornate robes of a newly created British order—the Grand Master of the Star of India—Lord Lytton then sat on a central throne, listened to a rousing rendition of "God Save the Queen," and called upon a herald to read aloud the proclamation of Victoria's new imperial status. Attendants then raised the royal flag, and a group of soldiers fired an enormous artillery barrage in salute of their new empress.

The deafening noise of more than a hundred cannon salvos jarred those present—and the carefully planned performance diverged from its script. Before the viceroy could address the assemblage and accept the princes' cheers and formal congratulations, the British troops in attendance performed a *feu de joie*, a rolling gun salute in which the firing moved steadily down a line of soldiers toward the back of the tent. According to Lord Roberts, the British military observer quoted above,

> This was too much for the elephants. As the *feu de joie* approached nearer and nearer to them they became more and more alarmed, and at last scampered off, dispersing the crowd in every direction. When it ceased they were quieted and brought back by their *mahouts* [drivers], only to start off again when the firing recommenced; but, as it was a perfectly bare plain, without anything for the great creatures to come in contact with, there was no harm done beyond a severe shaking to their riders.[5]

The strange paradoxes of colonial power—the birth of an empire proclaimed publicly by a (absent) queen of England, but denounced in practice by her (present) son; the uneasy interaction between British claims and theatrical gestures on the one hand and Indian realities (and pachyderms) on the other—all emerge in the hybrid

---

[4]Quoted by Davis, *Late Victorian Holocausts*, 37.

[5]Roberts, *Forty-one Years in India*, 334.

forms and unexpected outcomes of this ceremony. Such paradoxes are also evident in the wider context around the Durbar—where mass starvation and famine surrounded this oasis of grandeur and conspicuous consumption. As this episode suggests, European efforts to create powerful new empires certainly led to huge changes on the ground—but they did not always play out smoothly in practice, nor were the changes always the ones that had been intended.

****

We live in a world shaped by empire. This simple fact confronts all of us—women, men, children—every day. Look at today's news stories, on whatever day you are starting to read this book—pick a good newspaper, a high-quality news network, or a reputable website—and ask where empires and colonies, spoken or unspoken, are lying behind the stories. Where can you see them? Sometimes colonial power is directly visible, and is even unapologetic (in the rare stories about Gibraltar, Aruba, Guam and American Samoa, or the Falklands). But "empire" is now more often seen as a negative word, so governments usually prefer to deny that it applies to them. Yet in stories about French islands in the Pacific, China's western provinces of Xinjiang and Tibet, or the various British, Dutch, French, and US possessions in the Caribbean—even in news about the "reservations" set aside for Native Americans in the central and western United States and Canada's "First Nations reserves"—one finds millions of people willing to say that at least from *their* point of view, empire lives on, for the simple reason that they still live in colonies. And elsewhere too—almost everywhere if you know how to look—empire is visible through its various aftermaths. Sometimes empires live on through the borders they drew or their labels for categorizing people; sometimes the specific way an empire collapsed produced lastingly messy consequences. One need only consider the challenges facing Aceh or East Timor, or the differences between northern and southern Nigeria, or the horrific fighting in Darfur to realize that the footprints of empire are indeed all around us.

Almost any teacher of modern world history who wants her or his students to understand today's world is likely to emphasize the lasting importance of empire and colonies. Yet the benefits of such an emphasis are more than just **presentist** (useful in illuminating current conditions and our world today); empires and colonies are central to modern world history classes precisely because they have also been undeniably and fundamentally *historical.* Over the past 300 years, imperial relationships have structured the lives of hundreds of millions of people. (The same might be said of earlier periods, but this book concentrates on the period since 1750, leaving earlier empires mostly to other volumes in the *Connections* series.) Most of the people who lived during these centuries of high imperialism are now gone, but their heritage is still our own.

Consider Maps 0.1, 0.2, and 0.3, published a century ago in the authoritative *Cambridge Modern History Atlas.* One shows the extent of world colonial possessions in 1910, with bright colors marking lands claimed by several European empires (and by one Asian empire, controlled by Japan). Clearly the mapmakers saw this as a story involving most of the world in one way or another, as China and South America are the only large areas not shaded as "possessions." Even so, there are peculiarities. China is labeled as "Chinese Empire," for instance, suggesting that it too may be part of this story of colonies and possessions—although the editors apparently did not see it as meriting a brightly colored spot on the map. As a later chapter will show, moreover, by leaving South America almost entirely unmarked, the mapmakers chose not to show a slew of informal but basically imperial patterns of influence. Now consider the next images, a set of two maps that go farther back into time, depicting European colonies in 1815. This picture is obviously different: this time South America appears almost completely claimed as a "possession," while China and Africa are unclaimed—and for that matter, almost completely blank. Not only are they not labeled as "empires" or "colonies," they (especially Africa) are shown as almost entirely devoid of *any* markings.

Plainly these maps are useful resources for an historian. They are examples of **primary sources**, the raw materials of historical analysis. For historians—especially those who study the modern era—primary sources are usually documents generated at a time and place one wishes to study, and written (or drawn) in such a way as to cast light on the particular issues one has in mind. This book uses many such documents: it is based on the idea that if studied carefully and queried thoroughly, such raw materials can teach us a great deal about the world in which they were crafted. Here, for instance, the map of 1815 actually tells us not only about 1815, as the mapmakers intended, but also about the world of 1912, when the atlas was published. If one takes the time to ask a few questions about it, this map can show how cartographers of 1912 saw their world. How did they

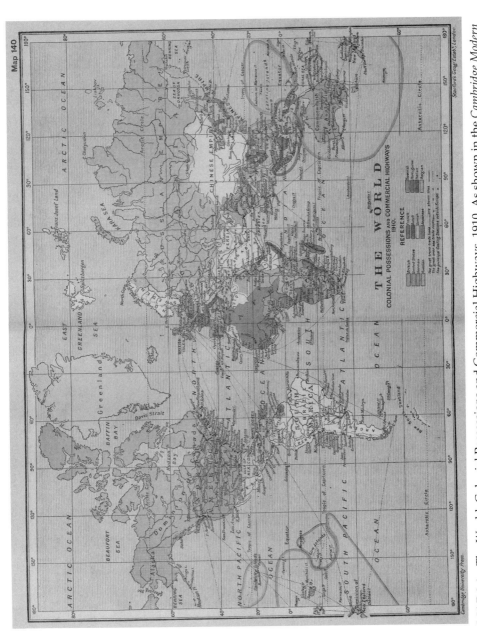

MAP 0.1 The World: Colonial Possessions and Commercial Highways, 1910. As shown in the *Cambridge Modern History Atlas* (1912). For color version, see: *http://www.lib.utexas.edu/maps/historical/ward_1912/world_1910.jpg*

7

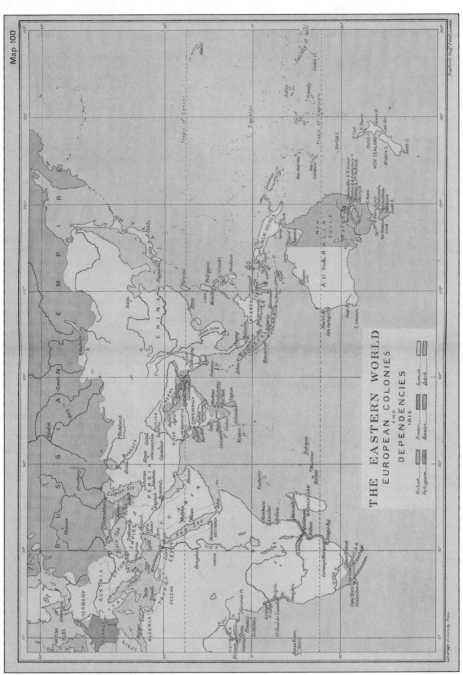

MAP 0.2 The Eastern World: European Colonies and Dependencies, 1815. As shown in the *Cambridge Modern History Atlas* (1912). For color version, see: *http://www.lib.utexas.edu/maps/historical/ward_1912/eastern_world_1815.jpg*

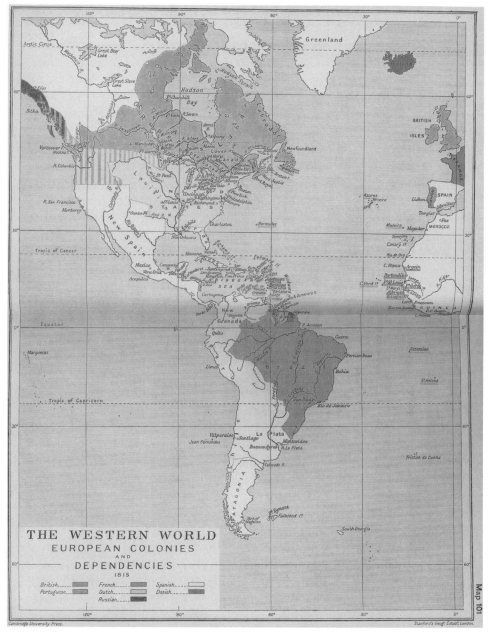

MAP 0.3 The Western World: European Colonies and Dependencies, 1815. As shown in the *Cambridge Modern History Atlas* (1912). For color version, see: *http://www.lib.utexas.edu/maps/historical/ward_1912/western_world_1815.jpg*

9

design their maps? Which elements of the picture did they include or emphasize? What information did they leave out? What sorts of maps did they think worth including?

Like historians, the Cambridge cartographers had to choose which stories to tell, and to figure out how to do so. Obviously they agreed that the story of colonies and empires, especially European empires, simply had to be told. And not only told, but *featured*, with multiple images that moved through time and covered the entire world. Thanks to these choices, their maps also tell us about a crucial historical story—a tale of change over time, one of global scope, of the dramatic appearance and disappearance of empires. This is what the mapmakers wanted to show, and their maps are truly startling: entire continents shift, change, fluctuate. Based on the maps' markings, a vast number of the world's people in 1815 (and even more in 1910) lived in either a colony or an imperial heartland. (Historians call such a place, from which an empire is controlled, its "center," or **metropole**.) Depending on time and place, the colonies could have been coming into an empire's possession (Africa) or breaking free (South America). The metropoles could have been in creation (Germany) or decline (Spain). No matter where a person lived, though, the *Cambridge Atlas* demonstrates the global sweep of empire, showing that in the nineteenth and twentieth centuries there was almost no escaping this story.

How did this happen? How did such enormous empires grow, and how did they influence the world? What did it mean for people to live through such momentous changes, in either the colonies or the metropole (not to mention the many people who moved back and forth, as mediators, emissaries, ambassadors, translators, soldiers, missionaries, merchants, or tourists)? Did each side even accept these labels, or understand these categories in the same way? Why do we need to know about this history of empire—whether our goal is to understand the deeper past on its own terms, or to see more clearly our own world, in which empire is still so present?

This book addresses these questions. *An Imperial World* offers a broad overview of global imperialism during the last three centuries. It is meant to be suggestive and thematic, to offer arguments and information that serve as a starting point for further exploration and debate, and not to be definitive or encyclopedic. With a combination of historical narrative, primary documents, and synthetic analysis, it sketches the historical development of various colonial systems and shows their enormous role in shaping the modern world.

The book is built around four case studies, explained below, each defined more or less continentally. Hence these cases emerge to some degree separately. But this story is global, so each case study simultaneously aims to trace connections among and between regions. Watch for the links between chapters, as colonial officials moved around the empires: a British administrator, for example, might be posted in India, Africa, and the Middle East before returning to London. Various imperial systems were also well aware of each other, and drew on tactics or models designed for other areas: Japanese colonial officials specifically sought to emulate European and American techniques of rule, for example. Likewise, imperial structures enabled movements of people and ideas among colonized areas: Mohandas Gandhi's years in South Africa before returning to India and Frantz Fanon's move from Martinique to take up anti-imperial politics in Algeria are just two cases in point. Other examples, like the thousands of Indian textile workers sent to Trinidad after being displaced by British tariff policies, involved large groups and had major social consequences in both places—the country of origin and the country of destination.

Although modern imperialism took many different and historically specific forms, a broad thematic and global approach can identify some of its key common features, and highlight the links and connections that developed between geographically far-flung areas. At its core, the colonial enterprise involved power—power expressed in innumerable contacts and exchanges between regions and peoples. The resulting crucible of empire reshaped all who lived through it, colonizers as well as the colonized: imperialism affected and sometimes transformed even those living comfortably in Paris, Amsterdam, or Moscow, apparently far removed from the colonial "periphery." Readers should thus view imperial states and their metropolitan citizens also in the context of an ongoing dialogue with colonized populations. Over time, this back-and-forth interaction—however unequal the two sides appeared on the surface to be—defined and shaped both parties, often in unexpected ways.

It is no accident that empires and colonies lie at the core of so many courses in world history. They show the importance of encounters—connections—between people from different parts of the world. Looking at such contacts is what world historians do, as many of the titles in this *Connections* series suggest. But unlike some other kinds of cross-regional or transcultural contact, colonial and imperial stories are often unpleasant, violent, vicious, and brutal—because they are about pure, raw power. The work to build empires—just like struggles to resist them—meant deep and bitter fights of all kinds, over the control of political power, economic resources, military might, and even over the content of the apparently nonpolitical realms of ideas, religion, the arts, and sport. To this end *An Imperial World* not only points to the structures of imperial power, emphasizing the "hard" side of modern empires—their military, economic, and political goals, and the practical techniques and institutional structures used by colonial authorities—but also explores their ideological underpinnings, along with the dizzying array of strategies devised by colonized populations to avoid, resist, transform, overthrow, or lessen their impact. It then surveys the enormous cultural and social impact of colonial systems in shaping the everyday lives of men, women, and children all around the globe, both in metropoles and in colonies, in ways both intended and not. To begin such an exploration, readers need to know what is being discussed.

DEFINITIONS AND CONTEXTS

The obvious place to begin is to ask, what is an "empire"? Dozens if not hundreds of books have been written to address this question, from a variety of viewpoints; but we will not spend much time exploring disputes over terms and definitions. This does not mean such semantic arguments are unimportant. They may seem abstract or theoretical, but they have real implications for how we see real historical people and places, and how we understand particular episodes. The arguments will emerge plainly enough if we discuss them not in the abstract, but concretely in the case studies that will follow. For now, a simple working definition suffices: **empires** are no more than a particular way of organizing political and social relationships. In some ways they resemble any other powerful government or **state**, as an entity that exerts sovereign authority over a large number of people and an extensive territory. Unlike other kinds of states, though, empires are characterized by a distinctive pattern of internal and external relationships. These relationships combine three crucial factors: **distance**, **difference**, and **domination**.

   Clearly it is difficult to be rigid or precise about these criteria, and much ink could be spilled trying to define any one of them. Each of the three applies to some states that are *not* empires; it is also possible to find unusual cases that seem to fit the definition in some ways but not others (hence all those books arguing about the word "empire"). As a working definition, though—an idea or conceptual tool that allows us to proceed with the historical task at hand—this definition goes a long way. The key notion is that a state needs to have *all three* of these characteristics to be considered an empire. First, it must be projecting political power over relatively great distances. Thus, a hypothetical empire of Flemish-speaking northern Belgium over the French-speaking south probably would not count. Second, its leaders must conceive of groups living in the faraway areas (the **colonies**) as being fundamentally different from those living in nearby areas (the metropole); and this underlying difference needs to be seen (by both sides) as deep, important, and either immutable or at least difficult to overcome. The physical distance between an imperial center and its peripheral colonies often underscores this sense of intrinsic difference, and makes rulers of a colonial government seem more alien and less connected with ordinary people in the colonies. Finally, an empire maps these differences onto political relationships that assert the metropole's superiority and ultimate decision-making power. In the words of one historian, **imperialism** (the system of rule by empires and its associated ideology) is a relationship in which one side— the dominated side—"not only is altered by the interventions of the dominating society, but loses its ability to reject those interventions. The Chinese, for example, were not in a position to tell the Japanese to go home in 1907 or 1932. By contrast the Japanese could and did send their European advisors away in the 1890s."[6] For the purposes of this book, therefore, an empire exists only if and when all three of these criteria—distance, difference, and domination—come together.

With this definition in mind, it is easy to find examples of empires in ancient as well as modern times. Certainly one might study the political entities created by Alexander the Great in the fourth century BCE, or that centered in Rome around the time of Christ, or the Mongol Empire that conquered most of Eurasia in the thirteenth century. Devastating military force established and supported all of these empires; they encompassed vast areas and incorporated a huge array of different peoples in relationships of clear subordination to an imperial center. After initially sweeping attacks that devastated the

[6]Louise Young, *Japan's Total Empire* (Berkeley, 1998), 11.

conquered areas—sources describe piles of skulls left behind by the Mongols' military machine, for instance—the new rulers forced oaths of allegiance from the survivors, and then incorporated distant areas in ways that enabled further conquest. Usually this meant regular, often onerous, tribute payments. Sometimes it meant the provision of people: the fearsome Mongol cavalry actually consisted mostly of Turkic soldiers drawn from among the first groups conquered. In some cases, early empires required a form of cultural assimilation. The Incas, for example, forced conquered peoples to speak Quechua as the language of empire. In an era before ethno-nationality came to define political identity, such assimilation could also take the form of religious conversion. The conquistadores who destroyed Aztec power in the sixteenth century focused on Christian conversion, even as the priests who accompanied them chronicled (and criticized) the brutal tactics used in New Spain. In many other cases cultural transformation seemed less important—the Ottoman Empire, perhaps more typically, did not require either religious conversion or linguistic uniformity from all its subjects, as variegated as they surely were.

The important point is that all of these empires, like the modern ones to be discussed in this book, made use of the newly conquered areas for the benefit of the imperial center, or metropole. Yet one also often finds complex processes of exchange and interaction—of connections—that reshaped both sides. This kind of dialogue, with give and take between sides, occurred even when on the surface it appeared to be happening in a context of radically unequal power relationships. The Mongols changed at least as much following their seizure of China, for instance, as their Chinese subjects shifted under Mongol rule.

This process of exchange, of mutual and often unexpected cultural exchange, is a key theme that this book will explore in its case studies of empire around the world since 1750. Of course modern empires were not the same as those of Alexander or the Mongols. Changes in military technology, for instance, especially involving firearms, by the eighteenth century helped settled agrarian societies, such as those in China and Russia, to conquer nomadic groups, rather than the reverse (as had been the case for millennia, at least in Eurasia). This decline of horse-borne archers in favor of gunners and artillery meant a fundamental shift in the balance of power between urban and steppe societies. Meanwhile new kinds of oceangoing vessels also made it easier for different powers to act forcefully on a global stage.

By the late eighteenth century, a few states in Europe had developed a new ability to project military power far across the oceans. Such underlying changes enabled modern metropoles to build more geographically dispersed empires, with colonial possessions that stretched around the world by the time the *Cambridge Atlas* appeared in 1912. Readers thus need to understand the historical contexts in which these modern empires grew, namely the "early modern" world of the sixteenth, seventeenth, and eighteenth centuries.

A WORLD OF EMPIRES, 1500–1750

Many college and university courses in world history begin in or around the year 1500. This choice is not accidental: during the half-century or so around 1500 new and expanded interregional contacts, through long-distance voyages (across both the Atlantic and Pacific oceans), military conquests, cultural missions, and trade relationships, rapidly created and then deepened the interconnections that linked populations in the Americas and Oceania with those living in parts of the so-called Old World of **Afro-Eurasia** (Africa, Europe, and Asia). Meanwhile the elaborate exchanges that existed both within the Americas and within Afro-Eurasia also expanded greatly in density and sophistication. This multifaceted deepening of systemic linkages, especially those that stretched far across the world's major oceans, yielded a newly globalized web of direct human connection.

At this time, namely around 1500, the world's largest, richest, most populous, powerful, and by many measures sophisticated societies could be found in Asia, including several major empires. Since 1368 the Ming dynasty had ruled the vast "Middle Kingdom," meaning a good portion of what is today China, claiming authority perhaps as far west as Tibet (historians argue about this), and sending ocean voyages as far as East Africa. The Ottoman Empire reached its peak in the mid-1500s, when its sultan controlled the Middle East, North Africa, and portions of southeastern Europe. The Mughal Empire, led by an Islamic dynasty, grew in the sixteenth and seventeenth centuries to govern an enormous and largely Hindu population in South Asia, including most of today's India, along with Muslim and Buddhist areas to the north. The list could go on, as other empires in Afro-Eurasia also dominated large areas, had sizable populations, and controlled strategic regions, markets, and natural resources—the Safavid Empire in Persia, for instance, or the Songhai in West Africa.

European voyagers of various kinds, latecomers to the networks that linked these centers of world wealth and population, in the 1500s worked to insert themselves into maritime trade routes that ran east and west.[7] They rounded southern Africa and crossed the Indian Ocean, avoiding Ottoman lands while seeking to carry home spices and other luxury goods all the way from Asia (and when possible taking a cut of local markets too). They did not, however, yet call themselves "European," operating instead on behalf of various Christian monarchs. Ships sailing for the Portuguese Crown led the way, seizing control of key trade centers at Hormuz (1507), Goa (1510), and especially Malacca (Melaka, 1511), a strategic port on the Malay Peninsula governing access to the "spice islands" and maritime trade with China. In 1517, a large Portuguese delegation reached the important Chinese port of Guangzhou. Unable to pronounce the city's name properly, the Portuguese called it *Cantão*, a label the British later transformed into *Canton*—a small but telling symbol of how colonial powers can transform identities.

In the late fifteenth and the sixteenth century, Iberian ships—those flying the standards of the monarchs of Spain and Portugal—also sailed west, crossing the Atlantic, soon followed by English, Dutch, and French vessels. Claiming ownership of Caribbean islands and building large plantations to produce agricultural goods that could be sold for cash overseas; establishing **settler colonies** (relatively large, permanent communities of families from—or identified with—the metropole, as opposed to temporary/seasonal outposts inhabited by [mostly male] merchants, soldiers, and/or officials) in Mexico and along the coastal areas and riverways of North America while pushing indigenous groups farther inland; and building vast mining complexes in the Andes and elsewhere to extract gold and millions of ounces of silver, these European empires grew suddenly richer and more visible on a world stage. This expansion could only happen, however, when powerful American empires—such as the Aztec and the Inca—came to an abrupt end in the 1520s and 1530s following encounters with Afro-Eurasian visitors, not least through the devastating impact of diseases such as smallpox, which spread in some areas ahead of

---

[7]See the *Connections* series book by Glenn J. Ames, *The Globe Encompassed: The Age of European Discovery, 1500–1700* (2008).

military advance.[8] Following this mass demographic catastrophe, most American lands, wealth, and surviving people were seized and controlled by new empires based in Iberia.

In the seventeenth century new competition and layers of interconnection complicated this landscape, as other states located in the previously marginal lands of Europe also became prominent players in preexisting Asian and African (as well as American) networks of wealth and trade. The Songhai domains splintered in 1591, and the Ming dynasty collapsed in 1644, replaced by a Manchu dynasty (the Qing). The Mughal, Ottoman, and Safavid empires also weakened, for reasons both internal and external, a process that continued into the period covered by this book and which made it easier for European countries to go on the offensive in Asia, Africa, and the Middle East, and in ways that previously would have been suicidal. Slave exports from Africa shot upward, mostly across the Atlantic; this transformed relationships between Africa's coastal and inland societies. It also sent millions of Africans into brutal conditions on the sugar, coffee, cotton, and tobacco plantations of the New World, where (unlike in Africa and Asia) the new European empires sought to maintain near-total control over local populations.[9]

Yet these "Europeans," like "Asians" or "Africans," could hardly be portrayed as united. They rarely cooperated, and certainly did not act as a single group. Continental identities, and their associated racial meanings and solidarities, emerged later, through the historical processes traced in this book. Conflict among Europeans and Asians alike, for example, broke out over access to, and control over, the lucrative sea lanes of the Indian Ocean during the sixteenth and seventeenth centuries—not with the intent, in most cases, of colonizing or conquering wide swathes of territory, and certainly not of attacking frontally the rich and still far too powerful Qing or Mughal states, but rather to secure rights to trade and to fend off their rivals. European states fought among themselves, and with other competitors, such as the Ottoman Empire, to control the western end of the globally dispersed trade network that connected China and its neighbors with Europe. They did so mostly by establishing small, fortified supply

---

[8]See the *Connections* series book by John Aberth, *The First Horseman: Disease in Human History* (2007).
[9]See the *Connections* series book by Lisa A. Lindsay, *Captives as Commodities: The Transatlantic Slave Trade* (2008).

points and trading posts (**factories**) in strategic coastal towns, as the Portuguese had done in Goa or Malacca—whenever possible maintaining good relations with local rulers.

Portugal took an early lead in setting up these trade outposts, but starting in the 1580s boatloads of Dutch merchants and soldiers whittled away at the Portuguese position. Iberian stations in the Indian Ocean, as in the Americas, faced continuing attacks from other European Christians as well as local groups—especially from the Dutch East Indies Company (the *Verenigde Oostindische Compagnie*, or VOC), which by mid-century had become a dominant presence in many Indian Ocean seaports, whereas a "West Indies Company" (*Geoctroyeerde Westindische Compagnie*) focused on the New World. The key port of Malacca, for instance, fell in 1641 to a combination of Malay and VOC forces, and the Dutch retained a presence there for almost 200 years. Amsterdam became a hub of global commercial networks—selling spices and silk from Asia, grain from Eastern Europe, slaves from Africa, and sugar from the Americas—as Dutch companies established imperial beachheads in the Americas, Africa, and Southeast Asia.

English and French sailors—even traders from Sweden and Denmark—all built their own South Asian and Indian Ocean settlements in the seventeenth century. The English Crown in 1600 chartered its own "East India Company"—the entity that ultimately took control of India and led to Queen Victoria's installation as empress and the Durbar of 1877. France followed suit not long afterward with *its* East India Company, as did other European countries. For most of the seventeenth century, however, such attempts to muscle in on prosperous Asian maritime routes were rebuffed. England, France, and other latecomers all found themselves at a disadvantage in the Indian Ocean and spice trades, and sought to compete, with no great success, with their Dutch counterparts. This relative weakness meant that sailors and merchants from the British Isles had to take a very different approach in Asia from the assertive one they pursued in North America. In 1622, for instance, the English East India Company agreed to bombard a Portuguese fortress at Hormuz, helping the Safavid emperor Abbas I expel other Europeans and reestablish Persian authority. (Abbas had promised them trade advantages, an incentive far more persuasive than any vague loyalty to "Europeans" or to fellow Christians.) This subordinate role continued even after England secured its key trading posts in Bombay (Mumbai) and Madras (Chennai) in the 1630s. (France established a main base in Pondicherry in 1674, keeping sovereign control there until 1954.) Many of these factories and concessions came about as much through negotiated agreements with local leaders as by force; so, for reasons of sheer practicality England, and later Great Britain, had to maintain initially a much less intrusive presence in India than the one it pursued after 1750.[10]

During the century before 1750, British and French attention also focused on each other. Through a series of globally dispersed wars the two countries fought for dominance, both within Europe and increasingly over colonial possessions around the world. These battles, part of what is sometimes called the "Second Hundred Years' War," began in the 1680s and continued at great cost for many decades, creating a context for the bitter imperial struggles and destructive world wars that came later. Indeed, these conflicts amounted to an early modern world war: following inconclusive fighting in the War of Austrian Succession, for example, the peace treaty of 1748 simply swapped colonial outposts seized by the other side. Britain gave up Louisbourg, a strategic port in present-day Nova Scotia that it had conquered in its effort to gain access to French Canada, while France returned a vital British colonial hub at Madras in India. This globally focused, Canadian-for-Indian port swap annoyed partisans in both empires.

The protracted warfare between France and Britain finally reached a global turning point in the late eighteenth century, shortly after the case studies in this book begin. The French state's defeat in the Seven Years' War (1756–1763) marked the end of its real presence in North America (its later support of the American colonies' rebellion notwithstanding) and the collapse of its effective power in India. Within a generation the French monarchy collapsed altogether under the combined weight of social protest and famine at home, slave rebellions and calls for political reform in the empire, and crushing debt run up in a century of worldwide warfare. From London's perspective, this victory over France in 1763, alongside the nearly simultaneous establishment of British East India Company rule in crucial provinces of India, laid the groundwork for Britain's rise to prominence as a fully global empire—a worldwide story not reversed even when Napoleon rebuilt French power and successfully conquered much of Europe.[11]

---

[10]In 1707, an Act of Union merged the kingdoms of England and Scotland to form a new political entity, "Great Britain."

[11]Great Britain of course experienced its own setbacks—most visibly, losing the thirteen American colonies and the Northwest Territory—but such defeats did not reverse its long-term trajectory of imperial expansion.

His efforts in the wider world, such as a dramatic campaign in Egypt and attempts to secure Persian aid to attack British India, were of less consequence in this global rivalry. Britain simply continued expanding its overseas colonies, and ultimately the British Empire grew to cover nearly thirteen million square miles (99 percent outside Britain proper), encompassing roughly four hundred and fifty million people, about a quarter of the world's population. That vast expansion is one of the core stories of this book.

CONNECTIONS AND COLONIES SINCE 1750

An important piece of this British imperial story is told in Chapter 1, the first of four case studies. That chapter focuses on India, and the next chapter explores Africa—two cases that frequently define modern imperialism. In both places imperial powers from Europe established colonial systems that asserted (although did not always achieve) sweeping dominance of local politics, culture, and economic, military, and natural resources. The third and fourth case studies introduce important complications. The Americas represent a story of not only direct but also indirect empire, in which power and influence could sometimes be levied even more effectively through informal and economic means. In other parts of Asia, lastly, one finds imperialism pursued by states (Japan, Russia/USSR, and the United States) that were *not* European, at least not fully so, and were also, ironically, avowedly "*anti*-colonial" in their self-conceptions and self-presentation.

All four of these cases thus explore the intricacies and varieties of modern empire. Together they show that imperial systems underwent important changes after 1750—not least in the simple fact of their vastly expanded geographic scope. By the 1870s European empires were adding more than 240,000 square miles *every year* to their possessions (that is, more land than is covered by France). Britain's world-spanning network of colonies is only the most dramatic example. Such enormous empires—and their attempt to rule directly over millions of colonial subjects—represented another key shift from earlier practices. The thirteenth-century Mongol Empire stretched far across Eurasia, for instance, but its supreme leaders, the Great Khans, did not attempt to know about, let alone control, their subjects' everyday lives. Such a task would have been patently impossible, given the large distances and number of people involved, and also the speed and capacity of available communications technology. Rather, the khans (like other early emperors) either struck a deal with the existing authorities in conquered areas, or delegated their power to a **plenipotentiary** (a representative who resided in a certain area—equivalent to Lord Lytton's role as Indian viceroy in the 1870s, but without Lytton's ability to send telegrams instantly to London). These representatives promised to act on the khan's behalf, and in his best interests—with the threat of lethal punishment if they did not live up to this trust. But in everyday life, the Mongol Empire remained a distant and some-what vague presence for most of the Great Khan's subjects (all the more after mid-century, when the empire evolved into four entities, three of which were nominally subordinate but effectively independ-ent khanates). As long as they paid an agreed amount of tribute to their particular khan, and as long as they did not organize military rebellions to break away, subjects within these four khanates could generally count on being left alone.

In the modern empires discussed in this book, colonial authorities often appear similarly remote from local populations, and certainly they failed to control the totality of colonial subjects' everyday life. These empires' stated goal, however, was far more ambitious than that of their predecessors. The **ideologies** of imperialism—the ways these colonizers unconsciously made sense of, and how they explicitly justified, the pursuit of imperial authority far from home—underwent a fundamental shift. In earlier wars of conquest, the seizure of new lands and people could be presented unapologetically, as serving God and saving souls through conversion of the natives and simultaneously serving a monarch or kingdom's economic, political, or military interests. By the eighteenth and especially nineteenth century one finds frequent invocations of new moral or cultural arguments—claims that armies conquered other lands, not for grandeur or wealth or to compete with other empires (although all of those mattered), but out of humanitarian concerns—that they attacked in order to help the people they conquered. This perhaps counterintuitive idea underpinned the notion of a **civilizing mission**, one in which modern empires sought not to slaughter or to dominate other peoples, at least not officially, but to remake and improve them (especially in secular ways that differed from earlier attempts at religious conversion). This stated goal in turn meant knowing more about colonial subjects' lives, hence the development of new information technologies and intrusive administrative techniques. (Admittedly, some early missionaries had displayed real ethnographic skill, and they too learned a great deal about the people they encountered.) A civilizing mission required sustained investment in efforts to change everyday culture, in ways the colonizers thought best—through work done in new schools, churches, and prisons, to name just a few places. Such ambitious goals of course presented huge practical problems, as the case studies will show; it also created new arenas for potential anti-imperial criticism and opposition, both at home and abroad.

Finally, these modern empires—in Asia, Africa, and the Americas— also arose in a new era of global interconnection, one that only expanded with a series of technological, economic, and political changes that occurred after 1750. The development of industrial capitalism both enabled and drove the search for colonies. Colonies played a crucial role in the industrial revolution: they produced the vastly expanded amounts of raw materials needed by new factories (cotton, for example), and also served as markets for finished goods. Industrializing economies then produced new materials like steel and developed technologies that used electricity, and these changes in turn helped build empires, in a literal sense. By the mid-nineteenth century people and goods (and soldiers) could move quickly and reliably across the world's oceans using steamships; the development of telegraph networks—which had reached every continent by the mid-1860s—meant communication between metropolitan centers and colonial peripheries, or between different empires, could take place nearly in real time.

The apparent association of these new technologies with Europe—although in reality their sources were far more complex and multiregional—and the simple visibility of these huge new empires seemed to some to prove they had reached a rightful position of dominance. Such imperialists welcomed facile but scientifically presented ideas of Social Darwinism (in which, supposedly, only the "fittest" countries would survive, a category in which they placed themselves) or equally "scientific" notions of racial difference (in which ideas about the cultural superiority of colonizing groups morphed into views of biological distinctions, which in turn mapped onto colonial systems of political hierarchy).

Such processes and attitudes cannot be seen as only or intrinsically European, although histories of empire sometimes present it that way. The pursuit of power, or the construction of colonies, was not a uniquely Western phenomenon. This book's final case study explores the late nineteenth-century drive by the Meiji rulers of Japan to expand outward into East Asia—to make the Japanese nation into an empire by projecting its power into other geographic spaces—a drive continued by their successors in the twentieth century. Wherever any empire arose, whether Asian or European or African or American, it pursued multiple goals. Some imperial aims were economic (new supplies of raw materials or precious metals; control over strategic trade hubs; markets for finished goods). Other motives appear to have been political (competing with other states that likewise want to carve out a "place in the sun"—and international prestige and respect—by building overseas or overland empires). Still others were military/strategic (occupying crucial ports or mountain ranges, or preventing others from doing the same) or ideological/cultural (proving national "greatness" and status, through the bald fact of conquest and by proclaiming a civilizing mission to benighted peoples). And of course all of these motivations overlapped, and fed one another.

In the nineteenth and twentieth centuries, though, one also finds other motivations for imperial assertiveness—by looking away from the colonies. Modern empires also pursued *internal* goals: they fought viciously overseas in hopes of using that struggle to overcome divisions at home. Many such states had developed new and more democratic forms of politics in the 1800s, hence their governments needed to be more sensitive to, or at least aware of, public opinion. In several cases aggressive colonial powers tried to persuade dissenting and dominated groups in the metropole that they should subordinate their grievances to the greater good of the nation's global imperial struggle—hoping to buy loyalty with the perceived glory of overseas conquest.

Ironically, therefore, the era in which most of the world's population came under the control of empires was also the same era in which those empires claimed to be bringing freedom to their own people. In Japan, for instance, the Meiji state remade rural peasants into supporters of the emperor, not only through nationalist propaganda campaigns but also through successive wars of imperial expansion. A similar effort characterized European attempts to undercut worker mobilization and weaken radical socialist and revolutionary movements by sending imperial navies across the sea. The international manifestations of such domestic politics are visible in the explosive growth of world colonies after 1870 (recall the *Cambridge Atlas* maps), and also in the number of armed skirmishes and the risk of all-out war between these imperial states as they competed testily for a diminishing pool of as-yet-unclaimed areas. The struggle for colonial possessions thus forms a crucial backdrop to other global conflicts of the twentieth century, such as the calamitous outbreak of the First World War, and also the birth of modern nations and nationalism: topics not directly addressed in this book but which hover behind the scenes.

So empire—its very existence, its growing extent, and its contested meanings—also played a key role within each imperial power, and suffused its history even at "home." At least in the modern period, it is impossible to understand these national histories without paying attention to the constant presence of colonies, even when they seem far away. The ongoing fact of empire shaped how people both in the metropole and in the colonies thought about themselves: nationally, racially, politically, and economically. Europe's supposedly autonomous cultural traditions, and their role as emblems of a new, wider "European" identity, emerged indeed from constant interactions with a wider world: through visits by travelers coming from the colonies and heading out again, through publications that circulated within a literary world, through food and clothing and slang and virtually anything else one could imagine. The historian Antoinette Burton, making this case while writing about Britain, says that such "traces of empire" exist virtually "everywhere" before 1914—"in spaces as diverse as the Boy Scouts, Bovril advertisements, and biscuit tins; in productions as varied as novels, feminist pamphlets, and music halls; in…the Franco-British Exhibition; and in halls as hallowed as Westminster itself." She concludes that "empire was, in short, not just a phenomenon 'out there,' but a fundamental and constitutive part of English culture and national identity at home, where 'the fact of empire was registered not only in political debate…but entered the social fabric, the intellectual discourse and the life of the imagination.'"[12]

Since at least 1750, then, and perhaps long before, the world has been fundamentally imperial. Understanding this fact sheds light on the front pages of today's newspapers; beyond that, it also illuminates in basic ways the global human experience of the last three centuries. The story of empires and colonies not only interweaves in crucial ways

---

[12]Antoinette Burton, "Introduction," in Burton, ed., *After the Imperial Turn* (Durham, NC, 2003), 3. (The inset quotation is from Benita Parry.) Westminster is the hall in which Parliament meets. Bovril is a meat extract, originally made from beef, sold in bottles and used widely: as seasoning in soups, stews, spread on toast, or diluted as a drink ("beef tea"). The Franco-British Exhibition of 1908 was a World's Fair gathering in London, jointly produced by the two countries. It included "colonial villages," exhibits with Irish, Algerian, Senegalese, and Indian themes.

with other key themes of modern world history—disease, migration, trade, slavery—explored in different *Connections* volumes, but it is also an independent and persistent thread in the contemporary world. Such a grand statement is not meant to diminish the vast variety of imperial cases, nor to deny the complexities, nuances, and contradictions embedded within their many colonial settings. Empires are at root about power in all its forms; but as the rest of this book shows, power works in unexpected ways. Sometimes it can be turned back upon itself, often it trickles out and manifests unpredictably, being wielded by many different players; and frequently there are more than two sides to a particular imperial story. Visitors from colonial powers sometimes donned local dress and tried to "go native," to the disquiet of their countrymen; colonized groups sometimes produced members willing to work on behalf of, to profit from, even to fight and die for, the empire that conquered them. Readers should watch for such paradoxes, and ask how such complications fit into—or whether they cast doubt upon—the wider narratives that have unfolded in the world since 1750.

CHAPTER

1

The Raj: British Empire in India and South Asia, 1757–1947

During the modern period British power in South Asia underwent trans-formations in style and substance—indeed, sometimes style was substance. These shifts were driven partly by changes in British fortunes relative to other European powers and partly by South Asian responses and resistance on the ground. At every stage, shifts in imperial ideologies and identities accompanied institutional, political, and economic changes. The meanings of colonialism could be ambiguous, and both Indian and British identities were shaped by the experiences of colonial rule. British officials used India as a laboratory for empire: administrative practices worked out there were applied around the world, while Indian foods and fashions—from curry to jewelry and clothing—became all the rage in London. Indian society also underwent dramatic changes. Many Indians faced new kinds of impoverishment, and massive famine and recurrent epidemics put unprecedented strains on local safety nets and social networks. At the same time, some indigenous groups, such as wealthy landlords and Brahmin elites, benefited from a privileged position in the imperial order. Some gained wealth, while others obtained an

education in the colonial system, and traveled widely throughout the empire—
such as the young lawyer Mohandas Gandhi, who practiced law for a time in
South Africa. Such wide-ranging mobility and exposure to ideas from Europe
and other parts of the empire helped inspire leaders such as Gandhi to organize
anti-colonial nationalist movements that ultimately destroyed the empire and,
by 1947, had gained Indian (and Afghanistani, Pakistani, and, later, Burmese
and Bangladeshi) independence.

Following the Durbar of 1877 that proclaimed Queen Victoria as
Empress of India, London achieved what appeared to be imperial
preeminence. With power asserted in India, the British Empire stretched
around the globe, and it defended itself with a navy that dominated
the oceans. As the largest empire the world had ever seen, Britain's
system was copied by would-be competitors, feared by peoples
facing conquest, and seen by commentators (and later historians) as
a defining case—the archetype of modern empire. India became a
model for other European states to emulate (or attempt to seize) and
a benchmark against which non-Europeans struggled—a place many
used to define themselves. India was the jewel in Britain's imperial
crown, and Britain's global policy protected this position of influence
and control. Officials, governors, soldiers, and politicians all worked to
make this dominance seem normal, natural, and unquestioned. But it
was a long road to Victoria's imperial coronation, and as the elephants
of 1877 suggested, British control was not nearly so firm as the empress
and her officials wished it to appear—hence the enormous efforts they
invested in designing ceremonies like the Durbar.

From a vantage point little more than a century before Victoria's
coronation, the British presence in India looked very different. Before
about 1700, London's position in South Asia was shaped more by
weakness than strength—weakness relative to European rivals and also
to the powerful Islamic Mughal state that controlled most of the Indian
subcontinent and its largely Hindu population. England first developed
a presence in India during the sixteenth and especially seventeenth
centuries, as merchants sought to profit from the Indian Ocean trade
routes that connected China with places to the west. In this period,
however, England played a relatively minor role, less prominent than
Portugal or the Dutch Republic in these commercial networks.

This position of weakness forced English emissaries and
merchants to adopt a conciliatory, nonconfrontational strategy in
their interactions with Indians. By the seventeenth century they

successfully negotiated agreements with local rulers to permit the establishment of trading outposts. Officially these merchants acted in the name of the English East India Company (EIC), a royally chartered but privately owned joint-stock company, although on the side they often also traded for personal benefit. In order to protect and expand these commercial ventures, these men (virtually all traders were male) frequently participated in local court life. Some assimilated into indigenous culture, adopting new ways of dressing, eating, and acting. They learned to speak Persian, the Mughal court language; some married local women, and a few took up the Mughal court tradition of writing lyrical romantic poetry. During this period, Britain did not attempt to invade or bend India to its will—far from it. Instead, Britons were willing participants in a broad and complicated world of **syncretism**, or cultural mixings, that characterized British presence through the mid-1700s.

Many of these early British efforts focused on the wealthy and important province of Bengal, in northeastern India. French and other European traders also set up outposts there and in other provinces and principalities. Bengal specialized in the production of inexpensive, yet top-quality cotton textiles—fabrics far better than European producers of the day could make. To obtain dependable supplies of this excellent Indian cloth, British traders set up more than 150 trading posts in Calcutta (Kolkata), the largest city in Bengal. As these exports grew, the local economy boomed at the expense of the central Mughal state. The continuing expansion of foreign trade in places like Calcutta—and the rapidly growing associated presence of foreigners—accelerated the political weakening of the Mughal emperor.

CONQUEST AND PROFIT: BRITISH POWER THROUGH THE EAST INDIA COMPANY (1757–1857)

By the mid-eighteenth century, British military power and assertiveness had grown in India and elsewhere, as Britain fought a decades-long global war with France, its main European rival. India—seen as a potentially rich colonial prize—played a part in this struggle. When British colonists in North America conquered a key French port in Canada during the War of Austrian Succession (1745–1748), for instance, London traded this new acquisition away in exchange for a French promise to surrender back Fort St. George, located at the wealthy Indian city of Madras, which they had conquered only a few years earlier.[1] And as Britain's Royal Navy grew stronger and more aggressive, British merchant ships slowly pushed out the Dutch to take the upper hand in Indian Ocean trade. Yet this shift on the ground in South Asia did not come about through direct action or military conquest by the British state. Instead, the expansion of Britain's role in India came principally through the efforts of the EIC, which enjoyed wide-ranging powers normally associated with states—such as levying taxes, concluding treaties, and recruiting soldiers to carry out armed military campaigns. In 1757 "John Company," as the EIC was informally called, took control of Bengal, and over the next century asserted its power and political control over a rapidly growing swathe of the Indian countryside, as shown in Map 1.1.

How had this happened? English traders did not conquer India on their own, but relied on their prior alliances with local bankers and Indian elites. These indigenous groups wanted to keep more of the wealth that arose from Bengal's booming trade—by reducing the amount of tax revenue that flowed onward to the central Mughal state. They therefore agreed to loan money to the Company's representatives, who hired mercenary soldiers and bought military equipment to prepare for a showdown with the emperor, which they duly provoked in 1757. In this struggle, the Company's army—comprised mostly of Indian troops, known as **sepoys**, and paid for by Bengali bankers—defeated the Mughal emperor's forces.

Military victory permitted the Company to seize the emperor's local treasury—which thanks to Bengal's prosperity was quite sizable, more than £5 million sterling.[2] This amount far exceeded the bankers' loans that had paid for the conquest, so the EIC made a quick profit. It then rapidly built on this success by expanding its army and bureaucracy and taking control of other areas across northern and central India. Sometimes it did so through military assault, but more often it simply made an arrangement with local princes, who were often only too happy to reduce their tax payments by cutting out the Mughal state. At first the EIC even said it was acting as the emperor's "protector"; rather than deposing him openly, the Company claimed to rule on his behalf.

---

[1] The French maintained other claims on India's eastern coast, such as at Pondicherry.

[2] This amounted to a very large windfall for the company. For comparison, the net annual public (government) income within Britain itself came to just under £8 million sterling in 1757.

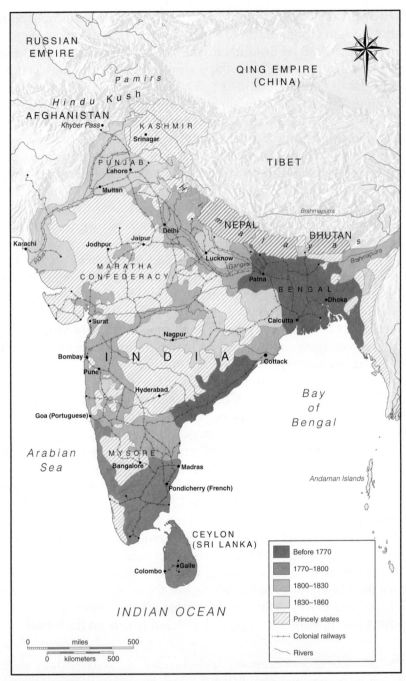

MAP 1.1   Imperial India. Shaded areas show British (EIC) expansion.

Over the next century, the EIC grew into something like an arm of the British state, assuming military and administrative powers over much of India. This piecemeal but steady assertion of colonial sovereignty was a hugely important shift. It led to deep changes in local economic patterns, social structures, and cultural practices—and it simultaneously changed the English too, both in India and in Britain.

By seizing Bengal, the Company established direct control over the economic engine of northern India: Bengali cotton textiles and thousands of the world's best weavers. At first, the Company made huge profits exporting this cotton cloth back to Europe. But since this cloth was so excellent and inexpensive, it threatened textile manufacturers in England with bankruptcy—and these manufacturers used their political muscle to fight back. They successfully pressured the English state—despite its vocal support for "free trade"—to adopt a protectionist economic policy that first restricted and ultimately banned the export of Bengali cotton cloth. This approach obviously protected English textile makers; with a safe home market, it also enabled them to flood Bengali markets with excess English fabric at very low prices—sometimes below the cost of production.[3] At these low subsidized prices, England's lower-quality cloth found a market in India (as it did in Latin America and elsewhere). In 1820 only 6 percent of English textile production had been sent to India; by 1840 this proportion (of a much larger total) had increased to 22 percent, by 1850 it was 31 percent, and by 1873 it exceeded 50 percent. Indian markets thus helped fuel the growth of British industry (and also plantation slavery in the United States, through the rapidly growing demand for cotton fiber).

One obvious consequence of this British expansion was the destruction of Bengal's once-powerful cloth producers, many of whom were driven out of business. Such bankruptcies in turn meant the sudden availability of now-unemployed weavers. These workers, along with many other Indians, were "liberated," as capitalist

---

[3]English cloth exports expanded rapidly in the early 1800s, as England's textile makers became one of the first economic sectors to reorganize in what is now called the "industrial revolution." This was not an English revolution per se—it was rather a global phenomenon, one that depended crucially on wider networks for both supplies and markets. It arose precisely from the connections that grew out of Britain's web of empire, with cotton fibers being imported from plantations in the New World (and other places such as Egypt, Uganda, and India), undergoing processing in textile mills in England (in Lancashire and other locations near port cities), and then re-exported for sale anywhere customers could be found.

entrepreneurs put it, to move around the world. Many went or were sent to other colonies, usually as indentured laborers, to work on agricultural plantations in the Caribbean, Africa, and elsewhere. The demand for such workers increased rapidly following the 1830s and 1840s, when slavery and the slave trade were banned in Britain's colonies. One scholar has estimated that more than thirty million Indians emigrated from South Asia between 1834 and 1937, mostly to British, French, and Dutch colonies. Some of these migrants died in the tea, sugar, rubber, or coffee plantations of Ceylon, Malaysia, or the Caribbean. Many who survived the rigors of such work ultimately returned to India—but at least six million South Asians did not, deciding to remain and settle permanently abroad.

This massive export of Indian labor only slowed in the 1910s when major protests broke out in India over the maltreatment of "coolie" workers in South Africa and Fiji. These protests helped force restrictions on the emigration of indentured servants, and in 1921 led to the establishment of a standing parliamentary committee responsible for protecting Indians throughout the empire. This outcome showed South Asians' growing ability to force changes on the colonial system, and foreshadowed Indian independence by expressing the political power of colonized populations. Even so, the previous mobility of generations of Indian workers had major consequences—it helped keep down agricultural wages in other regions, and permanently changed the demographic profile of many other countries around the world (see Table 1.1).

Within India too, the EIC created new social structures and economic patterns. In many ways Indian customs did not match

TABLE 1.1 A Colonial Diaspora: Indians Around the World (census of 1921)

Country (region)	Total population	Of South Asian origin
Mauritius (Africa)	383,069	265,524 (69%)
Guiana (Latin America)	297,691	124,928 (42%)
Trinidad (Caribbean)	365,913	122,117 (33%)
Fiji (Oceania/Pacific)	157,266	60,634 (39%)

Sources: Hugh Tinker, *A New System of Slavery* (Oxford, 1974), 370–372; and "Fiji," *United Nations International Human Rights Instruments* (HRI/CORE/1/ Add. 122) (November 25, 2002), 14.

accepted European practices, and after 1757 Company officials reshaped Indian society in a variety of ways to make it more familiar, drawing on models they already knew, from England or possessions such as Ireland. Under the Mughal system, for example, land taxes on Indian peasant farmers had been collected by a rural elite known as *zamindars.* The EIC altered this system of land use. It formalized the zamindars' position and, hoping to create a loyal group of Indian allies who had a stake in the colonial system, gave them formal title to the land (not just the right to collect taxes on it). In British eyes this made zamindars equivalent to the European gentry, landowners who collected local tax payments and forwarded them to the central state. But under the new system, Indian zamindars could move to the cities, becoming absentee landlords and hiring other people to collect the taxes—since their ownership of the land was now guaranteed, they did not need to be physically present on it. When local elites relocated to places like Calcutta and Madras, though, their absence altered the social system. Before the 1750s, for example, zamindars had organized or provided relief for hungry peasants in droughts and famines. Now, as the tax burden on peasants became heavier and less flexible, and as ties to higher social classes diminished, local safety nets disappeared.

As for the British, they moved away from the kinds of syncretic arrangements that had enabled the initial treaties and trade outposts of the seventeenth century. They increasingly saw themselves as the rulers of India and, thus, as a separate group that was distant from, and superior to, the indigenous population—even local princes. They stopped intermingling with local court society and instead established separate English enclaves. They ceased writing love poetry in Persian and marrying local women (although sexual contact certainly continued). They no longer established relations with local princes and trading partners by giving and accepting gifts. (These informal trade practices came to be seen as "illegal" and corrupt. Gifts from local traders were legally defined as "bribes," and the British Parliament outlawed them in the 1780s and 1790s.) The EIC was building a new kind of empire, one that intended to regularize, standardize, and control vast webs of Indian commerce and politics. As they created social distance from Indians, British EIC officials made Indian society and Indian languages formal matters to be "studied" and mastered, seeing India as an exotic arena that required specialized training and detailed education in arcane texts—not something that could be learned through informal everyday immersion of the kind practiced by early English traders.

While the Company's power grew rapidly after 1757, it never went unchallenged. In important ways, indeed, the EIC faced limits and came under attack fairly quickly. Many of its challenges arose from the recurrent, often violent, resistance of Indians who fought back—effectively raising the costs of empire. It also was weakened by the nagging voice of critics within Britain, some of whom held vehemently anti-imperialist beliefs, and others who supported the imperial project but felt the EIC could not be entrusted to carry it out responsibly. Both sets of critics agreed on the shortcomings of British policy in India. They lambasted the Company's actions as politically harmful, economically unproductive, and in many cases morally unsound.

A major famine that struck Bengal and its surrounding area in 1770 gave early impetus to such criticism, and spurred strong Indian resistance to British authority. The famine arose partly from environmental causes, as a shortfall of rain in 1769 led to a steep decline in local harvests. The critics, however, argued persuasively that the political and economic structures of colonial power also deepened the famine's human impact. Anti-imperialists accused the EIC of previously laying the groundwork for mass starvation by taking exorbitant profits in Bengal and single-mindedly continuing to export Indian grain even as the drought worsened. Large numbers of beggars appeared on the streets of Calcutta, and by the spring of 1770 starvation was rampant. Precise mortality figures do not exist, but estimates of the number who died range upward from 20 percent of Bengal's total population. Some hard-hit districts lost 50 percent or even more. In total, perhaps ten million Indians starved to death in this first grand disaster of British colonial rule.

Among its other consequences, this horrific episode shaped and in some ways extended English views of South Asia. India had long been seen by English visitors as a land of plenty, a wealthy country promising untold riches to a colonial conqueror; great Indian princes, after all, sat lazily about (or so British eyes judged) while living in grandeur. The starvation suggested, however, that India also hid manifold risks and hazard. In this and later famines British observers construed South Asians' supposed indolence as dangerously passive and fatalistic, as shown by their apparent unwillingness to do anything to stave off impending starvation (see Figure 1.1).

FIGURE 1.1 Famine in India. European pictures highlighted indigenous penury and helplessness, while underscoring the sense of separation between imperial observers and South Asian society. In this image from 1897, note the contrast between famine victims pleading for assistance and the well-fed English administrators to whom they appeal—and a similarly well-fed Indian servant, standing in the doorway. This drawing, published in the French press (*Le Petit Journal*), also stands as a political comment, underscoring as it does the failings of a competitor's empire.

After observing hundreds of Indians lying listlessly in the streets, James Alexander, the EIC's local representative in Patna, wrote in March 1770 that "such is the disposition of the people that they seem rather inclined to submit to death than extricate themselves from the misery of hunger by industry and labour."[4] Such depictions ignored the fact that Europeans like Alexander only saw these people at the very end of what had been a long, bitter struggle to survive. They left out the many ways Indians fought, against both the famine and the EIC—from begging on the street and submitting petitions for food aid to carrying out arson attacks on British facilities, from informal relief efforts organized by Indian notables to mass peasant migrations in search of work and food. One tax collector reported that from his (well-provisioned) perspective, the famine was a huge inconvenience: he faced thousands of peasants who had virtually nothing left, "and so clamorous are they in their complaints and lamentations that it is difficult for me to conduct business in the cutcherry [office]."[5]

Such judgments of Asian passivity lent credence to the view that Indians could not possibly survive on their own, and so required British help and protection—hence, an imperial presence. At the same time the Company came under attack by critics in England who argued that it had shown itself unfit to fulfill this responsibility. They depicted the Company as more interested in exploiting India than in lifting it up. The EIC refused to provide more than token famine relief, and in critics' eyes worked principally to protect its profit stream—by one reckoning, the Company had extracted £10.5 million from Bengal in the ten years before 1776. (The Crown, on the other hand, could not draw such profit from, for example, its American colonies, which had large European settler communities that needed repeated, costly defense to fend off French and Native American attacks.) Critics denounced this approach, contending that the EIC had been corrupted by the opportunities and temptations of absolute power. Leaving John Company in control, they said, risked damaging British institutions and morals, and threw serious doubt over Great Britain's international credibility.

---

[4]Quoted by David Arnold, "Hunger in the Garden of Plenty," in Alessa Johns, ed., *Dreadful Visitations* (New York, 1999), 96.
[5]*Ibid.*, 101.

REBELLION AND REPRESSION UNDER THE RAJ: BRITISH EMPIRE IN INDIA (1857–1947)

Such arguments pressured the British state to step in and steadily restrict the Company's authority. Parliament asserted its oversight rights in India as early as the Regulating Acts of 1773, and by the early nineteenth century the EIC had lost its economic monopoly. As Indian resistance continued to imperil Company authority, and as wider threats loomed from Russia and Afghanistan to the north, London perceived its political position in India as increasingly tenuous. Although the threat of armed force always underpinned British authority, in practical terms the EIC was attempting to use a handful of officials and a force of 311,000 sepoys (divided into separate armies in Bengal, Bombay, and Madras, and commanded by EIC officers from Europe), along with fewer than 38,000 regular British soldiers stationed in garrisons, to control a country with a population far larger than that of Britain. The risks of this approach were conclusively exposed in 1857, when colonial authorities faced a major armed rebellion (or "mutiny," as the British called it) by most of the sepoys in the Bengal army. This rebellion, although not joined by the mass of the Bombay or Madras armies, spread quickly across the Upper Ganges Plain and central India. It took British soldiers more than a year of bitter fighting and the use of scorched-earth tactics to reassert control.

The Company had faced an almost constant series of local uprisings before this: Indians never passively accepted British colonial rule. But by taking resistance to a new level, the rebellion of 1857 catalyzed a fundamental shift in the colonial order. Once the sepoys and their allies had been defeated (and their leaders put to death, publicly and sometimes spectacularly, along with mass executions for hundreds of sepoys who had "deserted"), the British state stepped in directly and Queen Victoria assumed control in India. The Mughal emperor, who by this time was little more than a figurehead, was formally accused of treason and put on trial for allegedly directing for supporting the "mutiny," deposed, and put before a military tribunal. Upon conviction, he was exiled to Burma, and Victoria formally took his place, assuming the title Empress of India in 1876—a shift codified in the grand Durbar of 1877. London thus claimed sovereign power in India, ruling directly in its own name, not through the EIC or on behalf of the Mughal state. This dramatic change required a fresh justification for British authority.

Colonial authorities continued to develop a vision for Indian society and introduced more structural changes. They still relied on European models, both to make Indian society more recognizable in British eyes and to reward allies and prevent future armed rebellions. Yet this new vision was not merely imposed by the English. At each stage it developed in tandem with privileged groups of Indians, who also benefited from their proximity to colonial power.

From the British perspective, the uprising of 1857 showed Indians to be untrustworthy and prone to social disorder. Interpreted in this way, the rebellion became a charter for continued British rule. After 1857 colonial officials represented India as a highly diverse but not yet civilized society, a country prone to divisiveness and lacking the kind of civic-minded patriotism needed to ensure social stability. Only British rule could guarantee basic law and order, they said; Indians were deemed unable to govern themselves. Victoria's local representatives portrayed themselves as the caring guardians of an immature and unstable society, and the colonial state as fulfilling a quasi-parental role, with responsibility for protecting and guiding India during the period of its supposed maturation. As Sir Edwin Arnold put it (in an article excerpted more fully later in this chapter), the British in India rule "for the sake of the Indians first, and for revenue and reputation and power [only] afterwards."[6] India was seen as a not-yet-civilized society, an undeveloped place, the equivalent of what England had been centuries before—meaning India was not different or unique, just less far along the same road that England had already traveled. The EIC was no longer appropriate for such a mission: British rule had to be caring and concerned with the good of India, not just focused on the profit of English investors.

The British state built on EIC policies that imagined India in terms familiar to European observers. In particular, they saw Indian society as functionally equivalent to the feudal order of medieval Europe. For this comparison to work, India had to have peasant-serfs, with fixed obligations to landowning nobles. These "nobles" in turn had to serve as vassals of regional princes, who themselves owed allegiance to, and provided military service for, a powerful monarch. Although this vision corresponded poorly to Indian reality, and did not at all reflect the economic and political control that was wielded from London, English observers painted India in terms shaped by this external lens.

---

[6]Edwin Arnold, "The Famine in India," *North American Review* 164:484 (March 1897), 261.

They wrote detailed histories that blamed the ("foreign") Mughal rulers for distorting India's true political, economic, and cultural heritage, and proclaimed Britain's duty to restore India's genuine traditions. Since feudalism, manorialism, and other European practices had never existed in India, this "restoration" really meant a process of invention: so British authorities after 1857 embarked on an elaborate program of inventing many of India's allegedly ancient traditions.

As already suggested, the English devoted considerable energy in India to inventing a European-style feudal nobility and regional princes—a process that had started with the EIC's redefinition of landownership and tax collection—and to making Queen Victoria into the central monarch that such a feudal system required (although with much more grandeur than actual feudal monarchs had had). Even before the Durbar of 1877 confirmed her as Empress of India, a series of smaller gatherings around the country had invited thousands of newly minted, precisely ranked Indian nobles to receive royal honors and privileges. These included the right to bear newly designed but supposedly traditional heraldry—shield-shaped banners with insignias and crests representing the imagined histories of their noble families. These recognitions were presented as ceremonial acts that restored and protected ancient Indian social customs, but they drew mostly on European iconography and often proceeded in ignorance of Indian families' actual histories. A particularly inventive English civil servant in Bengal, Robert Taylor, personally designed all of the elaborate heraldry that was distributed at the Durbar of 1877.

British authorities defended the political order of the **Raj** ("rule") as a system that protected ordinary Indians, especially the poor and powerless, far better than the Mughals and earlier rulers had done. Even under the EIC such justifications had been common. For example, colonial officials explained their approach to Indian family life and gender relations in terms of protecting disadvantaged women. When English visitors encountered the practice of **sati,** the ritual burning of Hindu widows on their husbands' funeral pyres, they were horrified—and fascinated. Company officials investigated the "problem" of sati thoroughly, investigating its causes and chronicling its frequency across India. As chronicled in a document that appears below, after much discussion, they decided in 1829 to ban the practice outright, using their own revulsion both to justify British colonial power and to stake a claim to moral superiority (see Figure 1.2). They

FIGURE 1.2   A sati in British eyes. A decade after the EIC banned the practice of widow immolation, a Protestant missionary to India, William Campbell, put a similar image on the title page of his 600-page book about Hindu customs (*British India in Its Relation to the Decline of Hindooism, and the Progress of Christianity*). How do such pictures present religion (or culture in general) in India? Why is sati given such a prominent position in descriptions of Indian customs? Why does this woman appear to be casting herself into the flames? And at whom were such images aimed—what is the target audience?

took this step most obviously to protect Indian women (in the words of Gayatri Chakravorty Spivak, this assertion amounted to "white men saving brown women from brown men"[7]), but also justified their actions by insisting that they wanted to restore and protect India's *genuine* customs and traditions—in which, they said, sati played no role.

Why would a widow burn herself alive? Obviously, British investigators could not ask a woman who had done so after the fact. Colonial observers assumed these women were victims, who must have been forced or coerced into taking their own lives. Yet investigators made little effort to ask other women about the phenomenon. They ignored the fact that the term "*sati*" also referred to the woman herself, not merely to the practice of immolation. (In common parlance it meant a virtuous or chaste woman, someone to be admired.) Investigators instead spoke mostly with upper-class (male) Brahmin religious authorities, asking questions about the scriptural bases in Hinduism for

---

[7]Gayatri Spivak, "Can the Subaltern Speak?" *Wedge* 7–8 (1985), 121.

and against widow immolation. This approach saw sati as a practice, not a person; and one rooted in and determined by ancient textual traditions—not the product of choices being made by individual women in the here and now. By approaching the question in this way, the **agency**, or free choice and power of the individual women involved (and also the men who influenced or coerced them), disappeared from these discussions.

Their specific conclusions aside, British investigators were asking these Brahmins to do something that had never been done before, namely to create a uniform, unambiguous set of religious "scriptures" on the model of Christendom. In the past, local Hindu thinkers had drawn upon different passages in different texts depending on the contexts and aims of a particular discussion. Beyond that, the Western principle of contradiction (a thing cannot simultaneously be and not be) was antithetical to Indian ideas of non-dualism—the view that dualistic contradictions (e.g., good and evil) are only apparent, not real. Now Hindus had to design something more like a Christian catechism: a standardized body of texts that would be uniform, knowable, and stable—not flexible. One group of Brahmin leaders agreed to support this approach by editing and changing the religious canon, not least because it brought them new power and influence; they thus acquired the ability to define Hindu scriptural truth. They agreed with the British that sati was alien to "true" Hindu practice, and they too depicted widow-burning as a recent, foreign corruption that should be banned. Where there had been no single Indian outlook or set of Hindu religious beliefs and practices, British intervention in this case defined one. Arguably, such collaborations of British and Brahmin authorities even helped to create "Hinduism," using Western models of a single core religious faith. Colonial authorities saw their actions as justified, both according to European morals and by purifying and protecting Indian tradition. The result, though, was a different India: one with a freshly textualized brand of Hindu religious practice, and with the co-optation of prominent Brahmins as allies, newly empowered to assert these claims to spiritual authority.

As this episode shows, colonizing India was a matter of spectacle as well as brute force, of vocabularies as much as arms, of finding allies as much as using physical coercion. Victoria certainly built a powerful practical empire in India after 1857; for more than two centuries Britain exerted enormous influence on virtually all areas of

South Asian economic, political, and cultural life. Perhaps especially under the Raj, India was exploited for London's benefit, and it was treated as a pawn in wider military and political struggles. India's integration into a global economic system—in a position of colonial subordination—left a lasting impact. Yet in order to function the Raj also needed local allies, men and women like these Brahmins, who participated in the British order for their own reasons. England's viceroys and colonial authorities could never rule through physical force alone, and Indian men and women also exerted a strong influence on the empire's policies, priorities, and personnel. Ultimately South Asians left a strong imprint on the rest of the empire, and even on the metropolitan center itself.

For their part, British officials continued to insist after 1857 that they were working for the benefit of India: building highways, railroads, canals, and telegraphs to enable rapid travel and communications, and to guarantee food security during droughts; establishing a productive agricultural system to bring prosperity to farmers by focusing on cash crops for export; protecting individual property rights and the rule of law; educating millions of young Indians in ideas of liberal democracy and market capitalism; and protecting the country's borders from the depredations of neighbors and other European powers. In the words of Sir John Strachey and his brother, Lieutenant-General Richard Strachey, all of this work had "increased to an extent absolutely incalculable the wealth and comfort of the people of India."[8]

The colonial system used in India had an enormous impact on British thinking about empire, as South Asian policies, precedents, and personnel filtered out into the world. Military incursions by British forces into Afghanistan and Egypt—and the construction and control of the Suez Canal—were heavily influenced by India's perceived security needs. British diplomats and soldiers built careers by shuttling from one part of the empire to another; many first learned the techniques of colonial power in India. One army officer, Tristram Speedy, started his career in the 1850s as a lieutenant in India before moving to Africa, where he fought in Ethiopia, before moving to New Zealand for the Maori wars. He then returned to Africa and again to India, leaving in 1871 to become police superintendent in the

---

[8]Sir John Strachey and Lt.-Gen. Richard Strachey, *The Finances and Public Works of India from 1869 to 1881* (London, 1882), 8.

Far Eastern port of Penang, in the colony of Malaya. Soon finding an imminent threat of armed resistance to British rule, he returned once more to India to recruit a force of Sikhs to serve as colonial police in British Malaya. Other Britons recruited Indian civil servants and traders to administer British territories from Hong Kong to Kenya, so thousands more South Asians joined the diaspora. Sometimes, too, the transmission belt ran in the other direction, as British officials brought other colonial experiences to India. Charles Trevelyan, for example, had served as permanent secretary to the Treasury during Ireland's potato famine and Great Hunger of the late 1840s, making his reputation by defending the untrammeled operation of free markets rather than providing relief for the hungry. He was appointed governor of the Indian province of Madras, and became finance minister for India in the 1860s—helping shape the colonial structures that exported large amounts of grain from India during deep famines that killed millions of Indians later in the century.

In addition to personnel, many colonial administrative and legal practices originated in India and then circulated to other territories. The political system of leaving local princes nominally in control, albeit under the supervision of an English "resident" (an approach that created huge problems in areas such as Kashmir when British imperial rule finally ended in 1947), was transferred to Southeast Asia. After fierce debate in the early 1870s, too, the Straits Settlements of Malaya, Singapore, and Penang adopted a new penal code and criminal procedures directly from India—rather than borrowing from English law. Part of the rationale was that Southeast Asia, like India, was said to resemble feudal rather than contemporary Europe. As a senior British civil servant put it, living in Malaya was "to live in Europe of the thirteenth century." Another pointed out that "The Malays, like every other rude Eastern nation, require to be treated much like children, and to be taught; and this especially in all matters of improvement."[9] A similar approach characterized imperial policy in British Africa, where Indian-style courts and legal codes governed Kenya and Zanzibar for the first half-century of British colonial rule, from the 1880s to 1930s. Until 1904, in fact, legal appeals from East Africa were sent directly to a high court in Bombay, not London.

---

[9]Both phrases are quoted by Thomas Metcalf, "Empire Recentered," in Gregory Blue et al., eds., *Colonialism and the Modern World* (Armonk, NY, 2002), 29–30.

This widespread use of Indian practices relied on the justification that in South Asia they had created peace and prosperity for Britain's colonial subjects, and also secured the empire's borders and thus safeguarded London's global interests. Yet in reality, under the Raj prosperity remained elusive for most South Asians. India's per capita income remained stagnant at best during the 200 years of British colonial control. By some estimates, indeed, Indians' life expectancy declined by as much as 22 percent between 1880 and 1910, at the very height of the Victorian Empire. Many of India's problems arose from the poverty created by its marginal position in an imperial economic system centered on London. Colonial officials encouraged Indian farmers to produce goods—cotton, wheat, indigo, opium—to be sold for cash on international markets. But in most cases, India served as a reserve producer for Britain, guaranteeing a steady supply to London if, say, American exports of cotton disappeared (as happened during the US Civil War). This meant that Indian farmers did not drive the market, but were subject to wild swings in commodity prices when, for example, wheat harvests soared in Canada and Argentina in the 1890s. And while India earned a profit on its exports to the rest of the world (it sent huge quantities of opium to China starting in the early nineteenth century), Britain turned around and forced it to pay high "home charges" for the administrative costs of running an empire—thereby balancing its own trade deficit with India's surplus.

The outcome was that many Indian peasants started planting cash crops for sale rather than growing food for themselves and their neighbors, yet usually wound up poorer. With the earlier changes in land ownership practices and newly rigid forms of tax collection, moreover, rural villages no longer had the support networks that had woven local society together. Poor farmers now faced grain merchants and moneylenders who saw them more as adversaries than neighbors. To make things worse, many new crops placed additional burdens on the environment—cotton is renowned for draining nutrients from the soil—which increased the rate of land depletion and accelerated the desperation of ordinary farmers to move elsewhere. Yet they could not readily move or expand their acreage, as colonial authorities were simultaneously applying another model drawn from the English past, that of **enclosure**. The state "enclosed," under private or state ownership, land and other resources that had previously been held in common, such as fields for grazing, wells for water, and vast forests for fodder and fuel. By forcing poor farmers to pay to use resources that previously had been free, this new system pushed peasants into deep debt and left many as sharecroppers.

Meanwhile the colonial government put most of its tax revenues—raised from agricultural levies—into military defense. British governors focused especially on efforts to fortify the northwestern frontier, where authorities feared a Russian invasion through Afghanistan, and also on the construction of thousands of miles of railways to improve transportation networks. Such work clearly served the state's needs first, enabling soldiers to be sent quickly to trouble spots and expediting exports to Britain and other international markets. It was less clear how this investment helped most Indians. Far less effort went into education and general public-welfare projects. Most obviously, the elaborate and very effective irrigation network that had been built and expanded under the Mughals was first neglected by the EIC, and after 1857 it decayed farther. When Victoria became empress, this system was near collapse, as millions of acres of previously irrigated land could no longer be planted.

The timing of this neglect could not have been worse, since, as already noted, a major drought struck north-central India shortly before the Durbar of 1877. As this drought grew into famine, the structures and ideologies of British colonial power proved as ineffective as the profit-driven approach of the EIC a century earlier. Following a poor English harvest in 1876, most of India's surplus grain had already been sent to Britain. The government's new rail and telegraph networks had nonetheless been intended to guarantee Indian food security by preventing any localized shortages from leading to starvation. Yet as the historian Mike Davis has shown, these information networks instead spread the news of drought very efficiently. In response, food prices quickly skyrocketed throughout the country, meaning that peasants, even in well-watered areas, could not afford to eat. In combination with ideological factors—specifically, the belief among colonial officials that market mechanisms should be allowed to work, and their fear that state-funded relief efforts risked creating a precedent of British responsibility for feeding two hundred and fifty million Indians—this price spike created the conditions for mass starvation.

The viceroy, Lord Lytton, continued to focus his attention on the Russian military threat in the north. He put a subordinate, Sir Richard Temple, in charge of famine response. Temple had organized another, generally effective famine relief effort in India only three years earlier; but his work in that case had been criticized in government circles as being "wasteful" of state resources. Hence, after 1876 Temple made relief as onerous as possible, allocating only tiny portions of food to the hungry, and usually requiring recipients to provide hard labor to eat. "Everything must be subordinated," he said, "to the financial consideration of disbursing the smallest sum of money consistent with the preservation of human life."[10] (Take a look again at Figure 1.1.) Of the approximately sixty million Indians affected by famine between 1876 and 1879, only about one million received any relief. Millions emigrated overseas as indentured servants, accelerating the formation of an Indian diaspora (and putting downward pressures on wages in other world regions). Moreover, India continued to export grain to international markets, despite the fact that by 1880 between six and ten million Indians had starved to death—followed by another six to eight million who died in a second wave of famine between 1896 and 1902.

The structural and cultural changes that occurred under colonial rule help explain how such horrific episodes could occur both under the EIC in the 1770s and again under the British state in the 1870s and 1890s. Yet as these colonial cataclysms reflect imperial ideologies, colonial priorities, and wider economic and social structures, they also provide a window to observe indigenous responses and tactics. This lesson is apparent if we consider yet another case of mass mortality that afflicted colonial India—an outbreak of bubonic plague in 1896 that spread from Hong Kong to India. Over the next quarter-century perhaps twelve million South Asians died from the disease, in addition to those who succumbed to the second wave of famine.[11] The turn of the twentieth century thus presents another colonial crisis of mortality—one that shows with great clarity both how the imperial state worked and how Indian citizens responded.

When the plague reached India in 1896, colonial authorities immediately launched a wide-ranging public health campaign to fight it. The government granted itself sweeping powers: to stop and

---

[10]Quoted by Davis, *Late Victorian Holocausts*, 39, who discusses this famine in great detail.

[11]John Aberth's book on disease, *The First Horseman* (2006), part of this *Connections* series, deals with this epidemic as one of its case studies.

segregate those suspected of being ill; to destroy personal property and demolish buildings if these were possibly infested; to stop trains and inspect travelers; and even to ban all population movements, popular gatherings, markets, fairs, or religious pilgrimages. These restrictions—which from the British point of view merely served the dispassionate, scientific interests of public health and safety—applied indiscriminately across caste and religious lines. Indigenous political leaders were ignored, or criticized for failing to support public-health measures. Often these local leaders were asked only to serve as translators for military search parties that scoured houses for corpses (many refused, often for reasons related to caste prohibitions). This lack of sensitivity to Indian beliefs and customs, and the arrogance of colonial doctors who saw no need to explain themselves, created a backlash. Many Indians resisted British ideas about how best to fight disease. Men refused to enter colonial hospitals, where they feared pollution by exposure to bodily fluids and lower-caste Hindus; women refused to submit to medical inspections, which violated basic norms of female seclusion, or **purdah**. Rather than observe new burial requirements, local men and women often hid the corpses of plague victims. Wild rumors spread, alleging that British doctors and hospitals intended to seize and poison Indians, or to extract an oil of their life-force (known as *momiai*), in a desperate attempt to forestall the imminent collapse of British rule and the total catastrophe that would ensue.

Such responses complicated the work of medical professionals and colonial officials. Massive riots in Bombay, Jawalpur, Calcutta, and other cities, along with passive resistance nearly everywhere, aimed to force a change in British tactics. Anonymous letters sent to the authorities suggested that another rebellion like 1857 was looming. Moreover, the anti-plague measures had not even been tried in the Muslim northern provinces, where the local British governor judged the danger of "popular discontent and tumult" in response to be riskier than simply letting the plague run rampant.[12] In the end, popular unrest succeeded in forcing medical compromises from the Raj. By 1898, the most intrusive public health measures had been reined back. The viceroy reduced military inspections of homes

---

[12]This quotation, and those in the next two paragraphs, are all from David Arnold, "Touching the Body," in Ranajit Guha and Gayatri Spivak, eds., *Selected Subaltern Studies* (New York, 1988), 391–426.

and corpses, ended compulsory hospitalization, and circumscribed attempts to change funerary practices.

All of these concessions helped. But much as higher-class Brahmins had cooperated with the abolition of sati in the 1820s, these anti-plague efforts found success only when British officials sought out local allies. By 1909, a government manual in Punjab summarized the two cardinal rules of public health. First, there "must be...no pressure or compulsion, in any shape or form...brought to bear on the people." Second, the "cooperation of the people and the active assistance of their leaders is...not merely a political desideratum, but an absolute necessity." The ultimate success of public-health efforts came more from the decision to rely not on British troops but on local notables—the "leading men" of Indian society—who for their own reasons were willing to persuade other Indians to observe the remaining health measures. The British state had to abandon its use of force to control Indian society, and to rely on indigenous groups who increasingly shaped local society and politics as they liked. As a result, later anti-plague campaigns faced nothing like the earlier resistance—because they took the form of Indians protecting Indians.

This shift brought a new class of Western-educated Indian professionals to prominence—men like Bal Gangadhar Tilak, who organized indigenous anti-plague efforts in Pune. Educated in English schools, Tilak was nevertheless sympathetic to the Hindu nationalist movement. (Later, in 1913, he established the Indian Home Rule League.) When plague reached Pune, he called for a "judicious combination" of Indian and Western medical systems—but under Indian leadership. Leaders like Tilak used the authority that came from both their Western training and their local status, attaining positions of power and influence that were possible only in such a colonial order. They then asserted this power both against the British and over the larger mass of Indians, whom some of them denigrated as "ignorant rustics" given to superstition and dirty habits. As the historian David Arnold has shown, these colonial public-health campaigns thus especially served the interests of a new Indian elite by giving it power over most of the population.

The growth of this hybrid elite—and its connections with both Western institutions and diasporic communities outside India— played a crucial role in shaping the nationalist movements that ultimately won Indian independence in 1947. Members of this educated elite helped invent yet another tradition: the apparently basic idea that "India" should be properly a single political unit, a modern national state made up of one Indian people. Although Hindu culture played a role in defining this national community, the idea of a unitary nation encompassed a dizzying variety of religious, ethnic, linguistic, and political groups in South Asia and gave them a basis on which to act against foreign (British) rule. Educated Indians formed politically focused organizations directed against the Raj. The Indian National Congress, established in 1885, was a political party that first dedicated itself to working within the colonial system for constitutional change. Others chose more direct paths to resistance. After 1900 activists organized Swadeshi circles, which focused on economic boycotts of foreign goods. The Swadeshi movement (from the word for "homeland") encouraged Indians to "buy Indian" and not to participate in the British colonial economy. This movement gathered momentum when the viceroy decided in 1905 to partition Bengal, dividing it into separate Muslim and Hindu areas and thus threatening the goal of Indian unity. Militant (especially Hindu) nationalists responded with a wave of violent attacks on British officials and outposts, while Muslims reacted by organizing their own action leagues, political parties, and religious associations (*anjumans*). The tumult provoked a harsh crackdown by colonial authorities—yet it also succeeded, in 1911, in forcing them to revoke the partition of Bengal.

The nationalist movement remained divided among these groups, but one leader emerged during the early twentieth century to play a particularly important role. The young lawyer Mohandas (Mahatma) Gandhi returned to India in 1915 after twenty-five years overseas. Educated in England, he had spent years living in South Africa, where he worked in the province of Natal as an advocate for immigrant laborers, many of them Indian. While lobbying for reforms in Africa he formulated his signature idea of *satyagraha* ("holding to truth," or using the force of one's soul to alter that of another—a notion that shaped his political campaigns of nonviolent action and civil disobedience). After returning to India, Gandhi expanded the Indian National Congress beyond a small English-educated elite, and reached agreement with Muslim leaders such as Muhammad Ali Jinnah (later revered as the founder of Pakistan) to form a more united front against the British. While radical socialist and Hindu groups called for different tactics and policies, during the 1920s and 1930s Gandhi's multifaceted effort to build Indian *swaraj* (self-rule) remained the key strategy of Indian nationalism.

Gandhi's approach was shaped by his personal experiences in the wider empire, and by his (and his colleagues') view of India's colonial position. He argued, for example, that it was immoral to ship Indian indentured laborers around the world, and organized Congress efforts to force an end to the practice. He also agreed with the analysis of Swadeshi activists that Indians should not buy British goods—especially not the kinds of foreign fabrics that had destroyed the Bengali economy. Gandhi was repeatedly photographed weaving his own homespun clothing, the wearing of which became an anti-colonial and nationalist symbol. Then when British authorities refused to reduce taxes during the Great Depression on necessities like salt, Gandhi organized marches and civil disobedience protests that inspired thousands of Indians not to pay, and encouraged them to withdraw wherever possible from interactions with the British state.

In the face of near-universal resistance, British officials slowly made concessions—expanding the right to vote to 3 percent of the Indian population in 1919, and to 10 percent in 1935. The momentum, however slow and halting, was clear. In 1936, colonial authorities accepted the inevitability of Indian self-government, and the following year recognized local elected assemblies and an Indian parliament. The indigenous colonial elite—with leaders like Gandhi and his Cambridge-educated colleague Jawaharlal Nehru—had shown itself able to speak effectively to both colonial and metropolitan audiences. Gandhi's personal example of resistance succeeded in generating sharp criticism of the British government, both in India and in England. Leaders like Gandhi, Nehru, and Jinnah also inspired Western anti-imperialists, forcing Britain's government to defend its policies to its own voters. As we shall see, this example held implications for other European empires and colonized populations in Asia, Africa, and elsewhere.

Indian nationalism stretched beyond Gandhi's call to nonviolent disobedience—since Indians, like any other people, followed complex internal dynamics and disputes. One obvious division, made deeper by British actions such as the partitioning of Bengal, fell along the religious lines between Hindus, Sikhs, and Muslims. Others corresponded to deep social differences of class (wealth), region, education, and urban or rural location. Yet by the 1930s, nearly all politically active Indians agreed on the central issue of independence, and different communal and religious groups cooperated to reach this core goal—even as their tactical choices varied widely. In 1929, one leading activist, the Sikh socialist Bhagat Singh, threw a bomb inside the Imperial Legislative Assembly in New Delhi. No one was hurt, intentionally—investigators concluded the bomb had been too small, and it was thrown away from any people. The message, though, was clear: in Singh's words, "It takes a loud voice to make the deaf hear."[13] (His execution in 1931—Indian nationalists call it a "martyrdom"—is recalled in a document below.) Subash Chandra Bose also disagreed with Gandhi over the priority of nonviolence, and he organized an army during the Second World War to fight the Raj: the Indian National Army (INA), or Azad Hind Fauj. In 1944 he famously told his supporters, "Give me blood, and I promise you freedom."[14] The decision to pursue military action drove Bose to make common cause with Britain's other enemies, especially Japan. The INA was comprised largely of Indian prisoners of war (who had been captured by Japan); they fought alongside the Japanese Imperial Army against British forces in Burma and Southeast Asia.

The full range of anti-colonial pressures forced Britain, weakened badly during the global war of 1939–1945, finally to withdraw from India. Victoria's empire thus ended—and independence came for South Asians—in August 1947. Elements of empire, though, left a deep mark. Once it became clear that Britain would leave, many of the tactical anti-colonial alliances came to an end. Social divisions—deepened by years of colonial power—shaped a vicious struggle for territory, resources, and population. The British Parliament approved dividing South Asia into two countries, along religious lines, so a commission drew lines on a map to partition "India" (for Hindus and Sikhs) and "Pakistan" (for Muslims). The complications of separating these intermingled populations, though, were huge. It did not work to divide provinces (as was tried in Bengal and Punjab), and the process immediately stranded millions of people in the "wrong" country (Hindus living in Sindh found themselves now residents of Pakistan; Muslims living in Kashmir learned that their Maharajah had agreed to join his principality to India). Riots broke out, and millions migrated across the new

---

[13]Bhagat Singh and D. N. Gupta (ed.), *Bhagat Singh, Select Speeches and Writings* (New Delhi, 2007), 12. The phrase quotes Auguste Valliant, an anarchist who bombed the French Chamber of Deputies in 1893.

[14]Subhas Chandra Bose and P. D. Saggi, *A Nation's Homage* (Bombay, 1954), 87.

borders, seeking safety in numbers. The Indian and Pakistani armies joined in, seeking the most possible for each side. Roughly 500,000 people died during this bitter struggle over partition. And grievances continue to rankle, with serious, ongoing consequences for regional (and global) security. Since 1947, Pakistan and India have gone to war four times over the terms of this colonial settlement. Three times they have fought over the disputed territory of Kashmir; a fourth war, in 1971, erupted when the geographically separate area of East Pakistan broke away, with Indian help, to form the country of Bangladesh.

British colonial power clearly reshaped India. It is easy to find physical manifestations of British influence, as in the self-consciously European architecture of Bombay's train station and university (see Figure 1.3). Yet cultural mixings are complex, and influences always run in multiple directions. Two centuries of imperial contact also fundamentally changed Britain, and today South Asians also have a major (and growing) presence in the United Kingdom. Native-born

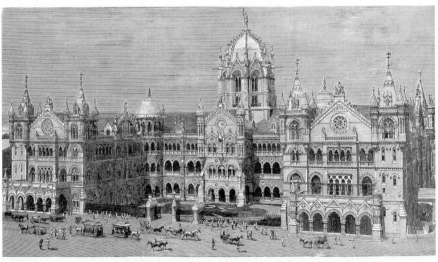

GREAT INDIAN PENINSULAR RAILWAY VICTORIA TERMINUS AND ADMINISTRATIVE OFFICES, BOMBAY
RECENTLY COMPLETED

FIGURE 1.3 Victoria Terminus, Bombay. Completed in 1887 to celebrate Queen Victoria's Silver Jubilee, the central train station in Bombay was designed by a British architect, Frederick Stevens, who took his inspiration from St. Pancras Station in London. Built in the "Indo-Saracenic" style—full of spires, turrets, and pointed arches—the station also features a huge octagonal stone dome, topped with a figurine of "Progress." Stevens included Indian elements, using South Asian palace floor plans and decorative elements (sculpture, railings, carvings). Victoria's name was dropped from the building in 1996, when the station was renamed in honor of Chhatrapat Shivaji, a seventeenth-century Maratha king.

Indians, Pakistanis, and Bangladeshis continue to arrive: census figures from 2006 found 339,000 South Asians living in London alone—by far the largest immigrant group in the British capital city. And joining the wider world of **Anglophone** (English-speaking) culture has changed the ways many South Asians think and express themselves. Today South Asian writers play a major role in English literature (from Indian natives like Salman Rushdie, Arundhati Roy, and Vikram Seth, to South Asian expatriates such as V. S. Naipaul, who was born in Trinidad, Jhumpa Lahiri, who lives in the United States, or Monica Ali, who moved at age three from Bangladesh to London).

South Asia served as an incubator for British political practices and ideas about empire, but it served too as a source of artistic inspiration, and a point of departure for creative expression. Brighton's Royal Pavilion, rebuilt between 1815 and 1823 in a phantasmagoric but Indian-derived style, may be the best architectural example (see Figure 1.4). But from Rudyard Kipling to George Orwell, a number of

FIGURE 1.4   Royal Pavilion, Brighton. Built for the future King George IV, this residence also appears in the "Indo-Saracenic" style. Constructed, starting in the 1780s, as a health retreat (initially in neoclassical style), it later changed appearance completely, first with the addition of a stable complex and then an expansion and restyling of the residential quarters. The latter redesign, carried out by the English architect John Nash, added a fanciful Indian-inspired exterior, full of domes and minarets (supported by a cast iron framework over the old building), and an elaborate chinoiserie interior—shaped by Chinese and Islamic, as well as Indian, motifs.

British authors made their careers—and set many of their best-known works—in India. Starting in the 1700s, South Asian fashions and foods swept through Britain, and Indian arts such as miniature paintings found an eager market. English aristocrats enthusiastically adopted the Indian sport of polo, which they encountered while on colonial postings in South Asia. And English adaptations of Indian cuisine—from curries to Mulligatawny soup—appeared in British cookbooks from the late eighteenth century on. They swept to commercial success in England during the Raj, and today "curries," as a synonym for "fast-food outlet," are present in virtually every British town. Moreover, such establishments do not serve only the 5 percent of Britain's population that is directly of South Asian ancestry. One recent survey found that chicken tikka masala—a dish that does not even exist in India, having been invented in England, for the British palate, by expatriate South Asian restaurateurs—has now surpassed fish and chips as the most popular choice among British consumers for the title of "Britain's national dish."

SOURCES

■ Remaking an Empire: Culture, Reform, and the East India Company (1829–1835)

British and EIC officials took an active role in matters of South Asian culture. They investigated and then, in December 1829, abolished sati. They built new colonial schools. Parliament also restricted slavery in India in 1833, the same year it legally abolished the practice in most other British colonies.[15] The passages below address two key cultural issues. William Bentinck, governor-general of Bengal (and after 1833, governor-general of India), first urges his executive council, comprised of three Britons, to abolish sati. Thomas Macaulay, a well-known British essayist and politician, then expresses his views on Indian education—first in a speech to Parliament, and later, following his move in 1834 to India (where he became the first non-voting "law member" of the Executive Council), in a policy memo to Bentinck.

[15]This change took phased effect in British colonies, starting in 1834. Slavery became illegal in EIC territories, including India, a decade later, in 1843.

What were the motivations—both practical and theoretical—behind these cultural efforts? How far did they (or could they) change India? How did they fit into wider British thinking about what an empire should do? What may we conclude about these writers' self-conceptions? How would their ideas appear to most Indians? Lastly, think about their audience: whom do the speakers address? Why do they insist they are acting selflessly, and in the interests of the local (Indian) population?

Bentinck, minute to the Executive Council, November 1829: I have now to submit for the consideration of Council the draft of a regulation enacting the abolition of satis....

The first and primary object of my heart is the benefit of the Hindus. I know nothing so important to the improvement of their future condition as the establishment of a purer morality, whatever their belief, and a more just conception of the will of God. The first step to this better understanding will be dissociation of religious belief and practice from blood and murder. They will then, when no longer under this brutalizing excitement, view with more calmness acknowledged truths. They will see that there can be no inconsistency in the ways of Providence, that to the command received as divine by all races of men, "No innocent blood shall be spilt," there can be no exception; and when they shall have been convinced of the error of this first and most criminal of their customs, may it not be hoped that others, which stand in the way of their improvement, may likewise pass away, and that, thus emancipated from those chains and shackles upon their minds and actions, they may no longer continue, as they have done, the slaves of every foreign conqueror, but that they may assume their first places among the great families of mankind? I disown in these remarks, or in this measure, any view whatever to conversion to our own faith. I write and feel as a legislator for the Hindus, and as I believe many enlightened Hindus think and feel.

Descending from these higher considerations, it cannot be a dishonest ambition that the Government of which I form a part should have the credit of an act which is to wash out a foul stain upon British rule, and to stay the sacrifice of humanity and justice to a doubtful expediency; and finally, as a branch of the general administration of the Empire, I may be permitted to feel deeply anxious that our course shall be in accordance with the noble example set to us by the British Government at home, and that the adaptation, when practicable to the circumstances of this vast Indian population, of the same enlightened principles, may promote here as well as there the general prosperity, and may exalt the character of our nation.

Source: Arthur Keith, ed., "Lord William Bentinck on the Suppression of Sati, 8 November 1829," in *Speeches and Documents on Indian Policy 1750–1921* (London: H. Milford, Oxford University Press, 1922), 223, 225–226.

Macaulay, speech to the House of Commons, 1833: It is scarcely possible to calculate the benefits which we might derive from the diffusion of European civilization among the vast population of the East. It would be, on the most selfish view of the case, far better for us that the people of India were well governed and independent of us, than ill governed and subject to us; that they were ruled by their own kings, but wearing our broadcloth, and working with our cutlery, than that they were per- forming their salams to English collectors and English magistrates, but were too ignorant to value, or too poor to buy, English manufactures. To trade with civilized men is infinitely more profitable than to govern savages. That would, indeed, be a doting wisdom, which, in order that India might remain a dependency, would make it a useless and costly dependency, which would keep a hundred millions of men from being our customers in order that they might continue to be our slaves.

Macaulay, minute to Bentinck, 1835: All parties seem to be agreed on one point, that the dialects commonly spoken among the natives of this part of India, contain neither literary nor scientific information, and are, moreover, so poor and rude that, until they are enriched from some other quarter, it will not be easy to translate any valuable work into them. It seems to be admitted on all sides, that the intellectual improvement of those classes of the people who have the means of pursuing higher studies can at present be effected only by means of some language not vernacular amongst them.

What then shall that language be? One-half of the Committee maintain that it should be the English. The other half strongly recommend the Arabic and Sanskrit. The whole question seems to me to be, which language is the best worth knowing?

I have no knowledge of either Sanskrit or Arabic—But I have done what I could to form a correct estimate of their value. I have read translations of the most celebrated Arabic and Sanskrit works. I have conversed both here and at home with men distinguished by their proficiency in the Eastern tongues. I am quite ready to take the Oriental learning at the valuation of the Orientalists themselves. I have never found one among them who could deny that a single shelf of a good

European library was worth the whole native literature of India and Arabia....

How, then, stands the case? We have to educate a people who cannot at present be educated by means of their mother-tongue. We must teach them some foreign language. The claims of our own language it is hardly necessary to recapitulate. It stands preeminent even among the languages of the west. It abounds with works of imagination not inferior to the noblest which Greece has bequeathed to us; with models of every species of eloquence; with historical compositions, which, considered merely as narratives, have seldom been surpassed, and which, considered as vehicles of ethical and political instruction, have never been equaled; with just and lively representations of human life and human nature; with the most profound speculations on metaphysics, morals, government, jurisprudence, and trade; with full and correct information respecting every experimental science which tends to preserve the health, to increase the comfort, or to expand the intellect of man. Whoever knows that language has ready access to all the vast intellectual wealth, which all the wisest nations of the earth have created and hoarded in the course of ninety generations. It may safely be said, that the literature now extant in that language is of far greater value than all the literature which three hundred years ago was extant in all the languages of the world together. Nor is this all. In India, English is the language spoken by the ruling class. It is spoken by the higher class of natives at the seats of Government. It is likely to become the language of commerce throughout the seas of the East. It is the language of two great European communities which are rising, the one in the south of Africa, the other in Australasia; communities which are every year becoming more important, and more closely connected with our Indian empire. Whether we look at the intrinsic value of our literature, or at the particular situation of this country, we shall see the strongest reason to think that, of all foreign tongues, the English tongue is that which would be the most useful to our native subjects.

Source: George Young, ed., *Macaulay, Prose and Poetry* (Cambridge, MA: Harvard University Press, 1952), 717, 721–723.

■ Anti-Imperial Critique: Victorian Empire through Indian Eyes (1886)

In the 1880s an Indian observer, Amrita Lal Roy, wrote an extended analysis of the British Raj for the *North American Review*, a popular US magazine. Roy grew up in Calcutta, before leaving to study medicine in Edinburgh. He left Scotland before graduating, though, and spent time in New York, where he was based while writing this article. He worked as a compositor and printer (and gave public talks critical of British imperial rule) before he returned to India. He then edited *Hindoo*, an English-language magazine published in Calcutta.

What are Roy's main lines of criticism? What does he see as the motivations for British power? How does Roy judge the kinds of cultural programs discussed by Bentinck and Macaulay? How does the colonial economy function? What kinds of officials are sent to India? What can you surmise about Roy's own class background? Why did he address this essay to an American audience?

There is a string of phrases about the English occupation of India which the genius of the English people has stereotyped into a cant. Security from foreign aggression, domestic peace, suppression of dangerous rites, protection for women and children, equality of all classes before the law, diffused education and extended commerce, railways and public works, and other benefits of the undefined entity called "civilization," introduced by a "superior" to an "inferior" race (whatever those words may mean); these are said to be the many blessings of English rule in that country. It is taken for granted in a general way that Englishmen saved India from anarchy and ruin, and gave her order and the beginnings of civilized life. A great many good people, on both sides of the Atlantic, who get their knowledge from the usual sources, honestly believe that she is very much better off with her present rule than she otherwise would be.

But the truth is this: India has given to England wealth and fame; England has brought upon India penury and shame. Instead of being a means of civilization, English rule in India is almost an excuse to keep up barbarism in the nineteenth century.... Instead of raising, it is degrading the people. The goods coming from it are at present remote and negative, while its immediate effects have been simply disastrous. The fiction of "England's mission" and "India's progress" is kept up by the agents of three interested industries—the military, mercantile, and missionary—aided by the cooperative journalism, in behalf of privilege and power....Distance and difference of language increase the difficulty of Indian thought and feeling on the question being known to the Western public. If I mistake not, this is the first time that...a native of India gives his version of her story in a publication of standing....

Never within the records of history have there been such widespread poverty and misery in India as her unfortunate people have had to bear since the planting of the English flag. Every walk of life has been gradually usurped by a grasping monopoly whose boast is that they are not of the people. The children of the soil are to-day, virtually, serfs, working away their lives for a scanty board. Free imports, which have enriched English capitalists, have killed the manufacturers of the country, maimed its industry, and made its trade pass into foreign hands, and the people have to look to Europe for the merest necessaries of life. As if this was not enough to keep down the wealth of the country, it is further exhausted by an increasing annual drain, now over £40,000,000, in the shape of exports, for which there are no corresponding imports.... Any signs of life in the country can be seen now in the seaports and a few centers of government alone, but the interior everywhere presents only ruins and destitution. The ruined industries have thrown increasing numbers upon an impoverished soil, only to struggle until nature fails, when they lay themselves down to die. Forty millions of the peasantry, or fully one-fifth of the subjects of the "Empress of India," are, on the telling of the official statistician, in a state of chronic starvation. To these even one meal of coarse grain in a day is a precarious luxury. The extravagance of the Government, its indifference to the needs and sufferings of the people and its oppressive taxes, have induced famine after famine, at the rate of one in every five or six years. Ten millions, by the official returns, have died of acute famine in the last twenty-five years, but in reality twice the figure would not very much overstate the fact. The national debt has steadily increased, is now near £250,000,000, while fully eighty percent of the people are more or less in the hands of the money-lender. Every means of raising money has been tried: free-trade England preaching to all the world untaxed bread as the first necessity of civilization, taxes India's native salt from 1500 to 2000 per cent. on its cost value; Christian England, sending missionaries to every corner of the globe, is compelled to eke out her Indian revenues by utilizing the opium habit of China; yet the average annual deficit of the Indian Government has for the last seventy years amounted to £1,000,000.... India is in pawn, and her people on the verge of bankruptcy....

The pretense that native anarchy and misrule made the "conquest" of India not merely a blessing, but a necessity, is false. It was the English themselves, who, by their artifices, prolonged and aggravated the native anarchy which they offer as an excuse for their own misrule....

If the English connection has been the means of removing a few social evils which grew, here and there, during a period of suspended vitality and temporary disorganization of the Indian nation, it has demoralized them wholesale, paralyzed their resources, reduced them to helplessness, tied them round with the red tape of a galling officialism, and flung them into the dungeon of pauperism, to be constantly jeered and insulted by their unsympathetic jailers. The process of healing a sore or extracting a tumor by killing the patient is bad surgery.... *Suttee* [sati] burning and self-immolation of devotees were never extensive practices in India, and attained their greatest limits during the early days of English rule, when the old authorities of the people had lost power, and the new rulers were too busy in removing the good things out of the country to give thought to its internal condition....

Book education, railways, civilization, a new life, and even a religious awakening, are not goods in themselves. To India, particularly, they have hitherto given nothing but a hope. The direct effects of each are evil. Indian railways today represent profits on foreign capital—often first made in India—native exhaustion, and the rule of militaryism. Many of them were built to facilitate the movement of troops. They have exported thousands of tons of grain from centers of starvation to centers of a trumped-up war.... Education has made those who are receiving it keenly alive to the miseries and indignities of their condition; open to insults from the ruling race by making them talk of "rights"; unhappy at having no other vent but sedition for their newly-awakened powers; while it haunts them with a sensation of one who discovers he has made a fool of himself. Of a new civilization we have got only the dregs; of a new religion, only an insufferable cant, and from the imported new life we have received only kicks....

And who are the gods manufactured to rule over us? Lads plucked from school, spoiled...and demoralized forever by a false success in early life. It is no exaggeration to say that the English schoolboy is a young savage. Compulsory Greek keeps him from study and hazing becomes his amusement. At an age when liberal studies should begin to expand his mind and social restraints should curb his egotism and form the heart, he is at once placed as a ruler over millions of men. Puffed up by fulsome eulogies of the prestige of his traditions and the greatness of his destiny, he begins to stalk with the air of a Caesar or a Napoleon, and can think only in the strain of *Veni, vidi, vici.* Comparing himself with the meanest and worst types of natives, with whom alone he comes in intimate contact, he fancies himself a veritable god. Restrained in education, with irresponsible license, he remains narrow in culture and his expression assumes a vapid dogmatism. Fully evolved, he is a curious compound of an overgrown schoolboy, an irresponsible savage, and a cynical philosopher....

There is a half truth in England's boast that she is the mother of free-dom. English liberty is a reaction against the English egotism which has made Englishmen the conquerors of nature and the oppressors of men. Freedom was born wherever England has been because the tyranny of English rulers is always the most unbearable.... It is for this tyranny that the Magna Charta was drawn and handed down from bleeding sire to son. It is against this tyranny that an English colony signed the Declaration of Independence in the blood of their own brothers of the cradle....

Come from a civilization of the past, ready to accept the civilization of the future, we have one appeal to make to the free citizens of this New World, whose life began in a protest against the oppression of which we today are the victims.... When the time comes for [Indians] to bring their case before the verdict of nations, let us hope that the American people, at least, will not let considerations of race, language, or commerce weigh against the eternal rights of man which they wrote in the Declaration of Independence.

Source: Amrita Lal Roy, "English Rule in India," *North American Review* 142:353 (April 1886), 356–358, 361–365, 368, 370.

■ The Beneficent Empire: British Images of Indian Famine (1897)

British officials responded vigorously to anti-imperialist critiques. During one of the largest famines ever to strike India, Sir Edwin Arnold attempted to explain—again in the pages of the *North American Review*—how this could happen on Britain's watch. Arnold was a well-known British poet and longtime editor-in-chief of the *Daily Telegraph*, then the world's largest-circulation newspaper. In his youth he spent several years in India—arriving as a 24-year-old teacher in 1856, shortly before the "Mutiny" against British rule, and staying through 1861. He learned to speak Hindi, Urdu, Sanskrit, Persian, and Turkish, along with several European languages. (He also moved to Japan late in life; a few months after this article was published, he married a Japanese woman who accompanied him back to London.) Arnold supported imperial expansion and exploration—under his leadership, the *Telegraph* funded Henry Stanley's voyage into Africa—and he wrote poetry inflected by, and meant to popularize, Indian literature and Hindu and Buddhist religion. He is now best known as the author of *The Light of Asia* (1879), a loose adaptation of the *Lalitavistara*, or life story of Siddharta Gautama, which he cites below.[16]

---

[16]Gautama, who lived around 400 BCE, is the key figure in Buddhism—a spiritual teacher who developed into the "The Buddha," or "awakened/enlightened one."

How does he address the economic, cultural, and political arguments made by Roy? What image emerges of India and Indians? How does Arnold characterize the role and motivation of British government, and how does he describe colonial officials? What is the orientation of India's economy, and how does this article explain the famine? What does Arnold's portrait imply about India's future? How do you think Indians would respond, and how would this essay resonate with an American audience?

I have gladly accepted a request to lay some of the chief facts regarding Indian famines, and the present visitation in particular, before the American public, that they may more justly judge the stupendous tasks undertaken by the Queen's government in India, the faithful spirit in which that government administers its prodigious charge, and some of the reasons why, without expecting any such complete success as is really impossible in saving the lives of the imperiled millions of our Indian fellow-subjects, American observers may perceive the sincere nobility of England's purpose, and may appreciate—nay, even admire—a self-imposed responsibility without parallel in the history of righteous and capable rule....

Neither have Western machinery nor scientific farming methods found any success [in India]. What can Sussex, or even Massachusetts, do with the husbandman who will insist on carrying a plough or a wheelbarrow upon his head, and whose fathers for 3,000 years past have stood upon a pointed stick drawn by a buffalo in order to make a two-inch furrow. The Hindu lives directly and placidly from the bountiful hand of Heaven, which he calls "Indra." Dwelling in his village he tills only so much of the culturable jungle as can be easily reached morning and evening by his slow-moving cattle. He has not the capital nor the mind for costly Western implements; and his winnowing-machine is still and always the wind blowing from Heaven....

[O]fficial documents in India have recognized the importance of the God of Rain, and the Queen's government alone, among all past and present rulers, has undertaken the daring, the extraordinary charge, to supply the shortcomings of Indra.... But ruling, as God knows we do, for the sake of the Indians first, and for revenue and reputation and power afterwards, the British in India have outdone all ancient works of artificial irrigation by such vast gifts to the land as the Ganges Canal, the East and West Jumna Canal, and those of the Bari Doab, of Agra, of the Lower Ganges, and the Soane, and the Sirhind. These cost tens of millions sterling and water millions of acres, otherwise arid, and far more quickly, too, than the bullock and the well, where the one leathern bucket, the mussak, asks six days to give to one acre its needful drink. Of course, where there is water there is always plenty. The Indian earth, lying red and yellow under the ever-fierce sun, demands but moisture to break into verdant foison, and the rich black soil of the Deccan will of itself hold water enough for every crop in ordinary years....

Her Majesty's government today, as before, adhere to the principle of "saving life by all the available means in its power." In accordance with such an unparalleled vow of duty, never accepted before in the annals of Empire, an all-embracing "Famine Department," has long been established, a "Famine Fund" has been instituted—officers of keen ability and devoted energy watch, inspect, enquire, and report constantly and ubiquitously, and the Indian people, so far as it knows or cares anything at all of politics, knows that the British Raj, as no conqueror, or power, or mighty Mahara ever previously attempted, this British Raj which keeps the *burra choop* for them—the "Great Peace"— and lets scrupulously alone their religions, their women, their liberties, and their property, stands also self-charged before Heaven with the resolve to rescue them from death and misery at cost, if needful, of the last rupee of the Sirkar's treasure chest, whensoever that wrath or indifference of Indra comes against it. The ancient governments offered little or no resistance, believing, indeed, that "the sky of brass and the soil of iron" was merely the Divine way of preventing the inhabitants of India from quite out-growing the productive capacity of their land.

You will hear in America echoes of those voices, ill-informed, egotistic, prejudiced, or positively treasonable and mischief-seeking, which say that India is unfairly taxed for army expenses, for home charges, and domestically. Do not believe this, until the true figures have been examined and compared with those of old times....Suffice it to remark [that]...the salt tax, so much clamored about, does not cost the individual peasant more than sevenpence a year, while the total fiscal burdens, producing thirty-seven millions sterling, may be set at four shillings per head....

Since, then, there lies no undue burden on these poor and gentle peasants; since India is naturally so fertile that, besides feeding her own two hundred and seventy millions she sends abroad in certain years thirty million hundredweight of grain and pulse, and twenty million hundredweight of rice; since Her Majesty's government stands openly bound to save her from famines at whatever imperial cost, how is it that we have failed in past visitations to rescue from perishing a terribly large number of people, and shall, too, probably witness the termination of this present dearth mournfully marked by another awful loss of innocent lives.... To answer this I must go deeper than all official documents, and explain some of the hidden social causes in India that render absolute victory... sadly impossible and never to be expected....

Starvation is essentially a slow disease the fatal crisis of which really arrives early, and oft-times unsuspected by the victim and his would-be helpers. The physical condition of the Hindu race is not a strong one. Lofty as those Buddhistic doctrines are, which Brahmanic India has adopted from *The Light of Asia*, about abstaining from the slaughter of animals, and from flesh-food, human bodies are all, I fear, imperfectly fitted by nature for an exclusively vegetable diet, which must, moreover, be consumed in large bulk to get adequate nourishment....

It must be mournfully added that the chronic insanitation of Indian towns and villages adds measureless perils to famine, weakening many who might have tided over a brief time of fasting to the finishing point of fate. British hygiene has done something for the cities in the way of pure water, civic regulations, medical dispensaries, and so forth. It might do more if properly supported by the sluggish native municipalities. But if the death rate of the Peninsula, even in ordinary seasons, were closely studied, it would be seen what a mere "bagatelle" the loss of even five million lives by famine is, contrasted with that "15 per thousand" which is the average *excess* rate of Indian mortality records over those of London or Boston. Nay, that Indian death rate often rises to 100 per 1,000, and the only medical solace is that the survivors must be protected by an inherited immunity. Graceful and picturesque and pastoral as must seem to the traveler that Hindu village existence, where all is so peaceful and so sunny, the sanitary expert shudders at what he sees—and smells—about the lively tank and around the gossiping well....

It will be seen in what a high and stern temper of honor and duty this British government in Calcutta sets itself to the periodical task of contending against nature for the vast multitudes of human life entrusted to it. And it will save lives by the million, while it perhaps loses—inevitably loses—so many millions for the reasons above displayed. But assuredly here is a spectacle of conscientious rule which effectually justifies our presence in India, which makes our Raj there a fact welcome to humanity and to civilization, and which may especially impart satisfaction to intelligent minds in the United States, since the credit of any such measure of success as these faithful Indian officials shall attain against odds so formidable belongs to the genius and to the energy of our common race.

Source: Edwin Arnold, "The Famine in India," *North American Review* 164:484 (March 1897), 257, 259–261, 263–265, 267–269, 272.

■ Colonial Subjects Look Back: Indian Memories of the Raj (1980s)

Zareer Masani, an Oxford-educated Indian scholar from Bombay, works as a producer at the British Broadcasting Company (BBC). In the mid-1980s BBC Radio sent him to travel through India interviewing elderly men and women about their experiences under British colonial rule. The first excerpt is from the reminiscences of Tara Ali Baig, a woman who grew up in a conservative area of Bengal. Her family belonged to the "new generation" of Indians, who had frequent contacts with colonial officials and held novel ideas about social questions, such as the proper role of women. The second excerpt is from an interview with Shiva Dua, the retired principal of a Delhi women's college and a former history teacher, who recounts her participation in the nationalist movement.

How do these women portray Indian views of British authority? How did British and Indian actors see one another, how did they measure status, and how did their priorities differ? What tactics were used to express political disagreement? Who had the power to control everyday social interactions? How does this compare with Roy's depiction of the 1880s? Why might these women reach different conclusions? How far do Indians seem to have united in their responses to colonial power? How might memories of the colonial period have shifted over the intervening forty years of independence, before Masani spoke with these women? Can you tell whether the recollections have been edited or influenced by others? How would you expect these interviews to be received in Britain?

Tara Ali Baig: We were certainly snobs too. A great many English people who came out in different jobs, whether it was as businessmen or as technical people, they were very varied in their level. Some people were definitely upper class, what you might call the top-drawer, but there were a lot of others who were not. The interesting thing was the snobbery that there was between themselves, as well as between them and the upper-class Indian, who looked upon them as something they had to endure, but didn't necessarily have to fraternize with.

It was particularly visible, for instance, in the big zamindari families, the landed gentry of Bengal, where there was a tremendous snobbery, in that they would not have anyone come to their house who did not have certain family qualifications. But where it was oftentimes hilarious was when the high official's wife, who may not have been all that top-drawer herself, wanted to call on one of these ladies. There was a great flutter in the zamindari house…and the kind of comments that there were between the Indian ladies when the Britishers had left, and among the British women when they were getting into their various cars, was often hilarious. The Indian women would say: "What sort of people are these? Their dress is so vulgar; they expose their legs. Look at those white arms; they look as if they haven't been cooked. And why do they wear those peculiar things on their heads?" And the British women would leave the place saying: "Really, isn't it shocking, these women are so backward. Didn't you see that they didn't even know how to drink from a cup?" There was all this kind of banter that would go on between the two sides.

Shiva Dua: My eldest sister was in the [Swadeshi] movement itself, and she wore nothing but *khadi*.[17] Since I was being brought up by her, having lost my mother at the age of three, I was under her influence, and she gave me only khadi to wear. When I went to school, I found everybody else wearing very fine foreign clothes, but it didn't affect me at all. I felt proud that I was the only child in a whole college of 600 children who was wearing khadi, and I felt I was something very different from the others.… In 1930, Mahatma Gandhi gave his call that foreign clothes should be burnt. The students' union in Lahore decided to go and collect foreign clothes from the city and have a bonfire. And they passed our house with the slogans "Boycott foreign clothes," "Burn foreign clothes." There was hardly anything foreign in our house; but Mother's belongings were still there, and one sari had come to me as my share of Mother's belongings. I wore it a couple of times with a kind of mental conflict going on over whether it should be worn or not. There were pulls in two different directions, but I had kept it very sentimentally, keeping it preserved. When the call came, and the crowd was just below our house, and the neighbors were throwing them things, immediately I decided that Mother was Mother, but the Mother Country was higher than Mother, and the sari must go, and I gave it.…

In March 1931, following the execution of the nationalist leader Bhagat Singh: That was a time when the whole country was simmering with anger and agitation. All we could do was let the Principal know that we too suffered the same kind of agony that the

---

[17]Coarse homespun or hand-woven cloth, made of hand-spun cotton yarn. Gandhi called on Indians to burn British fabric (which was produced by machines, in mills) and to wear only home-made khadi.

nation had been made to suffer. We decided to put on black clothes on the day after the execution, and we asked the washermen who lived on the premises to dye black veils for us. The Principal came to know; and she went and threatened the washermen with being thrown out and removed the entire 80 veils that were to be dyed black. So I went and collected a bale of about 100 veils, sent them to an outside dyer, and in the morning I took them to college. The entire hall was dressed in black, some in black saris and blouses, others in black veils.... It was a surprise for the Principal to find the entire hall absolutely black, but she never uttered a word. We wore that black for thirteen days, most of us.[18]

In 1932:   It occurred to some of us that we should ask the Principal to allow us to sing "Vande Mataram"[19] along with "God Save the King." She was absolutely adamant, and she refused. We felt very hurt, and we tried to explain to her that there was nothing seditious about singing "Vande Mataram." But she said, "No, that's politics." So we kept quiet and decided not to participate in the singing of "God Save the King." A few prize-winners—I was one of them—were sitting on the front benches. We decided that when they stand up for "God Save the King," we'll just keep sitting; and we just kept sitting. The Principal was so furious, she turned red; and we just refused to look at her. I don't know why she had the feeling that I was at the bottom of it. But at the end of the ceremony, she called me to her office and said, "Shiva, I didn't expect this from you." I said, "Have I done anything wrong by expressing a love for my mother country?" She said nothing and just kept quiet. Thereafter, I had a felling that my career would be affected, that she would never allow me to come back to the college in the third year. But I confess with great pride and admiration for the Principal that, not only did she accept me, but when she found that I had come out from the examination with very good results and that I had won a merit scholarship, she wrote a letter of congratulations and said, "I hope you are coming back to your college." And I went back to my college very happily.

Source: Zareer Masani, *Indian Tales of the Raj* (London: BBC Books, 1987), 57–58, 91–93.

[18]The duration of the customary Hindu mourning period.

[19]A nationalist anthem.

CHAPTER 2

The Scramble for Africa: European Colonialism and African Resistance, 1806–1945

African history appears to provide a textbook case of modern European imperialism: virtually an entire continent became colonial booty. This seizure of land, people, and resources happened very quickly—most of it happened during the space of a single generation, between 1884 and 1914. On its surface, African conquest is a story of competition among European powers, with Africa itself merely a backdrop for this saga. As shown most obviously at the Congo Congress in Berlin (1884–1885), European states frequently ignored African views and judged African precedents to be irrelevant. New maps of the continent featured colonial borders drawn in ignorance (or defiance) of pre-existing population distributions, geographical features, and economic trade patterns. Yet this European success was possible only during a very brief window of military and technological superiority—taking advantage of African vulnerabilities produced by environmental conditions and the prior depredations of centuries of slave trading, which had enriched coastal areas at the expense of inland groups. The economic exploitation of African resources after 1880 could thus take a particularly crude form, and modern empires subjected Africans to intrusive forms of surveillance and control. Nonetheless Africans fought back against these colonial states—and even when they suffered military defeats, local societies set about reworking the imperial order. Over time this system became a characteristically complicated hybrid—one that was brought to an end, soon after World War II, by a new breed of anti-colonial activists.

Today Robert Baden-Powell is best known for what he did after returning from Africa—especially for his work in 1907 to establish the Boy Scouts, an organization that prepared English youth, mentally and physically, for the demands of running an imperial state. Ten years earlier, however, Baden-Powell had still been learning about those demands firsthand as he built a career in the British colonial army. In 1896, while rising through the officer ranks, he published a book chronicling Britain's mission in the Gold Coast of West Africa (in modern-day Ghana). Baden-Powell told the story of how the colonial governor, Maxwell, ordered the army to march 150 miles inland to the town of Kumassi (shown on Map 2.2), hoping to force a local king to accept British rule. Why did Maxwell force Prempeh, the powerful ruler of Asante, to abase himself? "The danger of allowing treaty contracts to be evaded," wrote Baden-Powell, "is fairly well understood among European nations, but the results of slackness or leniency in their enforcement are nonetheless dangerous when the treaty has been made with an uncivilized potentate."[1]

Baden-Powell explained that the British army acted for reasons both pragmatic and moral. First, colonial officials worried about a potential loss of British prestige. While other European powers were seizing control of vast areas elsewhere in Africa, the Asante kingdom had not, in Baden-Powell's judgment, lived up to its obligations under a treaty signed twenty years earlier. This failure endangered Britain by encouraging Africans to ignore European authority. By hindering British rule it also kept colonists from bringing Africans the benefits of European civilization—specifically, ending the slave trade and abolishing the practice of human sacrifice. In Asante, Baden-Powell wrote, slavery was particularly detestable, as slaves were bought and sold

---

[1]The quoted phrases in this opening story are from Robert S. S. Baden-Powell, *The Downfall of Prempeh* (London, 1898), 19–20, 124, 128–129, 158–159; they are also quoted by William Worger et al., eds., *Africa and the West* (Phoenix, 2001), 209–213.

to be used as human sacrifices—a situation that cried out for change, by force if necessary. "Britons will never be slaves," he quoted from the anthem *Rule Brittania*, "and Britons are so peculiarly imbued with a notion of fair play that they will not see anybody else in a state of slavery either, if they can prevent it."

Baden-Powell thus stressed moral urgency to justify the mission to Kumassi—but his story looked different through African eyes. Certainly the Asante leaders found British tactics less than saintly, and they devised a range of responses to express their displeasure with, and resistance to, colonial power. From the start Maxwell and his soldiers were not welcomed in Kumassi. When Baden-Powell and others arrived at the king's ceremonial field, Prempeh and his entourage refused to come meet them. After a fruitless two-hour wait, British troops, along with a detachment of African soldiers brought from the coast, took matters into their own hands, marching to the royal palace and seizing the king and queen. Unceremoniously perching Prempeh in his state cradle, they marched him—with the queen, queen mother, and other Asante chiefs—back to the field, placing the king in front of Governor Maxwell and surrounding him with heavily armed soldiers.

At this point, Baden-Powell notes, "the doom of the [Asante] nation was pronounced in a set-scene, and amid dramatic incidents such as could not fail to impress both natives and Europeans alike." In an encounter reminiscent of the Durbar of 1877 in India, this ceremony invoked local and imperial languages of authority and subjection, as both sides acknowledged British sovereignty. The encounter was designed to leave Prempeh no choice but abject surrender, in the most humiliating terms. British soldiers forced him to bow and hug his knees as he walked up to the British governor. Maxwell then demanded Prempeh pay a massive indemnity, to cover the expenses of Britain's war and military occupation. When Prempeh produced only a small amount of money, his entreaties for mercy were ignored—soldiers arrested the entire royal delegation and sent them to the coast, where they served as hostages until their subjects paid the full amount. The arrest of the king and his chiefs neatly decapitated local authority structures, leaving a completely conquered society, and removing any doubt about British authority.

Colonial troops then surrounded the king's palace complex, seizing whatever valuables they could find (and later selling them at auction). Baden-Powell wrote of his fascination at seeing the gold-encrusted contents of "a barbarian king's palace." Yet here his story of British dominance and African victimization becomes more complex—because the soldiers sent to search the palace found a disappointingly small amount of treasure. Apparently the Asante had anticipated the possibility of British treachery and coercion. As Baden-Powell put it, "there were piles of the tawdriest and commonest stuff mixed indiscriminately with quaint, old, and valuable articles, a few good brass dishes, large metal ewers, Ashanti stools, etc. But a large amount of valuables known to belong to the king had disappeared…such as his celebrated dinner service of Dutch silver, his golden hat, his golden chair of state, and, above all, the royal stool, the emblem, par excellence, of the King of Ashanti." These missing items, Baden-Powell surmised, had been hidden in remote villages or in the bush—as were nearly all the contents of the nearby religious center at Bantama, where Asante kings were buried. As long as British troops had not captured the main symbols of authority—especially the Golden Stool—Asante sovereignty remained at a deeper level untrammelled, no matter what tactics colonial armies used or how humiliated King Prempeh might be.

Angry, the British soldiers reacted by burning Bantama to the ground. Baden-Powell concluded by putting on the best face he could, declaring that Britain had thus put an end to centuries of human sacrifice. By destroying Bantama, the "fetish superstition" that had gripped "the untutored children of the bush" had ended. By arresting the king, Britain had opened west-central Africa to civilized trade and exploration; protected its prestige, and persuaded other African chiefs to accept its protection; and, not least, prevented its rival, France, from expanding southward to control the wealth of Timbuktu and the Niger Basin. Such assertions sounded grand, and they resonated with Baden-Powell's British audience, helping him build the authority later parlayed into his role as founder of the Boy Scouts. In reality, however, these claims were overstated—nearly as empty as the treasure houses of Bantama. Yes, the king had been arrested, but in other ways Africans remained outside the reach of the colonial state. Prempeh sacrificed his dignity and even his person to Baden-Powell's soldiers, but the deeper symbols of Asante political identity and social integrity remained out of reach.

****

DIVIDING AFRICA: EUROPEAN DIPLOMATS
AND THE LEGALITIES OF COLONIAL CONQUEST

European empires came later to Africa than India, storming across the continent in a rapid burst of land grabbing and conquest in the late nineteenth century. This intervention was not completely unprecedented: Iberian forces had campaigned in North Africa in the fifteenth and sixteenth centuries, and soldiers representing the Portuguese Crown captured Ceuta in 1415—as an ongoing extension of the Crusades. Before 1880, though, Europeans had only a spotty presence in Africa—concentrated mostly in areas along the coasts, in outposts connected with oceangoing trading networks, and especially with commerce in slaves. The Portuguese established forts in West Africa in the fifteenth and sixteenth centuries, including in present-day Mauritania in 1445 and Ghana in 1482.[2] In the east they conquered Mombassa (holding it from 1591 until 1729) and established an even longer presence in Mozambique (one that lasted until 1975), along with a **factory** (trade station or outpost, with a secure warehouse used by "factors," authorized trade agents) on the island of Zanzibar. In the eighteenth century they also established *prazos*, large private estates with slave armies, several hundred miles up the Zambezi. A Dutch outpost in South Africa dated from 1652, and the Dutch, French, Swedes, Danes, Prussians, and English also set up trade stations along the west coast in the seventeenth century, although generally not in inland areas.

In the early nineteenth century this limited and mostly coastal European presence changed, as colonial holdings grew in size and imperial goals became more assertive. In 1806, during the Napoleonic Wars, British forces seized control of Cape Town; the loss of Dutch sovereignty was ratified by treaty in 1815. Such transfers both expressed and created tensions among Europeans. In this case Dutch Afrikaner (Boer) settlers in South Africa, especially those from poor and landless families, resented their newly subordinate position. Many fled north, creating ripple effects and military clashes as they confronted Bantu groups living farther inland. In North Africa, meanwhile, French forces in 1830 established a colony in Algeria that likewise extended inland from the coast, but faced complications

---

[2]Later, in the seventeenth century, Portugal lost most of its outposts on the West African coast to the Dutch.

created by the continuing presence of Ottoman Turks. By the 1860s, too, British explorers had located gold and diamond deposits farther south, creating powerful economic inducements for those interested in claiming wider swathes of African land.

Yet as late as 1880, roughly 80 percent of the African continent remained independent—outside the control of external empires—a situation that changed rapidly thereafter. By 1914, only Ethiopia and Liberia remained free of direct colonial control, and Ethiopia succumbed for a brief period after 1936 (see Maps 2.1 and 2.2).[3] How did such a dramatic change come about? On its surface, the "scramble for Africa" was shaped by European diplomatic agreements. At the Berlin Congress of 1884–1885, discussed at greater length below, all the great powers of Europe (with a few invited observers, such as the United States), agreed to carve up Africa into colonies. Without even the pretence of seeking African consent, this agreement marked a radical departure from established diplomatic practice. European kings had long acknowledged African leaders' sovereignty, and for centuries had negotiated treaties, alliances, and trade relationships with them. In the era of modern empires, however, the military-technological calculus, as well as wider economic and political contexts, had changed fundamentally; and in 1884 not a single African was invited to speak at the congress in Berlin.

This shift in colonial diplomacy was partly driven by developments within Europe—especially by a wave of state formation in the 1860s and 1870s that created powerful new countries such as Germany and Italy. The nationalist leaders and elites of these new states yearned for status and what they saw as a proper level of international respect. Empires represented one way to assure such standing—given the common view that a country's power was reflected in the size and wealth of its colonial holdings. As long as new states such as Germany and Italy lacked colonial empires, their leaders saw themselves lagging in the race with European competitors such as Britain, France, Portugal, the Netherlands, and Spain. They therefore sought places to build their own empires—a purpose for which Africa seemed particularly well suited.

---

[3]Invaded in 1935, Ethiopia finally succumbed to Italian troops in May 1936. In 1941, however, British soldiers arrived—this time in a very different context, and more as liberators than conquerors. Their intervention was shaped by global war against Germany and its allies, including fascist Italy. Great Britain recognized Ethiopia's full sovereignty just three years later, in 1944.

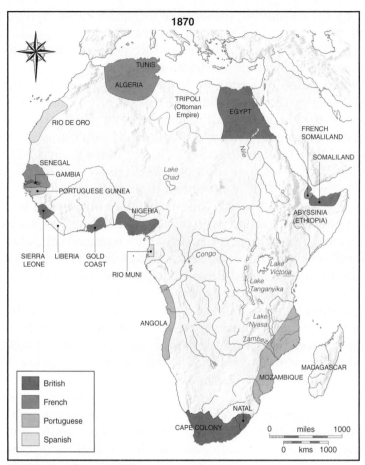

MAP 2.1   Africa ca. 1870.

Accordingly, European goals and tactics in Africa shifted in an interventionist direction. In the 1870s and early 1880s the Portuguese king claimed land stretching all the way across south-central Africa, from Angola in the west to Mozambique in the east. French forces pressed into northern Africa, occupying Tunisia in 1881, while British troops occupied Ottoman Egypt in 1882, bombing Alexandria into submission. Perhaps the most egregious imperial competition took place in the Congo River Basin, where Belgian and French emissaries vied to navigate inland and establish territorial

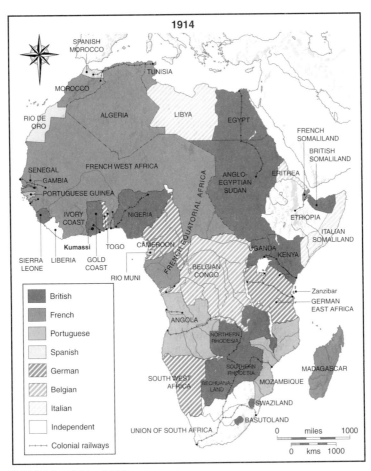

MAP 2.2   Africa 1914.

claims—overturning those made long before by Portugal. Seeking
to build a personal fief in central Africa, King Leopold II of Belgium
hired the British adventurer Henry Stanley to arrange treaties on
behalf of an "International Association of the Congo." The struggle over the Congo in November 1884 finally prodded European
powers to convene in Berlin—for a yearlong gathering to decide the
rules of the game, that is, to determine how European states could
legally build colonial empires in Africa.

The Berlin Congress convened with noble-sounding goals:
to establish free trade in the Congo Basin; to ensure its neutrality

during any European wars; to wipe out the slave trade; and to show the humanitarian benefits of European civilization through the enlightened administration of a modern colonial system. Unfortunately, it met none of these goals. Rather, the Congo became a place of monopoly trade and extraordinary (even for modern empires) torture and brutality. Almost all of Africa was drawn into World War I in 1914. Slave trading continued into the 1920s, and sometimes longer, often with colonial cooperation.[4] The congress's participants succeeded in only one aim: they drew a new map of Africa, dividing the continent neatly into new political units and spheres of imperial control. Some specific decisions favored one European power over another—Germany received areas formerly claimed by Portugal, while Leopold's "International Association" won recognition as the de facto government of a newly created Congo Free State (a place that was actually not free at all, as discussed below). But most important of all, the final treaty set clear rules, defining the procedures by which European powers could expand in Africa. Its Article 34 declared that any signatory wishing to take African land had to notify the other Berlin signatories, and to negotiate any intra-European disputes—but it included no such obligation to consult with, or even to consider the wishes of, local leaders or populations. The great powers thus arrogated to themselves the right to seize all the lands in which millions of Africans lived.

Rapid military conquest followed. French troops seized much of northern Africa, while Britain expanded its imperial holdings in the central and eastern parts of the continent. German leaders claimed land in the southwest and east, while Portugal, Belgium, and Italy launched colonial campaigns in other areas. From the European perspective, this process took place with remarkable speed and (usually) comradely good order, as relatively few conflicts broke out among the colonizing states. Those grabbing for land did generally observe the rules and overall map laid down in Berlin. From the African perspective, however, this rapid onslaught looked entirely

---

[4]It was not solely a colonial practice: Ethiopia only formally abolished slavery in 1942. Several emperors had issued earlier decrees and laws to restrict the practice, or to phase it out over time, to relatively little effect. Ending Ethiopian slavery was an avowed goal of Mussolini and the Italian forces, and in fact served as a public justification for conquest. Italy's occupation authority declared slavery outlawed soon after the 1935 invasion (initially, again, to little effect), and restated the ban more forcefully in 1936.

different. To Africans it appeared that Europeans followed no rules at all—and that colonizing states could not be trusted.

In Nigeria, for instance, a British governor had signed a treaty in 1873 granting the Opobo king, Jaja, control of commerce along the Imo River. This arrangement excluded European traders as middlemen, thereby guaranteeing the king great wealth—so he, not surprisingly, fiercely protected this concession. In 1885, however, negotiators in Berlin declared the paramount importance of free trade throughout the Niger River Basin. Two years later the British governor announced that Jaja's treaty was null and void, saying that legally he could no longer bar outside traders. When the king refused to accept this change, the British consul, Harry Johnston, tricked him into coming aboard a British warship to "negotiate." Johnston offered Jaja a promise of safe conduct, guaranteeing his security with the personal word of a British gentleman. The value of this assurance, however—and Britain's credibility—plummeted when Johnston arrested Jaja. British troops marched the king to the colonial capital of the Gold Coast, where he faced a quick trial and then exile thousands of miles away, on the West Indian island of St. Vincent. Johnston's treachery may have exceeded the imperial norm (although other chiefs, such as the Itsekiri leader Nana Olomu, faced similarly abrupt exiles). Yet his story shows a willingness to use anything-goes tactics when interacting with Africans—an approach that contrasts with the insistence of colonial officials on their "civilized" ways, and their assiduous attention to the Berlin rules, while interacting with European friends and rivals.

CONTINGENT CONQUEST: WINDOWS OF AFRICAN VULNERABILITY AND EUROPEAN OPPORTUNITY

How could Europeans have conquered Africa so quickly after 1885? Soldiers and officials such as Baden-Powell stressed colonizers' superior skills, weaponry, education, moral standing, character, and an indefinable "pluck," seeing the spread of imperial control as part of the inevitable spread of civilization and progress into a backward and benighted Africa. Yet there was nothing inevitable about this conquest, and many episodes show that Africans resisted as vigorously as they could—and sometimes they succeeded. In South Africa, for instance, in 1879 more than 20,000 Zulu troops managed surreptitiously to surround a force of about 1,700 British and African soldiers at the rocky outcrop of Isandlwana. Despite fighting mostly with spears, the well-trained Zulus used the advantage of surprise to deal the better-armed Europeans a crushing defeat. More than 1,300 colonial soldiers died at Isandlwana, including 858 British regulars, in one of England's worst colonial military defeats. Only fifty-five British troops escaped with their lives—and none who wore the official red-coated uniform. Chastened colonial officers and officials in Capetown had to regroup; a massive British punitive campaign later in the year ultimately crushed the organized Zulu opposition and captured the king.

An even more striking example of resistance comes from East Africa, where local rulers in Ethiopia successfully fought off decades of attacks by outsiders—by Anglo-Egyptians, Ottoman Turks, British regular troops, and finally, Italians desperate to claim a colonial empire. Successive Ethiopian emperors skillfully played the Europeans off one another to gain access to modern weapons, and then assiduously drilled and trained soldiers in their use. The military payoff became clear when Italy, in 1889, agreed to recognize the sovereignty of the Ethiopian emperor Menelik II. Unbeknownst to Menelik, however, the Italian translation of this treaty differed from its Amharic version. The Italians required (in their version) that all Ethiopian diplomacy be approved in Rome—thus making Ethiopia subordinate to Italy. Upon discovering this subterfuge, Menelik was furious; but unlike Jaja or Prempeh, he had the ability to fight back. Years of conflict culminated in 1896 at the battle of Adwa, where a well-trained Ethiopian army of 100,000 soldiers (equipped with at least five million rounds of ammunition) besieged and defeated a much smaller force of about 14,000 Italian troops. Each side lost around 10,000 men—but this meant that Italy lost 70 percent of its invading army, in contrast with an Ethiopian casualty rate of about 10 percent. A new treaty, signed at Addis Ababa, forced Italy unambiguously to recognize Ethiopian independence—this time with no unexplained translations in the Italian version.[5]

Despite the confident assertions of men like Baden-Powell, therefore, the overall fact of European conquest cannot be seen as inevitable. Rather, the rapid subjugation of nearly an entire continent

---

[5]The *Connections* book by Cyrus Veeser, *Great Leaps Forward* (2010), devotes a chapter to Menelik II's successful efforts to keep Ethiopia free of foreign control.

arose from a particular set of circumstances—an historically specific, or **contingent**, combination of personal, political, technological, and environmental factors that created a brief window of African vulnerability, and European opportunity, in the late nineteenth century. The personal and political side of this encounter has already been suggested; the episodes at Adwa and Isandlwana show that military force also played a key role. On this score, Ethiopia represented a rare exception: not only did it possess a rich military heritage and a dedicated and capable army, but unlike most African societies, it had the capital and political wherewithal at the crucial moment to provide its soldiers with the latest military technologies.

Unfortunately for other African states, during this period Europeans held a dominant (albeit temporary) position of controlling access to three crucial technologies. First, in constructing far-flung transportation and communication networks: new industrial facilities built steamships with shallow steel hulls that could sail farther inland—sometimes even boasting collapsible hulls that could be carried upstream around dangerous rapids. This technology enabled quick travel into new areas, opening the major river basins of the Congo, Niger, Nile, and Zambezi to European explorers, soldiers, and officials. Telegraph cables also offered immediate communications with colonial capitals and made possible a rapid military response to put down local rebellions. Second, improved medical technology brought another crucial advantage. Until the middle of the nineteenth century few Europeans welcomed a colonial posting to Africa; for many it was akin to a death sentence. Between 1695 and 1722, for instance, the Royal Africa Company sent dozens of Britons to Africa—but more than half died in their first year, mostly succumbing to diseases such as malaria and yellow fever. Only one in ten survived to return home to Britain. This situation changed dramatically in the nineteenth century, as quinine came into widespread production after 1850 and proved generally effective in preventing malaria. (A yellow fever vaccine followed much later, in 1935.)

Third and perhaps most crucial, new military hardware presented European armies with enormous advantages. Industrial factories churned out high-power explosives, poisonous gases and other chemical weapons, formidable automatic and repeating rifles, and by the 1920s, heavy artillery and airplanes. Many of these weapons were specifically designed for colonial conflicts, and they easily overcame the single-shot muskets that African armies had stockpiled. New rifles offered a vastly expanded killing power, through a combination of greater accuracy, lethal range, and rapid reloading. The "Maxim gun"—adopted by the British army in 1889 and quickly copied by other European forces—could fire up to 500 rounds every minute, the equivalent of roughly one hundred single-fire rifles. It was first used in combat in Africa, helping British troops slaughter Matabele warriors in the mid-1890s. As similar machine guns entered the forces of other European armies, the military disparity with Africans grew shockingly wide, especially once the Europeans agreed (in the Brussels Convention of 1890) not to sell such weapons to Africans, a monopoly that remained in effect until after World War I. Tiny groups of imperial soldiers could thus defeat entire African armies, no matter how brave or well-trained they might be: at the Battle of Omdurman in 1898, a badly outnumbered Anglo-Egyptian force nonetheless prevailed, mowing down 11,000 Sudanese warriors while losing only forty of its own number. As the British writer Hilaire Belloc put it in a grisly but well-known jingle, "Whatever happens, we have got/The Maxim gun and they have not."

Technology alone, however, cannot fully explain these patterns of African vulnerability and European expansion. Environmental changes in the late nineteenth century also played a critical role, as cycles of drought and disease first enabled and then followed the expanding colonial system. In Congo and Angola, for instance, famine and epidemic disease during the 1870s weakened local populations before Europeans arrived in force, while British power in South Africa likewise grew on the heels of a major drought between 1876 and 1879 that impeded resistance among both Bantu and Boer populations. As in India, moreover, once new empires appeared, they introduced crops that oriented farmers toward international cash markets rather than local food needs, and shifted the forms of land usage and property ownership, especially toward a plantation system for large-scale agriculture. Colonial economies did not cause the rains to fail, but they worsened the consequences when it happened; and imperial powers certainly took advantage of resulting indigenous vulnerability to expand their control over local lands during later waves of drought between 1886 and 1916. New tax burdens on colonized peoples, finally, made it harder for African farmers to recover when the rains did return.

The ecology of empire thus subjected colonial populations to new risks—partly by exposing them to new diseases and plagues, but mostly by weakening existing defensive structures and the reservoirs of strength that existed before colonial conquest. When another wave of drought and famine struck many parts of Africa in the 1890s, for example, red locusts and tsetse flies expanded into new areas, while livestock succumbed to a devastating epidemic of the viral disease rinderpest. By some estimates this pandemic between 1890 and 1892 killed 95 percent of East Africa's water buffalo and wildebeest, a shattering blow in an area with a culture and economy based on livestock husbandry. As poverty-stricken herders moved ever-greater distances seeking water and disease- and insect-free lands, they confronted new neighbors (sparking fresh conflicts over access to pastureland and water) and spread the diseases farther. Smallpox also accompanied this newly mobile population, and it soon swept through much of Africa, killing as many as two-thirds of the pastoral Masai. German doctors in Tanzania remarked that every other African they treated seemed to have a pock-marked face. A colonial railway in Uganda, finished in 1902, then unwittingly brought bubonic plague to central Africa; the disease probably arrived with construction laborers who brought it from India. As if more social strain were needed, in parts of Kenya the rains failed for three consecutive years in the late 1890s, leaving Gikuyu society tottering near disintegration; mortality rates ranged upward of one-third of the adult population. British officials made little attempt to provide food or medical relief until the damage had been done. When revolts broke out but failed, then—such as a series of uprisings in Zimbabwe at the turn of the century—they may fairly be said to have been defeated as much by famine and smallpox as by British machine guns.

EMPIRES OF EXTRACTION: ADMINISTERING AFRICA IN THE NEW COLONIAL ORDER

However they did it, by the 1890s European armies had conquered most of Africa—and colonial officials set about building a variety of imperial systems. Most started by designing administrative structures to guarantee control (by developing detailed knowledge of potential threats and responding rapidly to any rebellions) and maximize their ability to exploit African resources. In most cases, only a few thousand

Europeans were involved—only a handful of colonies, among them Algeria, South Africa, Kenya, and Mozambique, saw large numbers of European settlers. More typically, a handful of officials set up shop in separate enclaves, from whence they sought to supervise local society. Sometimes colonial emissaries administered African lands directly (an approach defended in a document below by the French governor G. L. Angoulvant); in other cases financial and practical considerations drove them to rule indirectly, through local allies or intermediaries, with a more limited colonial bureaucracy. Frederick Lugard, the British governor who wrote another of the documents below, defended this approach, contending that indirect rule reflected greater empathy for local populations and helped Africans learn to govern themselves like civilized people—under British tutelage, of course.

Scholars have debated how much such distinctions really mattered; the Ugandan historian Mahmood Mamdani argues that brute force and, ultimately, assertions of racial power lay behind either approach. Certainly the various European administrations had much in common. Even the French system of direct rule depended on local personnel at the grassroots level to collect taxes, administer censuses, and report on village developments. The supposedly indirect British approach, meanwhile, also subjected Africa to a broadly intrusive administrative structure, or **grid**, that aimed to know exactly what was happening in each colony—who was who, where they might be at any given time, and what they were doing and perhaps even thinking. Lugard's empathetic expressions meant less in practice, as British officials too mostly ruled Africans and expected them to change in the ways Europeans demanded. Colonial bureaucrats used all sorts of techniques to keep a firm hand, from detailed land surveys to censuses of local populations. African men and women had to carry identity and pass-cards when walking on the street (the much-hated *kipande* in Kenya was one example), and workers had to maintain labor books, in which employers wrote notes about their service, skills, and attitude. Colonial courts and police forces, anti-vagrancy laws, and even apparently well-meaning programs such as vaccinations for children and Christian church schools helped maintain control. They taught Africans to live according to European norms of health, hygiene, and morality, and aimed to prevent even the seeds of resistance.

Once European control had been established, colonial bureau-crats worked assiduously to maximize the economic benefits of empire. Some such efforts, it must be noted, had the potential to help Africans. New roads, railways, schools, and hospitals, for example, improved local infrastructures and enabled social welfare networks. Indeed, Europeans justified their presence by pointing to such projects, saying that modern imperialism was helping introduce Africans to the benefits of "civilization." And many colonial officials personally believed that they were doing good work, just as thousands of missionaries and aid workers made enormous personal sacrifices to help ordinary Africans, working for what they sincerely saw as a good and moral cause.

Yet taken as a whole, these economic developments helped colonizers far more than the colonized. Roads, railways, and telegraph lines served to permit the rapid exploitation of local resources, and enabled the speedy movement of imperial armies. High-caliber schools focused on training a small elite group to serve as colonial staffers—so a handful of the best students could be sent to schools in France and Britain, but only a few universities were built in Africa, and only rudimentary education was offered to most Africans. The remarkable advances in health care, meanwhile, focused first on saving the lives of soldiers, administrators, and missionaries. Ordinary Africans, those who did not work for the colonial apparatus, fared much worse: as late as 1924 colonial Nigeria could muster only one doctor for every 800,000 people. By the following decade, the country boasted twelve hospitals dedicated to the care of 4,000 European colonists—but only fifty-two others to watch over forty million Africans.

Although abolishing the slave trade lay at the heart of (especially British) justifications for empire, and the paternalistic language of protecting and upraising the weak underpinned European ideologies of rule in Africa as it did in India, such moral claims rang false alongside the brutal expropriations that accompanied colonial rule. Very quickly Europeans set about exploiting virtually the entire continent for its human, mineral, and agricultural resources. Trade patterns across the continent shifted dramatically: new maps of territory and sovereignty effectively oriented each colony to its own metropole. The borders between colonies cut across long-established intra-African trade routes, which dwindled over time, as railways moved goods from inland areas toward coastal ports—rather than into neighboring districts or upstream communities. And for the metropoles, wealth extraction became a key goal of African trade.

British land hunger in the south grew markedly after the discovery of diamonds in 1867 and gold in 1886—and the promise of riches accelerated London's confrontation with both Boer and Bantu populations. This confrontation came to a head in the viciously fought Boer War (1899–1902), when Britain achieved political control over South Africa, and control of its mineral wealth. To do so, the British had to defeat both Africans and other Europeans. Dispossessed Afrikaners—the descendants of an earlier wave of Dutch colonial settlers—waged a guerrilla war to fight off what they, like black Africans, denounced as British colonization. The British responded with scorched-earth tactics against the Boers, confining thousands to concentration camps where many died. In the end Afrikaners were relegated to agricultural lands, although their status as white Europeans did leave them in a better situation than defeated Africans. Afrikaners won full citizenship rights, even as they lived in separate enclaves from British settlers; when London created a semiautonomous "Union of South Africa" in 1910, its government helped squeeze out black African populations—to the benefit of all Europeans. As described in a document below, the Union government in 1913 passed a "Native Lands Act" which excluded indigenous Africans—but not Boers—from owning most property. It thus effectively expropriated most of South Africa from its own people.

Far from pumping major investments into Africa, European metropoles expected each colony to pay for itself, and more: to provide enough of a return, in fact, to pay for the next wave of conquest. Hence colonial governments squeezed every possible shilling out of their African subjects. All sorts of new taxes appeared. These included head taxes and "hut" taxes—which all families had to pay—and later, income and sales taxes. Many of these had to be paid in cash, a requirement that also forced fundamental economic shifts. Farmers had to grow cash crops for local or export markets, rather than food for their own consumption. Each colony thus specialized in goods it could produce most cheaply; cocoa, for example, was first imported in the 1890s from the Americas—but by 1911 Ghana had become the world's largest producer. Colonial Sudan soon ranked as one of the world's largest growers of cotton. Yet dominating such markets did not increase Africans' economic power—far from it. International markets determined the prices paid to growers, while middlemen and colonial taxes skimmed off most of the profits. Increasing economic specialization, moreover, meant less resilience in times of crisis.

As in India, local food production dropped as the colonial economy developed. Food had to be imported into areas that previously had been self-sufficient—rice, for instance, was now shipped into the Gambia, which previously had grown large quantities of it. The perils of this situation, in which farmers risked starvation if prices fell, and had no food reserves if the rains failed, became starkly clear during the terrible droughts and epidemics of the late 1890s.

The extractive policies pursued by colonial governments led to horrific consequences for African populations. Colonial rule reduced the population of Libya by 750,000 people; but the chief exhibit of colonial brutality in Africa—and the locus of British and American anti-colonial sentiment, as chronicled in a document below—lodged above all in the Congo Free State. This state, established in 1885 at the behest of Belgium's King Leopold II, was "Free" only in the sense that it did not technically belong to the Belgian government. Instead, it was Leopold's personal and absolute fief—a place he never once visited, but where his power knew no limits, and his representatives could do virtually anything they wanted. Initially Leopold had a difficult time figuring how to make money from his new realm, as early efforts to extract money from the ivory trade yielded only limited success. In the 1890s he had to borrow thirty-two million francs from the Belgian government to keep his Congo enterprise afloat. But Leopold's financial situation improved when global demand unexpectedly blossomed for rubber. The invention of the bicycle, specifically the pneumatic bicycle tire, created an overnight market for enormous quantities of the stuff. Soon thereafter automobiles came into use, too, producing additional demands for rubber—and happily for Leopold (although very unhappily for his African subjects) many rubber trees grew in the Congo River Basin.

So Leopold regrouped, focusing on rubber. He declared that all "unoccupied" land (meaning the forest lands, where rubber trees grew) belonged to the Free State, and that all adult residents had to work forty hours each month gathering rubber. He explained that this labor tax would teach Africans a proper work ethic. The resulting wealth could then pay back the loans he had received from the Belgian government. This system made a certain financial sense, so far as it went, and if one ignored its moral side; but moral issues could not be ignored when the Free State subcontracted its rubber harvesting to semiprivate charter companies. These companies had every incentive to maximize the amount of rubber they gathered, and faced almost no restrictions on their actions. As the international rubber market expanded, African women and men faced ever-higher rubber quotas, and ever-greater coercion by local company representatives ("sentries"). The prices they received in exchange for rubber, meanwhile, did not increase.

A vicious cycle resulted: as villages depleted nearby rubber vines, their inhabitants had to explore an ever-wider area. This put them in conflict with other villages, and took time away from farming, or hunting, or anything else that did not yield rubber. Meanwhile the sentries became more violent, using murder, mutilation, kidnapping, and rape to pressure local residents to find and harvest more rubber. The resulting anarchy and violence horrified missionaries, several of whom published detailed exposés of what was happening in the Congo (see Figure 2.1). These images and stories struck a chord

FIGURE 2.1   Congo atrocities: Nsala of Wala with his five-year-old daughter's hand and foot. Reportedly nothing else remained after rubber sentries killed and ate Nsala's wife, daughter, and a son. This shocking and tragic image was taken by a missionary, John Harris, in May 1904, and published soon thereafter by the journalist, and pacifist activist, Edmund Morel. Photographs, a relatively new form of evidence, played a key role in demonstrating the horrors of King Leopold's "Free State," and helped anti-imperialist groups such as the Congo Reform Association bring political pressure to bear. Photography's power resides in its apparently transparent character: evidence seems straightforward, honest, and undeniable. At the same time, pictures are also selected, and may be posed—a difficult point to keep in mind here, as Harris so powerfully maximizes the image's poignancy, and Morel uses it to resonate with (and horrify) his Western audience.

throughout Europe and beyond, even among those accustomed to the violent standards of colonial life. To prove that they had not wasted ammunition, for example, Congo sentries had to bring back the hands of their victims—one hand per bullet. Such gruesome tactics provoked horror both near and far, and in 1908 the widespread outcry forced the Belgian state to intervene and at last assume direct control over the Free State. By then, after a quarter-century of Leopold's rule, the population of the Congo had declined by half.

THE COLONIES STRIKE BACK: HYBRID CULTURES AND SHADES OF RESISTANCE

Such cases highlight the brutality of empires in Africa, and underscore the control wielded by colonial governments. Yet amid such carnage, Africans refused to submit passively to European conquest. Imperial efforts to transform African society yielded unexpected results—and the degree to which Europeans actually controlled their new colonies remained an open question. Missionaries stood at the forefront of Europeans' self-proclaimed effort to civilize Africa— an effort to justify colonial power through what the French called a *mission civilisatrice* (civilizing mission). Christian evangelism had a long, if intermittent, heritage in Africa,[6] and as a crucial component of the European self-image it fitted readily into this modern imperial project (see Figure 2.2). After about 1800, Catholic and Protestant missionaries alike focused in ever-greater numbers on converting the so-called Dark Continent, namely, the interior of sub-Saharan Africa. They took advantage of European colonial control—in some areas arriving even before soldiers or bureaucrats—to seek souls for Christ. As in the Belgian Congo, they sometimes acted as a thorn in the side of governments; certainly they did not always agree with state policies. Division and dispute was still common among Europeans, even as (from the African point of view) imperial powers appeared united in dominating colonized peoples.

Despite their apparently strong position, Europeans nevertheless sounded anxious when they talked about their empires—especially when they discussed their efforts to change African culture. Missionaries

---

[6]In the early sixteenth century, for example, powerful kings of Kongo, located along the West African coast (not to be confused with the Congo River Basin), had converted to the Roman Catholic faith and tried to use Portuguese help to Christianize their realm.

FIGURE 2.2   A black American Presbyterian missionary, William Sheppard, in full colonial garb, stands alongside Kuba nobles in the Congo. The photograph shows him carrying a spear but also wearing a pith helmet—suggesting complex inter-cultural and racial issues. Sheppard, an ordained minister, traveled to Congo many times between 1890 and 1910. First encouraged by the Belgian king Leopold to explore and to convert Africans to Christianity, he helped lay the groundwork for later critiques of Belgian rule. The US Presbyterian Church refused to send him to Africa without a white supervisor; yet to many Africans, Sheppard seemed as foreign as his white compatriots (they called him *Mundéle Ndom*, or "the black white man"[7]). Historians debate how far his letters and actions as an African American—including the acquisition of a large collection of Kuba art—reveal an outlook different from that of other Euro-American missionaries.

played a key role; but priests, ministers, and lay leaders who visited Africa worried deeply about the kinds of Christians they found, and the syncretic religious practices they saw developing on the ground. Even when missionaries succeeded in winning converts (and they had many difficulties), African and European Christians understood their faith very differently. African converts called themselves Christian, but most readily adopted those church practices that fitted with their view of the world—for example participating in infant baptism ceremonies,

---

[7]According to his traveling companion Samuel Lapsley, *Life and Letters of Samuel Norvell Lapsley* (Richmond, VA, 1893), 83.

which protected children against witchcraft, or feasts like All Souls Day that venerated ancestors. Frequently they refused to accept other parts of Christianity that Europeans saw as equally if not more essential, such as the belief in an afterlife spent by souls in heaven or hell. Such notions sat oddly for many Africans, who viewed their ancestors—and spirits of other kinds—as still very much at hand, a constant presence in everyday life.

Nineteenth-century missionaries lacked sympathy for such views, seeing Christianity as a complete package: as a faith focused on moral transformation defined along Western (they would say "scriptural") lines. It required adherents to denounce the evils of slavery, for example, and not to practice such customs as polygamy. Defining the faith in this more stringent way, though, meant that African converts tended to be socially marginal in their own society, or climbers who hoped to profit from an alliance with powerful outsiders. Many slaves converted, as did younger princes with no hope of becoming king; so did lepers, women who had given birth to twins, and other social outcasts. African Christians tended overall to be young and female: in one extreme case, women represented 80 percent of the Anglican communicants in Abeokuta in 1878. Even among such groups religious practices remained eclectic, as shown in two documents below—both Christian and Islamic ideas mixed with other spiritual practices to create locally unique amalgams. Indeed, with the rise of popular independent African churches in the early twentieth century, outside the institutional control of European church hierarchies, missionaries' hopes of bringing "civilization" to Africa wound up reversed: European Christianity, instead, became Africanized.

These issues merged when missionaries in East Africa joined forces with colonial bureaucrats to denounce the practice of female infibulation, or **clitoridectomy**. The debates that resulted are reminiscent of British colonial decisions in India, a century earlier, to ban sati. In the 1920s (in Kenya) and again in the 1950s (in Sudan), Europeans observing African customs judged the practice of female genital cutting to be morally abhorrent and physically harmful. Many Africans, by contrast—both males and females—saw it differently. Along with male circumcision, infibulation played an important role in communal life, marked a key coming-of-age ritual, and initiated girls into adulthood. Hence when several mission churches in the early 1920s banned the practice, Gikuyu villagers refused to comply.

They resisted, starting their own schools for children expelled from mission facilities. They openly ridiculed authorities, composing popular music and dances to denounce missionaries. (British officials tried, with limited success, to ban such songs and dances in 1929.) African members of local Anglican and Protestant congregations left in protest—many joined a new independent church, the African Orthodox Church, which started in 1928. European mission schools came under attack, protests broke out and disrupted religious services, and at least one missionary was killed in protest. In the end the effort to ban clitoridectomy—a campaign carried out in the name of helping African women, and of bringing the benefits of European civilization—had the unexpected effect of invigorating African religious culture, and persuading many Africans that imperial power could be resisted intellectually—if not yet militarily—by opposing the imposition of foreign, colonial social reforms.

So Africans did not passively accept colonial conquest, but resisted European incursions in a variety of ways. Colonial religious and educational work also gave rise to a number of cross-border oppositional movements—an example of colonized populations making unexpected use of colonial structures. The connections, training, and ideas provided by Europeans could be used to fight against, and even to overthrow, their imperial system. In 1915, for example, John Chilembwe, an African Christian convert from Nyasaland (present-day Malawi), led an armed uprising to protest colonial taxation and conscription policies. He resented the poor treatment of African refugees during a major famine, as white settlers seized the most fertile land while black Africans had to pay a crippling hut tax. He also denounced the conscription of Nyasa men into the British colonial army during World War I; African soldiers were used to attack the nearby German colony of Tanzania, while black troops in South Africa were forced to invade German Southwest Africa (Namibia). "We are imposed upon," said Chilembwe, "more than any other nationality under the sun."[8]

Chilembwe shaped his revolt in Christian religious terms. He had come into contact with Christianity through Joseph Booth, a radical Baptist missionary who preached as doctrine the politically dangerous idea that all men (and women) should be treated equally. In 1897

---

[8]The Chilembwe passages here and in the next paragraph are quoted by Robert Rotberg, *The Rise of Nationalism in Central Africa* (Cambridge, MA, 1965), 82, 86.

Chilembwe accompanied Booth to the United States, where he studied at Virginia Theological Seminary and learned about contemporary African American political movements. In 1900 he returned to Nyasaland to work for the American National Baptist Convention, and to teach his African parishioners self-reliance and self-respect. This message clearly threatened the interests of plantation owners and managers, including one William Livingstone (a distant cousin of David, the famous explorer). Livingstone harassed Chilembwe's parishioners and burned down his churches, and for many Nyasa, he came to personify imperial injustice. In January 1915 Chilembwe decided to take action. He called on his neighbors to follow John Brown's American example, to take up arms to fight for a morally just cause, even in the face of overwhelming odds—in Chilembwe's words, "to strike a first and a last blow, and then all die by the heavy storm of the white men's army." Two hundred followers responded, organizing themselves in detachments to attack European outposts. They torched mission posts, raided an ammunition supply depot, and killed at least three white men (including William Livingstone, whom they beheaded). At this point the rebels retreated for contemplation and prayer. Unfortunately for them, their opponents used this time to organize a counterattack, in which they captured and killed Chilembwe, and so ended the rebellion.

Chilembwe's willingness to take up arms against a militarily superior enemy may sound ill-advised, but it was far from unique. Many other rebellions broke out in the 1890s and early 1900s, forcing European governments to maintain a major military presence in their African colonies, thereby raising the financial costs of empire. In Sierra Leone, for instance, the British faced a major rebellion in 1898 when nearly everyone refused to pay a new hut tax of five or ten shillings per home. Rebels attacked British outposts and killed colonial officials and soldiers, as well as suspected informants and African collaborators. One district commissioner wrote that the rebels wanted to massacre all the Europeans along with African inhabitants of Sierra Leone's capital, Freetown, and that they had already destroyed the government's ability to maintain supplies and local trade. The military threat to Freetown grew serious when rebels advanced to within twenty-five miles of the capital, forcing authorities to send British troops from Lagos to reinforce the garrison. According to the unusually perceptive British governor, the whole saga arose out of "the growing political consciousness of the African, and his increasing sense of his worth and autonomy." "The native is beginning to feel his strength," Governor Cardew went on, "from the value that is set on him for the products of his country and his labour by the white man and in future the latter will not be able to trade so much on his simplicity and ignorance of the world as in the past."[9]

Europeans feared that such episodes would embolden other potential rebels—and they were right. All the major imperial powers faced such problems. Two years later, British officials faced another uprising in West Africa, when a different colonial governor, Frederick Hodgson, demanded that the Asante hand over their sacred Golden Stool—the stool that had symbolized Asante survival when it was hidden from Baden-Powell's group in 1896. Hodgson required that the Asante provide this stool for him to sit upon. Since no *human* had ever been permitted to do so (the Asante kings took the throne by being suspended over but not touching it), this sacrilegious request provoked deep anger. Although King Prempeh still lived in exile in the West Indies, the temerity of Hodgson's demand prodded his Asante soldiers to besiege the capital city. They nearly killed the governor, bottling him up in a fortress from which he barely escaped. A later punitive expedition finally subdued these Asante troops—and their lands became a British protectorate in 1902—but in a crucial way, the Asante prevailed: Hodgson never did find the stool.

Thousands of miles away in southwestern Africa, German officials in 1904 faced another rebellion among the Herero, a group of perhaps 70,000 livestock herders who had been particularly hard-hit by the rinderpest pandemic of the late 1890s, and their neighbors, the Nama. When rebels carried out guerrilla attacks that killed around one hundred German settlers and destroyed a large number of farms and cattle, they provoked a viciously strong response—one so strong, in fact, that some historians describe it as the world's first modern genocide. The German commander, Lothar von Trotha, opted to confiscate the Hereros' land and cattle and then to exterminate them, if possible completely. "All the Hereros must leave the land," he declared in an open letter to the rebels. "Any Herero found within the German borders with or without a gun, with or without cattle, will be shot. I shall no longer receive any women or children. I will drive

[9]Quoted by M'Baye Gueye and A. Adu Boahen, "African Initiatives and Resistance in West Africa, 1880–1914," in Adu Boahen, ed., *Africa Under Colonial Domination 1880–1935* (Berkeley, 1985), 143.

them back to their people or I will shoot them. This is my decision for the Herero people."[10] German troops surrounded the Herero on three sides and machine-gunned thousands. They left only one escape route: straight into the Kalahari Desert. Many did flee into the sands, only to die of thirst—German soldiers poisoned the few water holes that existed. Less than a quarter of the Herero survived in 1908; about 14,000 men, women, and children had been rounded up into prison camps, where German doctors carried out medical experiments on them. Only 2,000 or so managed to escape into South Africa.

Yet even this level of violence did not end African resistance, as the French found when facing their own rebellions in West Africa. The brutal policies of Governor Angoulvant (which he defends in the document below) stirred bitter resistance among the Baule (Baoule) and others. Open warfare broke out in 1908, and French troops needed the better part of two years to crush the rebellion, once again by using scorched-earth tactics and house-to-house raids to search for militants. By 1911, the population of Baule, which had stood around 1.5 million at the turn of the century, declined to barely a quarter-million. Many simply fled in response to imperial crackdowns—further reducing the labor force available to French authorities.

This litany highlights the depth and breadth of violent resistance across Africa—even in the face of near-certain death and defeat for rebels, given the dramatic military advantage held by Europeans around 1900. Africans also fought back against European colonists using nonviolent tactics that varied by place and time. The overall conquest, in short, may not have been stoppable; but it could be resisted in a variety of ways, and this fact remained a constant subtext within the story of African empire. Indeed, aspects of the imperial system itself ensured that control could never be total. European armies crushed organized resistance or rebellion (except in rare cases like Ethiopia), but generally, after the military struggle ended, only a few colonial officials remained to run things. Most did not understand local society—and many, convinced of their own superiority, did not try very hard. This led them into ham-handed tactics and bumbling selections of local allies, enabling African leaders to play Europeans against one another, or to use their outside help to fight local rivals. Even some who appeared to ally with Europeans—kings who accepted

---

[10]Samuel Totten and William Parsons, eds., *Century of Genocide* (New York, 2009), 23. A *Connections* series book in preparation focuses on genocides in the twentieth century.

protectorate status, or newly educated elites who took jobs in the colonial apparatus—should not be seen simply as "collaborators." In many cases they judged this to be the best—or only—way to preserve at least some independence, and did so grudgingly, seeking to protect as many lives and as much autonomy as possible.

DOUBLE-EDGED SWORDS: THE UNINTENDED CONSEQUENCES OF GLOBAL COLONIALISM

European empires created new social units and personal identities across Africa—sometimes in ways not intended (or even understood) by the people supposedly in charge. Most obviously, the act of fighting against Europeans, openly and covertly, helped unite African communities. It did so in paradoxical ways. Certainly colonial borders divided some groups—the Bakongo and Somalis each fell into no fewer than four different states—and **irredentism** (the effort to unite culturally related but politically separated peoples) and border disputes remained a factor into the post-colonial period. Yet at the same time, African nationalists argued passionately for the unity and independence of their countries—even though these countries had been defined by outsiders, and had never existed until Europeans, meeting in Berlin, drew artificial borders on a map. The fifty or so colonies that they created shaped Africa's politics in lasting ways.

European power also shifted social relationships within Africa. As new forms of wage labor emerged, for instance, trade unions appeared. The rural countryside faced neglect as colonial budgets focused on the cities—the places where, not coincidentally, most Europeans lived. Relations between men and women shifted, and Europeans' presence complicated mating patterns. White men sometimes forcibly seized African women, and marriages rarely resulted from such unions. But these men could, if they chose, also offer material inducements to a sexual partner (money, food, access to power and privilege). French colonists in North Africa, for example, regularly took temporary African "wives," and returned these women to their families after a preset interval, usually with some sort of payment. Both approaches obviously unbalanced marriage markets—and created sharp resentments among African men as well as women.

New groups also emerged within African society to help run the colonial system—since European empires could not function without indigenous personnel as intermediaries, foot-soldiers, or local supervisors. Sometimes these figures came from traditional elites who chose to retain some authority by cooperating with a colonial state. In other places new groups, like the brutal sentries in Congo, arrived from other parts of Africa. A third possibility involved elites from outside the continent altogether—such as the Lebanese, Syrian, and Armenian traders who had long formed **diasporic** communities (substantially sized, culturally and socially coherent immigrant populations living far from their perceived homelands) that played an important role in Africa's economy. The wider expansion of global empires in the late nineteenth and early twentieth centuries also brought thousands of other trained workers (and administrators, doctors, and lawyers) from elsewhere. The decorated World War II veteran and psychiatrist Frantz Fanon, for example, a native of Martinique who came to Africa after finishing medical school in France, galvanized Algerian resistance in the 1950s[11]—just as the Indian lawyer Mohandas Gandhi had done for colonized groups in South Africa before World War I. Both men personified the potential for cross-regional alliances of colonized peoples. Immigration from India in particular remained a controversial issue in the early twentieth century among black Africans as well as colonial officials, who feared a local backlash if Indians received any special status. Some Britons also wondered about the wisdom of entrusting the "civilizing mission" to Indian staffers who had, in European eyes, not yet been fully civilized themselves—and who might conceivably unite with Africans in a grand anti-colonial alliance.

Finally, and crucially, colonial systems also produced highly trained indigenous groups that were meant to administer and preserve the imperial order, but whose members graduated from European schools and then—as in India—worked to bring down that order. This topic is treated more fully in a forthcoming *Connections* volume on decolonization, but a generation of early twentieth-century African leaders such as Solomon Plaatje (who wrote one of the documents below) used the wider intellectual framework provided by colonial schooling—and their connections to other colonized places such as India and the Caribbean—to define and articulate new visions for a post-colonial future. At first members of this African elite worked within the colonial system, taking jobs in government agencies and

---

[11]A forthcoming book in the *Connections* series discusses the influence of Fanon's writings on black protestors of the 1960s in West Africa, France, and the United States.

social-assistance programs, while organizing independent social and political groups to seek incremental reform. Highly educated and mostly urban, they initially appealed for help from imperial authorities. Rather than taking direct action to protest the Native Lands Act, for instance, South Africans like Plaatje in 1913 sent petitions to British MPs in London. When colonial authorities refused to listen to such grievances, and showed no signs of being motivated by Christian morality or their stated desire to help Africans, these groups grew disillusioned with quietist reform; and they possessed the leadership, training, and resources to act in other ways.

As they articulated African grievances, these leaders organized a diverse set of groups to work for change, often in new organizational forms shaped by the colonial experience: trade unions, political parties, literary clubs, religious groups, and youth organizations. To undercut the moral claims of colonial governments they used strikes, boycotts, petitions, and appeals directly to international audiences. After missionary reports helped end Leopold's reign in the Congo, for example, investigative journalists elsewhere looked for similar abuses. African anti-colonial leaders also drew on their military experiences as a key resource. Many African soldiers had fought in World War I, and they did so again in World War II, suffering grievous losses in the African campaigns and on the European fronts. They thus knew European military tactics and weaponry (overcoming a disparity that had aided European conquest in the 1890s) and they knew the butchery of trench warfare—underscoring the hollowness of European claims to moral superiority.

This new, colonial generation of African leaders also developed connections with other parts of the world. Gandhi had developed his techniques of nonviolent resistance in Natal; Africans likewise learned from their experiences in India, Europe, and elsewhere. Benjamin Nnamdi Azikiwe, the first president of independent Nigeria, followed such a path: after graduating from Catholic and Anglican mission schools, he studied for a decade in the United States before returning to Africa in 1937. He dropped his European first name and during World War II visited Calcutta, where Indian nationalists urged him to stand up forcefully against European imperial governments, and to fight for Nigerian independence. Leaders such as Azikiwe and Plaatje organized pan-African congresses in Europe and worked with the African diaspora in America—all of which contributed to the amazingly rapid collapse, when it came, of the European empires in Africa.

In one sense the colonial era in Africa reached its high-water mark in 1935-1936, when Italy invaded and finally defeated independent Ethiopia. This conquest left only a single African country, Liberia, free of direct colonial authority—and as the product of its own peculiar history, Liberia served only imperfectly as a symbol of African freedom. (Outsiders had established the country in 1847, when freeborn blacks and former slaves returning from the Americas had declared independence—yet these returnees, their black racial identities notwithstanding, finagled treaties with local kings just as the Europeans had done, and asserted a basically colonial status over the "uncivilized" Africans they found.) Yet even as the continent appeared to succumb completely to European power, this Italian invasion also galvanized a wider response, laying the groundwork for a push that finally expelled all the colonial empires. It catalyzed the wider African diaspora, Western anti-imperialists, and most importantly, Africans themselves. As Kwame Nkrumah, a student of Azikiwe who later became the first president of Ghana, later wrote about hearing the news in 1935, "At that moment it was almost as if the whole of London had declared war on me personally."[12] This was the turning point, and within thirty years all European governments in Africa had been forced to withdraw—among them the British from Ghana, the former Gold Coast, where Baden-Powell had so proudly chronicled the European conquest of Kumassi. After eighty years, African colonies had gained their independence—and Prempeh's heirs had their revenge.

SOURCES

■ Mentalities of Rule: Administering French West Africa (1908)

Rather than governing through intermediaries or empowering native elites to rule in its name, the French colonial state maintained direct administrative control over an extensive empire in northern and western Africa. Here Gabriel-Louis Angoulvant, soon after being transferred from the small territory of French India in 1908 to become governor of Ivory Coast (Côte d'Ivoire), explains this approach to empire.

---

[12]Quoted by Ali Mazrui, *The Anglo-African Commonwealth* (Oxford, 1967), 105.

A widely resented "head tax" had been imposed in Ivory Coast a few years before, and Angoulvant resolved to force local chiefdoms more fully to comply. This, however, meant abrogating the terms of treaties signed in the late 1880s, in which France had promised not to intervene in African politics, landholdings, or social customs. When Angoulvant tried to disarm local populations, they fought back; in a general rebellion led by the Baule people between 1908 and 1910, French colonial officials were pushed entirely out of the interior of the country and confined to a small strip of land along the coast. Angoulvant called in reinforcements from Senegal and cracked down harshly: burning villages, herding their inhabitants into larger settlements that could be closely monitored and guarded, imposing taxes retroactively, and deporting nearly all the chiefs he could find (many were sent into the deserts of Mauritania). Angoulvant's efforts gained him a promotion: in 1916, he rose to become Governor-General of French West Africa.

Who is Angoulvant's audience? Why does he see it as necessary to repress all indigenous resistance? What, in his view, is the state of African society—and what (in the long term) does French empire mean for Africans? How does he justify French presence? Would other Europeans support his reasoning? How, for instance, does the French theory compare with Britain's imperial system in India? How do you think an African would respond to this argument? What evidence does Angoulvant (sometimes inadvertently) provide that shows how Africans responded to French power? How firm does French rule appear?

One of the greatest difficulties we have encountered in establishing our influence lies in the natives' attitude of mind, or in short in the moral condition of the country....

Among the natives of the center of the Colony and the lower Ivory Coast the previous state of anarchy, with the solid advantages it brought to savage peoples, is still all too persistent, and where it has ceased it has left deep traces; its gradual disappearance is causing too many regrets for there to be no after-effects. These are manifested by the survival of internal disputes, feuds and rivalries, which are too often translated into sudden attacks, fights between villages, or individual crimes. Order, which in this country should ideally develop through the sacrifice of particular liberties for the sake of the liberty of all, seems to the masses to mean painful, almost intolerable, interference with all their conscious aspirations.... The native is so incapable of reflection that he does not spontaneously compare the present with the past, does not consider that we have brought him peace, the right to circulate freely, to enrich himself by his labor and to enjoy its fruits. We are the masters, and so people whose power must be respected but whose actions, however full of justice and goodwill, arouse no affection.

To make ourselves understood we must totally change the Negro mentality. It is not those who lived through the periods of anarchy who will follow us, welcome us, and love us. If we had any illusions about this they would be destroyed by the way our favorites—those who have been able to serve us and earn our special interests—often hasten to profit from their position at the public expense. Let's face it; at present the native is still hostile to our institutions and indifferent to the efforts we are making to improve his miserable lot.

This is a sad conclusion but we must recognize it; even if does not modify our aims it should dictate our actions. For a long time yet our subjects must be led to progress despite themselves, as some children are educated despite their reluctance to work. We must play the role of strong, strict parents toward the natives, obtaining through authority what persuasion would not gain.

The most urgent task is to check every sign of insubordination or ill-will....

I was quickly struck, when talking with administrators or reading their reports, by the false ideas which natives have about our occupation. In many parts of the Colony they regard it as temporary, and do not hesitate to say so. Again, when making contact with certain tribes I was greatly astonished by the lack of deference in their chief's attitude toward us, and by the independence of character which even led them to try to discuss with us the advisability of our best-justified measures....

What I want us to avoid, in this country where minds have still to be conquered, is making a display of fruitless sentimentalism. We ought not to start off by seeming to set great value on the natives' wishes; the essential thing is to follow, without weakening, the only road capable of leading us to our goal. Make no mistake, these wishes of the natives are essentially unproductive, and hindrances to progress....

The native policy to be followed in this country must therefore be, literally, benevolent but firm; its firmness will be shown by the suppression of all resistance (which does not mean that we may depart for a moment from the humane principles by which our colonial policy is inspired). If it is important to avoid abuses and excesses by individuals, to aim always to appeal to the native's reason and to win his goodwill, to use patience, diplomacy and forbearance, it is as dangerous to show weakness as it is unwise. It is desirable to avoid the use of force, but if it is used against us we must not be afraid to use it in our turn; I am determined to teach the natives a very sharp lesson whenever, wearying of our gentleness, they think they can flout our authority....

In short, I cannot repeat too often that the first condition for achieving anything practical and useful in our Colony is to establish our authority on unshakeable foundations. If there is the slightest crack, all our work will be at risk; hence we must not tolerate even the slightest breach in security. In native countries events may have extraordinary reverberations and the slightest incident, especially if troublesome for us, is at once blown up and misrepresented. Administrators must thus keep an attentive watch, and even eavesdrop. Demonstrations of impatience or disrespect for our authority, or any deliberate lack of goodwill must be suppressed without delay. Populations must be kept in suspense, held on the right lines by repeated visits from those whose mission it is to command them. It is essential that bad characters, who are generally the only instigators of disorders, should be isolated and eliminated.

Now I have indicated the attitude to be adopted toward the [overall] populations I can raise the question of native administration....We may consider our purpose as almost fulfilled when we can administer with the help of native elements, instead of finding them in our way....

Not that I have the slightest notion of attempting here any experiment in indirect administration. Except in a few northern districts the Ivory Coast does not have, among its own natives, any subjects capable of even roughly discharging the role of native official, of holding even the slightest fragment of public authority. Long years will be needed before we can find individuals who are at once relatively well educated, energetic, active, honest, loyal, ready to face the dangers involved for a native in exercising of power in his own country, and sufficiently disinterested to serve us as administrative auxiliaries, even at the price of close and continuing control.

We must thus confine ourselves to practicing direct administration, which is in any case the most moral system in Negro countries, for it involves far fewer of those excesses which are the undeniable consequence of any participation by natives in public affairs.

Source: John Hargreaves, ed., *France and West Africa* (London: Macmillan, 1969), 201–205.

■ Empire and Its Discontents: Investigating the Belgian Congo (1905)

Many social reformers criticized the brutality of the Belgian colonial system in central Africa. Following missionary and traveler reports, an investigation by the British consul Roger Casement (who also wrote a document excerpted in the next chapter), and several vehemently anti-imperialist publications by such well-known figures as Arthur Conan Doyle, Joseph Conrad, and Mark Twain, King Leopold II finally allowed an investigation. He insisted, however, on selecting the three men to carry out this work: a Belgian government lawyer, a judge working in the Congo Free State, and a respected Swiss jurist. They traveled throughout the Congo Basin during the winter of 1904–1905, and published their findings later that year. The excerpts below were compiled and published by the Congo Reform Association (CRA), a group of prominent Americans (its vice presidents included Samuel Clemens [Mark Twain]; David Starr Jordan, the president of Stanford University; and Booker T. Washington).

Given that Leopold appointed them, are you surprised by the commissioners' tone or conclusions? In which areas do they support the Belgian authorities—and why? What kinds of criticism do they make? What do they see as the root causes of any problems? Who appears to have authority (physical and moral) in the Congo? What are the goals of Leopold's colonial system? What reforms do the commissioners suggest? Do they think the king should cede authority, or grant independence to the local population? How does their view of local chiefs compare with Angoulvant's? What does it mean that criticism of colonial policy in the Congo came from British and American observers (missionaries, writers, and politicians)? Can you judge whether the CRA has fairly represented the situation in Congo, or accurately restated the commission's findings?

"In this sinister and mysterious Continent a State has become constituted and organized with a marvelous rapidity, introducing into the heart of Africa the benefits of civilization. Today security reigns in this immense territory. Almost everywhere the white man, where not animated with hostile intentions, can penetrate without escort or arms."

"Towns resembling our most coquettish seaside resorts, which lighten up and animate the banks of the great river; and the two rail-heads of the Lower Congo railway—Matadi, where the ocean steamers arrive, and Leopoldville, the great fluvial port, with the activity of its dock-yards, make one think of busy European cities."

"With a limited number of officials the State has accomplished the task of effectively occupying and administering its great domain. By the wise distribution of its government stations it has succeeded in coming into contact with what is practically the whole native population. The villages are now few which fail to recognize the authority of 'Boula Mat-adi' [the colonial administration]."

[*Ed.*: The commission discusses the agents who are authorized to collect rubber in payment of tax obligations.] "When the agent was reasonable he endeavored to conciliate the interests of the State, or the companies, with those of the natives, and sometimes he obtained much without violent measures; but numbers of agents only thought of one thing, to obtain as much as possible in the short-est possible time; and their demands were often excessive. This is not at all astonishing, at any rate as regards the gathering of the produce of the Domaine.[13] For the agents themselves regulated the tax and saw to its collection, and had a direct interest in increasing its amount, since they received proportional bonuses on the produce thus collected."

"As soon as the territory near to the villages was exhausted, and, consequently, the labor of the native become more painful, force was alone able to conquer the apathy of the native."

"[Protestant missionaries] brought before the Commission a multi-tude of native witnesses who revealed a large number of crimes and excesses alleged to have been committed by the sentinels. According to the witnesses, these auxiliaries, especially those stationed in the villages, abuse the authority conferred upon them, convert themselves into despots, claiming the women and the food, not only for themselves but for the body of parasites and creatures without any calling which a love of rapine causes to become associated with them, and with whom they surround themselves as with a veritable bodyguard; they kill with-out pity all those who attempt to resist their exactions and whims. The Commission was obviously unable in all cases to verify the exactitude of the allegations made before it, the more so as the facts were often several years old. However, the truth of the charges is borne out by a mass of evidence and official reports."

"Of how many abuses the native sentinels have been guilty it would be impossible to say, even approximately. Several chiefs of Baringa brought us, according to the native custom, bundles of sticks, each of which was meant to show one of their subjects killed by the capitas."

"The accusations against the sentries seem to be well founded. More-over, the agents examined by the Commission or present at its sittings did not even attempt to refute them. The least unfavorable opinion

---

[13]The *Domaine de la couronne*, or royal estate, was established secretly in 1896 to include a huge area between the Kasai and Ruki rivers that included the Congo's most valuable rubber-gathering areas. From this area all revenue flowed directly to King Leopold. Its existence was only acknowledged publicly in 1902, just before this document was written.

about the sentries was that of the Manager of the ABIR Company,[14] who said, 'The sentry is an evil, but a necessary evil.' We cannot share this view."

"There is no despot more cruel than a black given control of other blacks, when unrestrained by ties of race, family or tradition."

"The intermediary between the white man and the natives ought to be; as far as practicable, the village chief.... These, indeed, govern often in a paternal manner; in every case their rule is accepted by the populations; the natives hold them in much respect and affection and it is very rarely indeed that they complain of them. We refer here only to the chiefs of villages or of small groups of villages."

"Chiefs have been utilized to get labor from the natives and imposts, but only by making them personally responsible for all shortages and for all the faults of their people, without recognizing their being possessed of any rights or authority over their people. Many have disappeared or lie hidden, others refuse all contact with the white man."

"The imprisonment of the chiefs has completely destroyed their authority, the more so as they have been forced to the performance of servile tasks." ...

"Often also, in the regions where evangelical stations are established, the native, instead of going to the magistrate, his rightful protector, adopts the habit when he thinks he has a grievance against an agent or an Executive officer, to confide in the missionary. The latter listens to him, helps him according to his means, and makes himself the echo of all the complaints of a region. Hence the astounding influence which the missionaries possess in some parts of the territory. It exercises itself not only among the natives within the purview of their religious propaganda, but over all the villages whose troubles they have listened to. The missionary becomes, for the native of the region, the only representative of equity and justice."

Source: Congo Reform Association, *Report of the King's Commission of Inquiry and the Testimony Which Compelled It* (Boston: n.p., 1906), 19–20, 22–23, 26–28, 30, 40.

■ Race and the Imperial Economy: An African View of the Native Lands Act (1916)

In 1913, ten years after the Boer War established British sovereignty but preserved significant Afrikaner autonomy, the South African assembly passed—and the British parliament, with little discussion, approved—the Native Lands Act. This law sharply restricted ownership of land

---

[14]The Anglo-Belgian India-Rubber and Exploration Company, one of the main companies holding a rubber concession in the Congo.

along racial lines, contributing to the geographic stratification of society and helping lay the groundwork for an apartheid system in South Africa. It was resented and resisted by black Africans, who found themselves excluded from land ownership in 93 percent of the country. A near-simultaneous law also restricted mixed-race and "colored" land ownership, especially by Indian immigrants—but London intervened a year later to reverse this so-called Coolie Law, while restrictions on native Africans remained in place. (The amount of land set aside in reserves and trusts for black Africans did grow, but in 1936 still stood at a modest 13 percent.) In this excerpt, Solomon Tshekisho Plaatje chronicles the effects of the Native Lands Act. Plaatje, who from 1912 until 1917 served as the first Secretary-General of the South African Native Congress (which later evolved into the anti-apartheid African National Congress), was a writer as well as politician—he also published *Mhudi*, likely the first novel by a black South African.

As Plaatje describes them, what are the law's economic consequences? What is its social impact in black African society? How does Plaatje judge its intent? Would a British parliamentarian see it differently? What audience does Plaatje have in mind for his book—and why does he make a point of noting the previous service by black Africans in British military campaigns?

Awaking on Friday morning, June 20, 1913, the South African Native found himself, not actually a slave, but a pariah in the land of his birth.

The 4,500,000 black South Africans are domiciled as follows: One and three-quarter millions in Locations and Reserves, over half a million within municipalities or in urban areas, and nearly a million as squatters on farms owned by Europeans. The remainder are employed either on the public roads or railway lines, or as servants by European farmers, qualifying, that is, by hard work and saving to start farming on their own account.

A squatter in South Africa is a native who owns some livestock and, having no land of his own, hires a farm or grazing and ploughing rights from a landowner, to raise grain for his own use and feed his stock. Hence, these squatters are hit very hard by an Act [the Native Lands Act] which [has just come] into operation....

The locations [reserved for Natives] form but one-eighteenth of the total area of the Union. Theoretically, then, the 4,500,000 Natives may "buy" land in only one-eighteenth part of the Union, leaving the remaining seventeen parts for the one million whites....None of the non-European races in the Provinces of Natal, Transvaal and the "Free" State can exercise the franchise.[15] They have no say in the selection of members for the Union Parliament. That right is only limited to white men, so that a large number of the members of Parliament who voted for this measure have no responsibility towards the black races....

The section of the law debarring Natives from hiring land is particularly harsh. It has been explained that its major portion is intended to reduce the Natives to serfs; but it should also be noted that the portion of the Act that is against Natives acquiring any interest whatsoever in land aims directly at dispossessing the Natives of their livestock. Section 5 provides for a fine of £100,[16] or six months' imprisonment, to a farmer convicted of accommodating a Native on his farm. And if after the fine is paid, the Native leaves the stock on the farm, for a number of days, while he goes to search for another place, there will be a fine of £5 per diem for each day the cattle remain on the farm.....
It would seem that the aim of Section 5 is not only to prohibit native occupation of land, but, in addition to it, makes it impossible for him to be a cattle owner....

Well-to-do Natives [in the Cape Colony] mainly derived their wealth from this form of occupation. It enabled them to lead respectable lives and to educate their children. The new prohibitions tended to drive these Natives back into overcrowded locations, with the logical result that sundry acute domestic problems, such as disordered sanitation caused by the smallness of the location, loss of numerous heads of cattle owing to the too limited pasturage in the locations, are likely to arise. These herds of cattle have been the Natives' only capital, or the Natives' "bank," as they truthfully call them, so that, deprived of this occupation, the down-grade of a people...must be very rapid....

This prohibition seems particularly contemptible when it is remembered that the majority of the Natives...are Fingoes,[17] and that their fathers in the early days joined the British in fighting most of the Kafir wars, side by side with British troops. They shared in all the massacres and devastating raids committed upon the British

---

[15]The right to vote.

[16]This figure approximated the average income for a citizen in Britain. Per-capita income in South Africa in the early 1900s stood at roughly one-third this level. But this "one-third" comparison itself aggregates the vastly different incomes of European settlers and black Africans. The penalty thus represented an impossibly large fortune for nearly all "Natives."

[17]The Fingoes fled from Natal to Transkei in 1820s, only to fall into slavery among the Gcaleka Xhosa—hence in the 1830s they allied with the British, and converted to Christianity, to fight alongside the British when they attacked the Gcaleka in wars against "Kafirs" (unbelievers).

settlers by unfriendly native tribes. As a mark of recognition of their loyalty to the Government, and of their co-operation with the British forces in the field of battle, this country was given, in the name of Her late Majesty Victoria, to their chiefs by a British Governor. But in spite of this treaty, the people have been gradually dispossessed of the land during the past three-quarters of a century. Hence the occupation, now crystallized into ownership, passed bit by bit into white hands. Hitherto the right to live on, and to cultivate, lands which thus formerly belonged to them was never challenged, but all that is now changed. Naturally the ingratitude meted out to these people by the authorities in return for services consistently rendered by three successive generations of them will be a blow, not only to the economic independence of a loyal and patriotic people, but to the belief in British sense of justice.

Source: Solomon Tshekisho Plaatje, *Native Life in South Africa, Before and Since the European War and the Boer Rebellion* (London: P.S. King, 1916), 17, 20–21, 149–150, 153–154.

■ Colonial Crossings I: Missionary Cultures of Health and Religion (1893)

European colonists justified their presence in Africa by pointing to the various benefits of "civilization"—first and foremost, the introduction of Christianity and improved public health. Missionaries flooded the continent after the Congress of Berlin, sometimes assisting but also complicating the task of colonial authorities (as shown in the CRA report, above). Yet many ideologists of empire saw missionaries' work as essential. The excerpt below comes from a book by Frederick Lugard, a British military officer, East Africa Company official, and (later) state administrator in Nigeria and Hong Kong. Lugard was born in India, to missionary parents (his father, a minister, worked as an army chaplain in Madras). He fought in Afghanistan, Uganda, and Nigeria against both local armies and European competitors, and his successful effort to establish a British presence in Nyasaland and Uganda—fighting off French as well as African attacks—is chronicled in the book quoted here.

How does Lugard, an official interested in military, economic, and political matters, see missionaries' role, status, and social function? To what extent has mission work changed Africans' spiritual life? How does it intersect with indigenous religious practices and beliefs—and with wider economic and social structures? What does Christianity mean to Lugard, to his reading audience, and to Africans—and how does it shape the way this document is presented?

A word as to missions in Africa. Beyond doubt I think the most useful missions are the Medical and the Industrial, in the initial stage of savage development. A combination of the two is, in my opinion, an ideal mission. Such is the work of the Scotch Free Church on Lake Nyasa. The medical missionary begins work with every advantage. Throughout Africa the ideas of the cure of the body and of the soul are closely allied. The "medicine man" is credited, not only with a knowledge of the simples and drugs which may avert or cure disease, but owing to the superstitions of the people, he is also supposed to have a knowledge of the charms and *dawa* which will invoke the aid of the Deity or appease His wrath, and of the witchcraft and magic (*ulu*) by which success in war, immunity from danger, or a supply of rain may be obtained. As the skill of the European in medicine asserts its superiority over the crude methods of the medicine man, so does he in proportion gain an influence in his teaching of the great truths of Christianity. He teaches the savage where knowledge and art cease, how far natural remedies produce their effects, independent of charms or supernatural agencies, and where divine power overrules all human efforts. Such demonstration from a medicine man, whose skill they cannot fail to recognize as superior to their own, has naturally more weight than any mere preaching. A mere preacher is discounted and his zeal is not understood. The medical missionary, moreover, gains an admission to the houses and homes of the natives by virtue of his art, which would not be so readily accorded to another. He becomes their advisor and referee, and his counsels are substituted for the magic and witchcraft which retard development. . . .

In my view, moreover, instruction (religious or secular) is largely wasted on adults, who are wedded to custom and prejudice. It is the rising generation who should be educated to a higher plane, by the establishment of schools for children. . . .

One word as regards missionaries themselves. The essential point in dealing with Africans is to establish a respect for the European. Upon this—the prestige of the white man—depends his influence, often his very existence, in Africa. If he shows by his surroundings, by his assumption of superiority, that he is far above the native, he will be respected, and his influence will be proportionate to the superiority he assumes and bears out by his higher accomplishments and mode of life. In my opinion—at any rate with reference to Africa—it is the greatest possible mistake to suppose that a European can acquire a greater influence by adopting the mode of life of the natives. In effect, it is to lower himself to their plane, instead of elevating them to his..... The whole influence of the European in Africa is gained by this assertion of a superiority which commands the respect and excites the emulation of the savage. To forego this vantage-ground is to lose influence for good. I may add, that the loss of prestige consequent on what I should term the humiliation of the European affects not merely the missionary himself, but is subversive of all efforts for secular administration, and may even invite insult, which may lead to disaster and bloodshed. To maintain it a missionary must, above all things, be a gentleman; for no one is more quick to recognize a real gentleman than the African savage. He must at all times assert himself, and repel an insolent familiarity, which is a thing entirely apart from friendship born of respect and affection. His dwelling-house should be as superior to those of the natives as he is himself superior to them. And this, while adding to his prestige and influence, will simultaneously promote his own health and energy, and so save money spent on invalidings to England, and replacements due to sickness or death....

I am convinced that the indiscriminate application of such precepts as those contained in the words to "turn the other cheek also to the smiter," and to be "the servant of all men," is to wholly misunderstand and misapply the teaching of Christ. The African holds the position of a late-born child in the family of nations, and must as yet be schooled in the discipline of the nursery. He is neither the intelligent ideal crying out for instruction, and capable of appreciating the subtle beauties of Christian forbearance and self-sacrifice, which some well-meaning missionary literature would lead us to suppose; nor yet, on the other hand, is he universally a rampant cannibal, predestined by Providence to the yoke of the slave, and fitted for nothing better, as I have elsewhere seen him depicted....

That is to say, that there is in him, like the rest of us, both good and bad, and that the innate good is capable of being developed by culture.

Source: Frederick Dealtry Lugard, *The Rise of Our East African Empire* (Edinburgh: William Blackwood & Sons, 1893), 1, 69–75.

■ Colonial Crossings II: African Cultures of Religion and Health (1929–1937)

Conversion was never a simple process. Medical work, like mission work, resulted in complex interactions, as seen in this first account, by a Lithuanian-Jewish psychoanalyst, Wulf Sachs, of his two and a half years of work with an African patient he met in the slums of Johannesburg, South Africa. Sachs, a socialist, moved there in 1922; his patient John Chavafambira migrated in the 1920s from Manyika, in Rhodesia (present-day Zimbabwe), and in 1933, when he met Sachs, worked in two worlds—serving as a house servant for Europeans and also as a *nganga*, or African healer. The excerpt opens with his thoughts on Christianity; it encloses his and other Africans' words in quotations, while Sachs provides the clarifications in (italicized) brackets.

How does Chavafambira differ from Lugard on the position of European missionaries (and on the power and persuasiveness of European healthcare)? What would a missionary make of Sachs' account? Does he offer a different view of Africans? How much power do Europeans actually have? Finally, why do you think Chavafambira sought Sachs' help? Does the fact that a Western psychoanalyst retells his story affect your confidence in this source?

The second excerpt, part of a letter to the editor of *Mwigwithania* ("*Reconciler*"), offers another view of the social position and meanings of Christianity, this one in British East Africa (present-day Kenya). *Mwigwithania* (1928–1931) was one of the first publications written by—and for—an emerging Gikuyu intellectual elite. Johnstone (later Jomo) Kenyatta, who became the first president of post-colonial Kenya, was its founding editor. At the request of Special Branch (part of the British police), Arthur R. Barlow, a Presbyterian missionary who knew Gikuyu (also spelled "Kikuyu"), translated each issue of this journal into English for the colonial authorities; he added the alternative words that appear interspersed in parentheses. Charles Ngundo, author of this particular letter in late 1929, is more obscure. We know only that he came from Nyeri district, and likely had studied at the Tumutumu mission, a Protestant school run by the Church of Scotland.

In Ngundo's view, what social identities and values matter most—and how are they determined? Where does Christianity fit in this moral economy? What is Ngundo's attitude toward Europeans? Toward the government? Toward other Gikuyu? Why would the British police be so interested in this journal? Are you confident of the translator's ability, or does the journal's voyage into English raise specific queries or concerns?

Finally, note that you now have multiple African voices on this topic. How does Ngundo compare with Chavafambira? Can you identify any elements they share in common? Do they express contrasting engagements with religion (and missionaries), medicine, or politics? Does one or the other seem a more credible source in addressing these questions—and if so, why?

[Wulf Sachs, quoting John Chavafambira:] "We used to talk a lot about Christians. Even now we do. We don't think a lot of Christians. We don't believe in Jesus. We used to pray in olden times to our native god, and to the *midzimu* [ancestral spirits], for rain. It always helped. Now we pray to Jesus and rain never comes. We have no corn, no land, nothing. We all hate the Christians; they talk, talk, and nothing comes to us from it. I am only waiting to go home and learn how to pray to our god and will never pray to Jesus, and won't be a Christian any more. I became a Christian when I was quite small. I was still stupid. My mother was a Christian and also my second father, and all the children were baptized. My children were not baptized and never will be. My father also does not believe any more in Christianity. He became a native doctor. The Christian priests are even so bad [*he probably meant stupid*] that they are against native doctors and native medicines. When a missionary comes to our houses at home, they chase him away. Nobody wants to talk to them. In the kraals nobody wants to be a Christian any more. Why should they be? [*And here he became rather agitated.*] The white people came to our country, it is the natives' country [*he was emphatic about it*], took everything away from us—the land, the cattle—and made us work. We cannot move without a pass, have to pay taxes; and they have given us Jesus. We don't want him. I read in the Bible that the Jews also refused to have Jesus, and believe in God. We are also the same; I won't send my children to church, but I will send them to school to learn native and English." ...

One day, he said, a strange man came and joined the circle. He was a silent, taciturn man, who listened to their talk but said nothing. He came often, although he was not a patient. He eventually broke his silence with a bitter attack upon Christianity, remarking, at the end, that the missionaries were no longer popular among the kraal-folk, who were turning away from the churches.

"That is true," a chorus of voices attested, though the majority of those present were Christians belonging to various denominations.

"I am also a Christian," the stranger said. "I belong to the Apostolic Church. But my *midzimu* are angry with me because I don't kill any goats to them, and the minister talks of hell where I will go if I remain a heathen. I want so much to know what is this heaven and this hell."

"Yes, and they also tell us that *lobola*[18] is a sin," someone put in. "To have more than one wife is a sin. How can one marry without *lobola*? And how can one wife work the land?"

"They say if you make a sin you go to hell," the stranger interrupted again. "I would like to know what it is, hell." His face was stubborn and dull. Fear of hell seemed to have drained all life out of him.

Tentatively, someone tried to explain. But he failed. For the conception of hell is utterly foreign to the African mind. When people die, they become *midzimu*, and continue to live in the places in which they lived in the flesh. They actually continue to live, only in a different way, and are in constant and intimate contact with the living. The dead and the living form a chain which must not be broken. There is no division of the worlds between them; so that the idea of hell, of "the other world," is utterly incomprehensible to them.

"And why do they want us not to talk to our *midzimu*? You are a *nganga* [healer]," they said to John; "why don't you ask them?" "When I go to church," another said, "it is the Catholic Church. I look at all the statues. I like to look at them and think they might be my *midzimu*."

"Yes, that is right," John remarked. "The same happens to me in my church. I pray, I think of my *midzimu*, and the faces change even if I don't close my eyes. The woman with the child turns into my mother, Nesta."

John sat silently pondering this thought, till Maggie broke in loudly: "Well, I don't want any other *midzimu*, and I don't like the priests. I won't be a Christian."

But John loved the statue of Christ. He even referred to him as the Great Healer. Was he perhaps, he wondered, the great-great-great-grandfather of all the *ngangas*? He knew that Christ was born in Africa, and wished that he could have proved that Christ was a real African, black as all Africans. But he knew from the Bible that Christ was a Jew, and he had not seen a black Jew.

Strangely enough, John never commented upon the multiplicity of denominations. He did not understand the differences between them, but assumed that, as there were many tribes, so there were many *midzimu*, all representing their various people in the One Supreme Being that all acknowledged. Just as in the kraals each *midzimu* had to have a man or woman through whom one could communicate with the

---

[18]*Lobola*—a payment from the groom's family to the bride's family, usually translated as "brideprice." Europeans saw this as a simple purchase amount, and looked down on what they called the straightforward buying and selling of women. These payments, however, also served as a tangible means of creating connections and alliances between the families involved, and could extend over many years.

ancestors, so the ministers and pastors and priests were people who talked to the *midzimu*, to Christ, or the Trinity.

So John had his simple solution to the problem of the many denominations: a problem that the missionaries feared would prove a stumbling-block to their converts. Paradoxically, the diversity of Churches was to the latter a natural and normal thing....

"[But] why," he expostulated, "does the priest speak against us native doctors, and leave the people unprotected against evildoers, *abathakathis* [witches], *ticoloshes* [demons], and all the other bad luck?"...

"There are good doctors from [many of the African] nations...I think in Transvaal the best doctors are the Ba-Venda, the second the Shangaan; the Zulus are the best poisoners; of the born fortune-tellers, Sotho and Shangaan are the best. But Manyikas have the strongest medicines. In Rhodesia are the best medicines. Many native doctors come to Rhodesia from other places, just to get the best medicines. My real father was the very best doctor in Rhodesia. I agree that the white people are also good, but they don't know about *abathakathi*; they can't make thunder; they don't know how to protect people. I cannot operate, but what is the good of cutting? The white people cut the woman if the baby goes the wrong way. My father would put his hands on the stomach with some medicine, and then the baby would come!"

Source: Wulf Sachs, *Black Hamlet* (Baltimore: Johns Hopkins University Press, 1996), 173–179.

[Charles Ngundo, to the Editor of Mwigwithania:]   *One does not part from one's Clan or Circumcision-Guild....*

...take note that neither are we able to (or, neither will we) forget at any time (or, ever) our Kikuyu customs.

For, prior to everything else, amongst the Kikuyu, when a child is born, Land is found for him (or, it), and he is made to know that the Land is the primary (or, principal) thing (element) in the Inheritance apportioned to us by our God. We ought more abundantly earnestly to return thanks before the Almighty Who gave us this gilf [sic] – the Circumcision-Guild and the Clan....[We do so as follows:] when the Child arrives at the time (age) for circumcision, his (or, her) Father brews beers. When this is finished, he then brews a greater quantity and invites (calls) those who were circumcised at the same time as himself, his Circumcision-Guild, and says to them, "Your child is now old enough to be circumcised", so that they may know it is so. And when they have finished drinking the beer, very many Prayers are offered in the village concerned, and in this way the Clan and Circumcision-Guild know that the Man (i.e., the parent) has arrived at the stage of eldership, and the child also knows (distinguishes) who are its Fathers who were circumcised along with its Father. So I ask this question – How is a Man to be recognised to be an Elder nowadays? And how are children to be distinguished? By what sign will they be able to know, This is my Father?...

And now, if you like, [I] will show you the Christian way. It is like a Man who wishes to remember his Circumcision-Guild, to show (to them) their Child. Let him make a feast of very much Food and Tea; and let this feast be given this name – the Festival ("Siku-kuu") of the Circumcision-Guild, or Feast of the Circumcision-Guild. And let them come and eat and drink tea, for such is a Christian feast, in place of the beer of the Circumcision-Guild, so that their children may have an opportunity ("see a place") of recognising (distinguishing) their Fathers properly (or, clearly), and so that you Christian may not abandon (or, cast off) your clan. As regards the Chomba (Europeans, foreigners), note that from this month of April, for instance, until another (next) April they will ("must") make a feast, and the Chomba drink within that village in order to remember the time of birth of this child (i.e. the child of the head of the house) and they regard it as praising (or, thanking) God for bringing the child to the time (date, "place") of its birth (i.e., birthday). But remember that when our Fathers do those things note that it is just like that (or, this?), when they invite (call) the Clan or his circumcision-guild, and when they have done drinking very many prayers are offered and thanking (praising) of God, the giver of the child, to return great thanks to Him in respect of the time of its birth. And it is here that I feel grieved, for I hear (it said) that "One does not part from one's Circumcision-Guild or one's House";... for if you abandon (cast away) the sign (mark) of the circumcision-Guild and the family ("house"), from whence will the name of this country (and tribe), Kikuyu, be retrieved?

Source: Charles Ngundo, "Letter to the Editor," *Mwigwithania*, 1:12 (May 1929), pp. 5–6. KNA DC Machakos 10B/13/1. Published by permission of the Kenya National Archive.

CHAPTER

3

Hidden Empire: Dependency, Domination, and Neo-colonialism in the Americas, 1783–1933

*Nowhere did imperialism undergo more dramatic change than in the Americas, where colonial relationships shifted from formal, direct empire to a more informal, indirect kind of economic control known as **neo-colonialism**. At first, in the eighteenth century, European colonialism in the Americas followed a pattern similar to that of previous case studies. A fierce global rivalry between Britain and France played out partly in the New World, as the two empires fought sporadically over colonial possessions in North America; meanwhile the Spanish and Portuguese empires dominated Mexico, Central, and South America. In the decades after 1750, however, European wars and indigenous revolutions forced these financially and militarily overstretched metropolitan states to withdraw, in whole or in part. By 1830 the European empires seemed, on the surface at least, to have suffered near-total defeat, as independent states arose throughout the mainland of the Americas. Formal decolonization thus came early to the Western Hemisphere, with many colonies achieving political independence by the mid-nineteenth century—ironically, just as other parts of the world (such as India and Africa) were coming more fully under the* *control of these same European powers. (The Caribbean, where Spain's first American colonies had been established, followed a different path: here formal empire had a longer run.)*

Yet political independence (on the mainland) did not always bring freedom to former colonial subjects. In an ironic twist, some of the new American states themselves developed into imperial powers: the United States seized enormous amounts of Native American territory and warned European powers to stay out of the hemisphere, while starting in the 1840s, the Mexican state fought a long war against indigenous ("Indian") rebels.[1] Across Latin America, moreover, a new kind of hidden, informal colonialism appeared. Revolutions carried out in the name of national liberation benefited small, wealthy elites, drawn especially from the descendants of colonial settlers. These elite groups maintained strong ties to European and US banks and multinational companies. By the late nineteenth century, systems of informal, economic control—based on complex arrangements for loans, debt, and the provision of aid, and frequently coupled with behind-the-scenes political influence—replaced older, formal empires. Scholars today debate the historical extent and full implications of this "dependency," but the Latin American case highlights the global character of financial networks, and shows vast flows of capital as well as personnel among world regions. Neo-colonial relationships, based on the indirect exercise of power, may be less obvious (and thus harder for local populations to target or resist), but can be no less pervasive in their effects.

"Sam the Banana Man" may not sound like the name of a typical colonial official—but in the world of informal Latin American empire, Samuel Zemurray (Zmuri) reigned supreme. Zemurray, an entrepreneurial immigrant to the United States (from Bessarabia, present-day Moldova) who rose by age thirty-two to own a major fruit company

---

[1]Even terminological debates, as embedded here, can point to past global interactions—and misunderstandings. "Indians," although a name used in this chapter (because it was widely taken up, by all sides, in the North American historical contexts under discussion; likewise "*Indios*" in Central and Latin America), originates from a fifteenth-century mistake: Christopher Columbus erroneously thought the people his ships encountered inhabited the "Indies," meaning the exotic lands east of Persia. More recent substitutions, such as "Amerindian" (for "American Indian") or "Native American" in the United States, "First Nations" in Canada, or "indigenous peoples" [*pueblas indigenas/povos indigenas*] in Spanish- and Portuguese-speaking America, have attempted to undo this historical misjudgment. Yet for various reasons—such as the simple fact that no single, quasi-racial label accurately encompasses all the groups involved—the debate continues. Ironically, the word "American," first coined in the sixteenth century, initially applied only to these indigenous groups—it only later came to include, and then still later to mean, European and other settlers.

in Honduras, wielded as much practical power as any British viceroy. His grip helped reshape the economy of Central America, and he dominated local politicians as thoroughly as any overseas empire could have done. Yet he reached this position of nearly untrammeled authority without the support of—sometimes even working against— his own country's government.

After making his fortune as a young man by working on the Alabama coast, Zemurray moved to Honduras, where the local government, dominated by wealthy elites lacking any connection to the rural masses, faced major problems. Above all they were trying to run a state that had been hobbled by large loans owed to foreign, mostly British, banks. These fiscal problems drove the Honduran state in the 1890s to welcome outside investors, especially North American fruit companies, along its thinly populated northern Atlantic coast (see Map 3.1). It offered tempting incentives, in hopes of producing a stream of tax revenue to pay off its loans: cheap land and labor, low tax rates (just 1.5 cents per banana stem), and generous concessions for any company willing to build railways, ports, and steamships. Such infrastructural investments, officials assumed, would create— at no cost to the state—the beginnings of a national communication and transportation network.

This decision transformed the country, as Zemurray and other wealthy foreigners swept in and virtually took over the reins of authority. Although the three major *fruteras* (fruit companies) fought among themselves over land, resources, and influence, together they came to control the Honduran economy and government "to an unprecedented and incredible extent,"[2] as one amazed diplomat put it—especially after Zemurray merged his firm, Cuyamel, with the larger United Fruit Company to form a single corporate behemoth in 1930. As early as 1911 Zemurray had owned more than 400,000 acres in Honduras, served by 450 miles of purpose-built railway lines. The people of Honduras, however, did not realize much benefit from Zemurray's success. The low tax rates and long-term concessions offered by the Honduran state left its coffers emptier than expected—and infighting among officials only worsened the government's financial position. In 1912 Zemurray even financed his own coup d'etat—working against the US State Department to

---

[2]Quotations in this and the next paragraph are from Thomas O'Brien, *The Revolutionary Mission* (New York, 1996), 48, 85, 87.

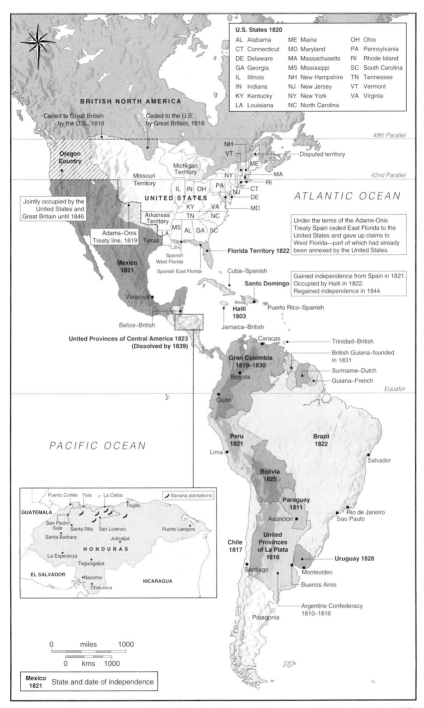

U.S. States 1820

AL	Alabama	ME	Maine	OH	Ohio
CT	Connecticut	MD	Maryland	PA	Pennsylvania
DE	Delaware	MA	Massachusetts	RI	Rhode Island
GA	Georgia	MS	Mississippi	SC	South Carolina
IL	Illinois	NH	New Hampshire	TN	Tennessee
IN	Indiana	NJ	New Jersey	VT	Vermont
KY	Kentucky	NY	New York	VA	Virginia
LA	Louisiana	NC	North Carolina		

BRITISH NORTH AMERICA

Ceded to Great Britain by the U.S., 1818

Ceded to the U.S. by Great Britain, 1818

49th Parallel

Oregon Country

Disputed territory

Michigan Territory

42nd Parallel

Jointly occupied by the United States and Great Britain until 1846

Missouri Territory

UNITED STATES

ATLANTIC OCEAN

Adams–Onis Treaty line, 1819

Arkansas Territory

Texas

Under the terms of the Adams-Onis Treaty Spain ceded East Florida to the United States and gave up claims to West Florida—part of which had already been annexed by the United States.

Mexico 1821

Spanish West Florida

Florida Territory 1822

Veracruz

Spanish East Florida

Cuba–Spanish

Santo Domingo

Gained independence from Spain in 1821. Occupied by Haiti in 1822. Regained independence in 1844.

Haiti 1803

Puerto Rico–Spanish

Belize–British

Jamaica–British

United Provinces of Central America 1823 (Dissolved by 1839)

Caracas

Trinidad–British

British Guiana–founded in 1831

Gran Colombia 1819–1830

Suriname–Dutch

Bogota

Guiana–French

Equator

Quito

PACIFIC OCEAN

Peru 1821

Brazil 1822

Lima

Salvador

Bolivia 1825

Paraguay 1811

Rio de Janeiro
Sao Paulo

Asunción

Puerto Cortés Tela La Ceiba

Trujillo

♩ Banana plantations

GUATEMALA

San Pedro Sula Santa Rita San Lorenzo

Santa Barbara

Juticalpa

Puerto Lempira

Chile 1817

United Provinces of La Plata 1816

H O N D U R A S

La Esperanza

Tegucigalpa

Uruguay 1828

EL SALVADOR

Nacome

NICARAGUA

Santiago

Montevideo

Choluteca

Buenos Aires

Argentine Confederacy 1810–1816

Patagonia

0	miles	1000

0	kms	1000

Mexico 1821   State and date of independence

MAP 3.1   Sovereignty and empire in nineteenth-century Latin America. The inset map shows Honduras and its "banana coast."

bring Manuel Bonilla, a deposed president, back to power. When this plan succeeded, Bonilla repaid the favor by granting Cuyamel Fruit a twenty-five-year tax waiver. The fiscal shortfalls produced by such decisions forced the state to seek direct loans from the fruteras, making its ministries even more beholden to men like Zemurray. Almost all Honduran officials received payments, either openly or under the table, and local powerbrokers (some of whom controlled large personal armies) also had a place on the fruteras' payroll. It all led to political chaos: between 1901 and 1933, Honduras had no fewer than fourteen governments and, by one count, 159 rebellions. The US minister to Honduras noted in 1925 that the powerful fruit companies opposed any attempt at political stabilization because "their interests appear to be best served when the country is in a state of turmoil and the Government financially embarrassed—conditions which permit the companies to obtain valuable concessions, exemptions, privileges etc."

Certainly companies like United Fruit (the forerunner of today's Chiquita Brands) often seemed more powerful than the state. Frequently they acted like a government: the three largest fruit companies invested seventy million dollars in Honduras, largely on infrastructure projects—building railways; dredging riverbeds; constructing new factories, water plants, and radio networks; and even designing a banking system to control virtually all foreign exchange. United's omnipresence earned it the nickname *Mamá Yunay* ("Mommy United"), as banana money enabled the rapid growth of towns along the Atlantic coast and drew thousands of people from the highlands. (Between 1905 and 1927, Honduras' coastal population grew 2.5 times faster than the country as a whole.) The new arrivals came in response to incentives, seeking the good life offered by jobs at the fruteras. For many this new life meant prosperity, in the form of higher wages and access to new consumer goods—what the writer Ramón Amaya-Amador called in 1930 "the marvelous life that moved to the captivating rhythm of the Dance of the Dollars."

Yet depending on the fruteras to develop Honduras meant the resulting development primarily served company interests—not necessarily national interests, much less the interests of poor women and men who worked in the banana forests. New rail lines, for instance, connected banana-growing areas with booming export hubs on the coast, rather than linking existing inland cities and towns. Hence they developed excellent connections to international markets, making local products available to faraway customers (and subjecting growers to far-flung competition and price fluctuations). They did not, however, accelerate trade along existing Central American land routes, nor did they integrate the Honduran economy. Workers, meanwhile, lived in company towns, buying necessities from company stores (often by running up debt) and following a work regimen and corporate culture imported from the United States—a gospel of efficiency and time management that was not always universally welcomed. (Partly for this reason, the fruteras imported thousands of English-speaking black workers from Jamaica and British Honduras to take some of the new jobs. Their presence alongside Spanish-speaking and Native American groups created new tensions, especially when local planters and workers started organizing against the conglomerates.)

The biggest overall change, though, came as the Honduran economy shifted in the 1890s away from small peasant farms toward a system dominated by massive company-owned landholdings. The world market for bananas grew exponentially, but it had far less competition as the trade came to be dominated by just a few enormous companies (see Table 3.1).

In this new world virtually all of the banana workers were paid wages, often on a **piece-rate** basis (based on how many bananas they picked or processed), rather than receiving a hourly or daily wage or working as contractors to grow crops on their own land. This approach meant the companies owned the land, trees, and bananas, and by paying workers a fixed wage-rate that was quite low

TABLE 3.1   Global Banana Trade, 1900–1932

Year	Total exports (bunches)
1900	19,848,692
1913	50,111,764
1929	97,233,972
1932	87,888,200
Of which:	51,600,000 (58.7%) United Fruit
	15,559,887 (17.7%) Standard Fruit

Source: Steve Striffler and Mark Moberg, eds., *Banana Wars* (Durham, NC, 2003), 4.

and encouraged productivity, it kept most of the profit when fruit prices went up—and when prices went down, it could fire workers to reduce costs. In some places companies like Zemurray's owned or leased twenty times more acreage than they actually cultivated (ostensibly a protection against crop disease, this practice also prevented others from using the land). The companies pursued **vertical integration** of the banana market, too, meaning control over all parts of the production process—from growing to cleaning to shipping to marketing. Such integration enabled the fruteras to squeeze out smaller competitors, since ownership of rail lines and steamship routes meant they dictated the terms of access to wider markets. By 1929 United Fruit produced up to 91 percent of the bananas it shipped from some districts, and the few remaining independent growers increasingly felt like hostages of "Mommy United." Even when they had production contracts, they complained that United played games with the system, such as rejecting their fruit as "low quality"—something the company only did, growers pointed out, when US banana prices dropped below the level at which their fruit would earn the fruteras a profit.

Such policies produced anger at all levels of Honduran society. Since the companies had little interest in industrial welfare policies or training programs, requiring only a steady stream of unskilled labor to work in the orchards and fields, it may not be surprising that many workers developed grievances. United Fruit also alienated officials when it regularly shifted production into new regions—but destroyed its old rail lines and other infrastructure to prevent squatters from using company land. In 1913, the year after Zemurray's coup, waves of strikes broke out against the fruteras, inaugurating more than twenty years of labor unrest. A general strike in 1920 forced Standard Fruit to raise its piece-rates to yield an average daily wage of $1.75 per worker, soon after Zemurray likewise tried to buy peace by raising wages 33 percent. Even so, by the mid-1920s communist organizers found an increasingly receptive audience in Central America, and labor militancy accelerated during the Great Depression. Ambitious local *caudillos* (military leaders) shook bribes from the fruit companies, turning around to use this money—and the support of angry workers—in attempts to overthrow the discredited central state. The fruteras responded by asking the US government to protect American business interests; US Marines intervened in Mexico, Panama, Nicaragua, Cuba, El Salvador, the Dominican Republic, and Honduras in the decade and a half after 1916.[3] Standard and United Fruit also started their own security forces, complete with spy networks and thug squads.

It all led to enormous polarization and hostility. As one planter put it in 1937 in a letter to the US president Franklin Roosevelt, "for some time now the inhabitants of this north coast of Honduras have been feeling asfixiated; this asfixiation has been caused by the extortion of the *United Fruit Company,* a ruthless banana company that day after day is absorbing the energies of these young people who are striving for greater progress and well being."[4] By this point the Honduran state, controlled by a tiny and wealthy elite, had devolved into a tool of American business—a situation that largely discredited the government among its own people. All of this occurred even as Honduras remained technically independent. As the story of Sam the Banana Man shows, the economic, social, political, and cultural consequences of informal neo-colonial control could be just as pervasive as those brought about by formal imperial systems.

NATIONAL LIBERATION AS ELITE FREEDOM: CULTURAL MIXING AND SOCIAL DIVIDES

The curious form of indirect empire that emerged in Honduras would not have been an obvious outcome to an observer of Latin America in 1750. In the eighteenth century, both North and South America appeared headed for the sort of colonial domination already chronicled in India and Africa. In the northern parts of the so-called New World, France and Britain played out their global imperial rivalry—the two sides waged five major wars during the century between 1689 and 1783, their armies fighting for roughly half of this time. Each war had an important American component, but the

---

[3]Not all US citizens welcomed this interventionism. In the words of the humorist Will Rogers, "Now you can't pick up a paper without reading where our Marines have landed to keep some nations from shooting each other, and if necessary we shoot them to keep them from shooting each other. America has a great habit of always talking about protecting American interests in some foreign country. Protect them here at home. There are more American interests right here than anywhere. What would we say if the Chinese was to send a gunboat up the Mississippi?" (Will Rogers, "On American 'Moral Leadership' and Foreign Adventurism," *The Journal for Historical Review* 17:2 (1998), 32, online at www.ihr.org/jhr/v17/v17n2p32_Rogers.html.)

[4]Quoted by O'Brien, *The Revolutionary Mission,* 105.

struggle was global. Consider the treaty of Aix-la-Chapelle, agreed to in 1748 to end the War of the Austrian Succession: As noted in Chapter 1, Britain swapped away an important Atlantic port that it had conquered in French Canada in exchange for France's returning the Indian port city of Madras. Such trades made sense from London's imperial point of view, but greatly annoyed British colonists in the Americas who had fought to end French rule. Many within this colonial elite felt abandoned by the metropole, and within a generation they too rebelled against the British Crown— this time with France's support.[5] Paris and London both understood the renewal of war in the 1770s as merely the latest episode in this worldwide struggle. From this imperial perspective, the key figures of American national mythology—from the Minutemen to patriots such as Patrick Henry and Paul Revere—played at best a supporting role in the drama. Certainly George Washington's poorly equipped colonial army could not have prevailed without assistance: his final victory at Yorktown in 1781 came only with the help of French ground troops and a French naval blockade.

Yet, whatever the cause and whoever facilitated the outcome, these battles did lead to the end of direct European control in much of North America. France's hands-on rule ended for the most part in 1763, leaving only a few islands in the Caribbean and French Guiana in South America. Its American possessions still included, however, the French empire's crown jewel, the wealthy colony of Saint-Domingue on the island of Hispaniola, until its slaves and others broke away in 1804 to become an independent country (Haiti). With that defeat, and the sale of its claim to Louisiana in 1803 to the United States, France's American empire all but disappeared.[6] Britain also lost much of its American empire when it agreed in 1783 to recognize US independence. It kept Canada (vast in territory but not population),[7] plus a few

---

[5] A treaty established this French-American military alliance in early 1778, a few months after American forces proved their viability by defeating a British army at the Battle of Saratoga. This alliance stretched globally: French naval and ground forces attacked their British counterparts in India and Martinique, as well as in Europe and North America, between 1778 and 1783. Notably, the treaty of 1778 obligated American revolutionaries to protect all French landholdings in America.

[6] Ownership of the Louisiana territory had long been disputed, but Spain controlled the western portion after 1763. France regained this area, at least nominally, shortly before its sale to the United States in 1803.

[7] In 1790 the new United States counted a population of 3,929,000. Canada, by comparison, had just over 161,000 people.

toeholds in Central and South America, along with its Caribbean and Atlantic possessions (including Barbados, Jamaica, and Bermuda). Later, and much farther south, it also claimed the Falklands and a few other small islands. Even Canada, although nominally subordinate until 1931, became more autonomous as Britain faced rebellions there pressuring the Crown to provide better support for its remaining outposts. In a food shortage of the late 1780s, for example, Britain's generous Canadian relief policies far exceeded the aid offered by the new US government to its citizens—and also vastly exceeded what Britain was doing at the same time for millions of colonial subjects facing a massive famine in India.

Spain and Portugal, meanwhile, which had long dominated the areas farther south, grew much weaker in the eighteenth century. European rivals had attacked their worldwide trade routes and colonial holdings, and both empires' financial position worsened. As Madrid's debt load skyrocketed toward catastrophe, Spanish colonies enjoyed more autonomy. Affluent settler elites in South America increasingly saw colonial silver mines and other natural wealth as their property, not the king's (and certainly not the property of indigenous Indians). These settlers resented royal attempts to reassert imperial control, and indigenous rebellions also challenged Madrid's authority. In the 1780s, a major revolt in the Peruvian Andes nearly succeeded before being brutally suppressed—but even this serious threat produced only a temporary alliance between American-born colonial settlers and their metropolitan sponsors. Settlers' power also grew thanks to European events; especially when, in 1807–1808 during the Napoleonic Wars, French troops marched in to occupy both Lisbon and Madrid. The Spanish king, who found himself under house arrest, had to leave the colonies more or less on their own until 1814; Portugal's royal family fled to Rio de Janeiro, turning Brazil into its own (weakened) imperial center. Following Napoleon's defeat, neither Iberian power could rebuild its prewar empire, and in the 1820s wealthy white settlers in Latin America turned definitively against their faraway rulers. Brazil gained its independence from Portugal in 1822, one year after Mexico left Spain; by 1828 the rest of the Spanish empire had likewise been transformed, most of it fragmenting into sixteen independent countries as shown on Map 3.1 (leaving only two Caribbean colonies, whose fates are discussed below).

The most famous of these independence campaigns came in the 1820s, when the general Simón Bolívar evoked comparisons with

George Washington by leading a military struggle against Spain. Bolívar earned his status as an icon of national freedom when he won victories in the areas now comprising Ecuador, Peru, Colombia, Panama, Venezuela, and Bolivia (the last of which was named in his honor). Yet while his victories led to the expulsion of Spain's monarchical empire and the establishment of democratic republics, Bolívar's troops fought especially for the freedom of a subgroup within Latin American society—the American-born and relatively wealthy colonial settlers of Spanish descent, known as *criollos*, who protected their own interests even as they acted in the name of the "nation." Other groups, such as Native American, African, and **mestizo** (mixed-race) communities, usually were kept at a distance. Indeed, Bolívar's supposedly national army relied largely on British soldiers and loans to win its struggle—a fact its leaders did not openly proclaim, but one they preferred to arming the potentially dangerous mass of exploited Indians and blacks. Freedom from Spain brought few benefits to these indigenous and lower-class groups; after 1830 they still faced constant exploitation. The criollo-dominated state did little to protect them, and indeed often allowed outsiders free rein to squeeze whatever they could (as seen in the harrowing document from Putumayo, below). This narrow approach to building a national government held serious risks: as in Honduras, it could amount to a recipe for political unrest and instability.

The nineteenth-century split between supposedly democratic Latin American governments and their people—a divide that fell along mutually reinforcing lines of race, class, ethnicity, and politics— only underscored the degree to which local society had been shaped by the characteristic intermixing and exchanges of earlier colonial systems. The major cultural encounters had been between European (especially Spanish and Portuguese) settlers and indigenous groups, on the one hand, and African slaves, on the other—but such lines had never been entirely clear, thanks to the blurring that came with cross-racial interactions and connections of all sorts, biological as well as cultural. For example, Levantine Arabs, especially Christian Arab merchants from Lebanon, had also moved into Haiti and Latin America, playing an important role in long-distance trade.

Such encounters expanded after independence, as economic migrations brought hundreds of thousands of new workers to the region. Millions of African slaves, of course, had already been forced to work on plantations in the Caribbean and Latin America, and continued to do so in the largest plantation societies, such as Cuba and Brazil, until the 1880s. But the influx of new slaves diminished substantially after the 1830s, when the major European slave-trading countries outlawed this traffic. Wealthy planters in the Americas cushioned the economic blow by finding other sources of cheap labor, again from places far away—adding to the pastiche of cultural interaction. Between 1838 and 1917, nearly 430,000 South Asian laborers (mostly indentured servants from India) arrived to support the agricultural economy of the West Indies, most of them working on the sugar plantations of Guiana, Trinidad, and Jamaica. Other immigrants came from Europe (especially Portugal), while many more journeyed from China.

The statistics are incomplete but suggestive: in just two countries, Cuba and Peru, roughly 225,000 Chinese laborers arrived during the quarter-century after 1849. They too intermingled and became part of this complicated social world. In Cuba, Chinese migrants joined white Cubans for initiation into local Afro-Cuban religious societies such as the Abakuá. In the words of George Lamming, a black West Indian writer, such patterns of influx and intermixing formed a unique social realm—however confusing it might appear to outsiders—and created one of the most cosmopolitan places on the globe. "For what do we see?" Lamming asked rhetorically, using the West Indian cricket team as an illustration. "Short and tall, yes; but Indian, Negro, Chinese, White, Portuguese mixed with Syrian. To the English eye ... the mixtures are as weird and promising as the rainbow. And the combination of that team is not a political gimmick. That is the West Indian team; for it is, in fact, the West Indian situation."[8]

EMPIRES OF FORCE AND FREEDOM: TERRITORIAL EXPANSION AND INDIRECT INFLUENCE

By 1830, much of the New World appeared to have won its freedom—at least on the surface, and according to its new leaders. Organized movements in North and South America had fought successfully for political emancipation from European empires. Yet as suggested by Bolívar's reliance on British bankers—and by the angry attitude of Honduran farmers toward their own government—the story of

---

[8]George Lamming, *Pleasures of Exile* (Ann Arbor, 1991), 37.

decolonization was not always so simple. Political independence did not necessarily mean much to ordinary people; certainly it did not always mean freedom in everyday life. In at least two fundamental ways the tendrils of colonial control—although in some ways less formal and harder to see than before—continued to structure daily life in the Americas.

First, several of the independent countries that emerged after 1770 ironically turned into new colonial powers—building overland (and sometimes overseas) empires through the direct conquest of lands with alien populations. In Mexico, for instance, criollo elites built a powerful centralized state, crushing indigenous Indian revolts along the way. This was not easy, and in places like the Yucatán, which had successfully declared its independence from the Mexican government in 1841, it took decades. In 1847 Mayan soldiers and others took up arms against white Yucateco settlers when the latter tried to subjugate indigenous peasants, confiscating land, raising taxes, and forcing poor Mayans to harvest sugarcane and henequen (a fiber used in making rope). When faced with large-scale rebellion, the settler elite quickly put their economic interests above political independence. In exchange for help against the Mayans, they agreed in 1848 to merge again with Mexico. Even with Mexican troops, guns, and money entering the fight, the so-called Caste War continued for more than a half-century. For years any white settler who ventured into Mayan areas of the Yucatán forest faced near-certain death. Mexico's army finally crushed organized Mayan opposition in 1901, but indigenous groups in the Yucatán continued to resist the power of the Mexican state. Smaller skirmishes continued for decades, some occurring as late as 1933 (and unrest still persists in Chiapas).

Yet however imperial the Mexican government may have been (during a brief period of conservative control in the 1860s it even saw the investiture of an Austrian archduke, Maximilian, as emperor), its colonial policies paled in comparison with its northern neighbor. The United States steadfastly denied that it wished to become an imperial power—its leaders insisted that the United States, unlike major European empires, sought only freedom for itself and others—but during the nineteenth century it nevertheless pursued an aggressive program of territorial expansion. This meant, first, taking control of Native American areas by any means available. Sometimes the US government obtained such control by purchasing land in supposedly voluntary transactions: exchanging token gifts such as beads, for example, or simply bargaining over the heads of the land's inhabitants, as in the purchases of Louisiana from Napoleonic France in 1803, or Alaska from tsarist Russia in 1867. Sometimes it meant seizing territory by force, as in many Indian campaigns, or in the Mexican war of 1846–1848. (Admittedly, in this latter case the treaty of Guadalupe Hidalgo did obligate the United States to pay Mexico for some of its lost land; the money helped Mexico attack its Mayan rebels.) In other places, like Texas, the United States did what Mexico had done in the Yucatán: making common cause with settler elites who were for various reasons willing to give up their own independence.

This expansion of US authority meant that Native Americans found themselves pressed ever farther north and west as US politicians and settlers steadily claimed their land. In one particularly egregious example, in 1838 Cherokee Indians living in northern Georgia faced expulsion westward with a forced march along the "Trail of Tears," so named for the high death rate it produced. At first such forced emigrations came with solemn promises that they would be final, that beyond a certain line, all land would remain perpetually "Indian Territory," not open to white settlement; but such promises always fell victim to the next generation of white expansion. After the United States fought and won its war against Mexico in the 1840s, it claimed land stretching all the way to the Pacific coast—meaning that Native Americans could no longer be pushed farther west. With the discovery of gold in California, moreover, large numbers of settlers moved across the continent, while Indian areas seemed potentially valuable, and exploitable. (In Latin America, too, major resources turned up in indigenous areas: diamonds in Brazil, diamonds and gold in Guiana, and later, large deposits of oil in Mexico and Venezuela.)

Hence American soldiers and bureaucrats focused on consolidating Indians into small, carefully circumscribed internment areas. These areas, known as **reservations**, were generally selected for their lack of arable land, known mineral resources, or anything else of value to white settlers.[9] Realizing this, Amerindians did not want to move onto the reservations either, and often had to be forced (or killed if they refused, as in 1890 in a massacre at Wounded Knee,

---

[9]Such judgments could, of course, prove mistaken. Congress created the first US Indian reservations in 1851, in the ostensibly barren territory of Oklahoma. Eight years later, the first subsurface oil was discovered; a major oil boom began a generation later, in 1897, following completion of Oklahoma's first commercial production well.

South Dakota). On reservations the US government set about bringing them into "civilization"—and thus, officials insisted, showing how US authority meant freedom and democracy, not the oppression and exploitation of (other) empires. It was part of a wider state-building project, but one that in Native American areas counts as imperial and colonial: American institutions aimed to survey, control, and integrate these culturally diverse societies into a broader economic and cultural sphere, overseen by faraway elites in Washington DC. With rhetoric reminiscent of British India or French North Africa, US officials depicted American Indians as children—requiring a firm hand and knowledgeable teachers to be raised properly. This tutelary approach went so far as to take Native American children away from their families and place them in government-run schools, to teach them the virtues of American civic life, economic values of market capitalism, and highlights of Euro-American, especially Anglo-Saxon, culture. Any children caught speaking Lakota or other indigenous Indian languages, or trying to return home, learned the other side of "civilization"—being liable to severe beatings and other punishments.

The conquest of Indian lands was only one way that forms of colonial authority, projected outward from new metropoles, structured daily life in the Americas. The second major tendril of empire has already been suggested by the story of Sam the Banana Man: the growth of informal mechanisms of indirect control and influence. This system of neo-colonialism developed in ways that especially benefited the United States. The United States, in other words, did not always need to achieve formal conquest to have its way. As early as 1823, the US government essentially proclaimed the Americas to be its own sphere of influence—declaring in the Monroe Doctrine that outside states (especially European powers) would no longer be permitted to interfere in the New World. At first the US military was far too weak to enforce these brave words, and ironically it relied initially on support from the Royal Navy (as its revolutionary forebears had relied on France). Yet the underlying principle remained in effect as the United States grew in military might, economic power, and political stature. It also took on new diplomatic meaning when European merchants and producers became more interested in Latin American markets, and in possible canal routes to the Pacific.

Push came to shove in 1898, when the now-much-stronger United States needed just three months to defeat Spain and seize its remaining overseas empire—especially the Caribbean islands of

Cuba and Puerto Rico, and the Pacific chain of the Philippines and Guam. (At the same time it also annexed the independent islands of Hawaii.) Spanish authority had already been weakened nearly to the point of collapse (a Cuban insurgency had started in 1895, the third major anti-colonial uprising in thirty years of intermittent war), but US military governors took credit for victory and quickly set about "emancipating" local men and women from Spanish rule, as General Leonard Wood, the soon-to-be military governor of Cuba (and later, governor-general of the Philippines), explains in a document below. In Cuba, the largest of Spain's remaining American colonies seized during the war, the United States declared itself a protector, not a permanent occupier. Cuba would govern itself as soon as possible, Wood asserted, although for the time being it had to remain under American "tutelage." In this sense the Monroe Doctrine lived on, as the US government asserted its duty to protect Latin America from European powers, and thus, to safeguard the region's freedom. As critics pointed out, though, the doctrine did nothing to restrict US intervention. It served instead to justify American supervision and oversight throughout the hemisphere—establishing a system that was arguably more patronizing, and sometimes more intrusive, than direct imperial control would have been.

The US effort to civilize its southern neighbors included educational work in schools, spreading American ideals of efficiency, enterprise, progress, and democracy. It involved nongovernmental missionary efforts like those in Africa—aiming at spiritual conversion and moral uplift, usually understood in Protestant Christian terms. It further included aggressive public-health campaigns, some run by independent groups (the Rockefeller Foundation worked to eradicate hookworm in Costa Rica) and others by American authorities. Leonard Wood, for instance, focused personally and intensively on issues of hygiene and disease. Wood had graduated from Harvard Medical School before starting his military career as an army surgeon (joining the US Army on the Western frontier in its war to contain Indians—and earning a Medal of Honor during its campaigns against the Apache leader, Geronimo). As a physician as well as soldier, he now forced cleanups of Cuban cities—sometimes at gunpoint—and assiduously investigated outbreaks of yellow fever and malaria. Such efforts led to a dramatic decline in disease mortality: an undeniably positive outcome for Cubans, to be sure, and also one that protected newly arrived North Americans.

Most of all, US companies, officials, soldiers, and teachers sought to introduce new categories through which Cubans, Puerto Ricans, and Filipinos would see their lives and their place in the world. "The Cuban people have generations of bad training ... to outgrow," said one American visitor. "[They have] new habits to form, new customs to adopt, before they can reach the condition of civilization which they ought to have."[10] Puerto Ricans, too, had to be civilized in American terms—US officials were horrified to learn that half the island's births occurred out of wedlock. This barbarism was blamed on oppressive Spanish rules and Catholic patriarchy; hence new civil marriage laws and free access to divorce were put in place, aimed, ironically, to make marriage more popular (especially among women), and thus to create a society that better lived up to Protestant-American ideals of morality.

Strident rhetoric trumpeting this work came from those supporting imperial expansion. Albert Beveridge, a US Senator from Indiana, justified it all in quasi-racial patriotic terms, lauding what he called "The March of the Flag" in a campaign speech of 1898. In this and other speeches (one of which is excerpted in the next chapter), Beveridge stressed the righteousness of the American colonial mission, praising its Anglo-Saxon and Christian character. He also noted the strong commercial impetus underlying the push for expansion. US industries produced more than the US population could consume, he pointed out, so they needed to find new markets. Moreover, the Spanish colonies—starting with Cuba, "the richest spot on the globe"—possessed vast resources, which could enable even greater US production. "In Cuba, alone," he remarked, "there are 15 million acres of forest unacquainted with the axe, exhaustless mines of iron, priceless deposits of manganese, millions of dollars' worth of which we must buy, today, from the Black Sea districts.... The resources of Puerto Rico have only been trifled with. The riches of the Philippines have hardly been touched by the finger-tips of modern methods. And they produce what we consume, and consume what we produce—the very predestination of reciprocity.... They sell hemp, sugar, coconuts, fruits of the tropics, timber of price like mahogany; they buy flour, clothing, tools, implements, machinery and all that we can raise and make." The United States needed to pursue a monopoly in these markets, he concluded, because "the

---

[10]The evangelical writer Howard Grose, quoted by Louis Perez, *On Becoming Cuban* (Chapel Hill, 1999), 249.

conflicts of the future are to be conflicts of trade—struggles for markets—commercial wars for existence."[11]

As time passed, US companies did conquer these markets—and the economic, social, and cultural presence of American models became overwhelming. The United States seemed to be everywhere. In Lima, the capital city of Peru, missionaries from the YMCA taught Peruvians American-style sports as well as Protestant Christianity; US companies sold Chevrolet automobiles and Palmolive soap; young people drank Coca-Cola (see Figure 3.1); and cinemas screened the latest films by Cecil B. DeMille. Things North American—from baseball to yacht clubs to English names to a parliament building modeled on the US Capitol in Washington DC—likewise permeated Cuban culture after 1898. By the 1950s, as an anthropologist discovered when he visited the small provincial town of Bejucal (pop. 11,000) in rural Cuba, "The clothing factories employ American-made sewing machines and use American-made yarn and dyes.... The people buy and consume large amounts of American-grown rice, beans, lard, hams, and canned goods. The farmers use American-made plows, machetes, and other hand tools, tractors, pumps.... The people of Bejucal watch television on American-made sets, listen to American-made radios, watch American movies, dance and listen to American music."[12]

Such efforts at dominating local markets as well as minds extended to the highest levels. Following William McKinley's assassination in 1901, the new US president was forty-two-year-old Theodore Roosevelt, who had used his military exploits in Cuba to achieve national renown. (He made his name in 1898 by joining Leonard Wood's famed Rough Riders and storming Spanish positions.) In 1903 Roosevelt essentially decided to take control of Central America's politics. Judging the region critical to US strategic and economic interests, he forced the building of a canal across the isthmus of Panama—and then kept this canal under US control. In what he later declared "by far the most important action I took in foreign affairs during the time I was President," Roosevelt refused to accept defeat when the Colombian Senate initially rejected the idea, calling the US offer of $10 million (plus annual payments of $250,000) insulting. Rather than offering more money, as the Colombians asked,

---

[11]The quoted passages in this paragraph are from Albert Beveridge, *Meaning of the Times and Other Speeches* (Indianapolis, 1908), 52–54.

[12]George Stabler, quoted by Perez, *On Becoming Cuban*, 379–380.

Have a Coca-Cola = ¿Qué Hay, Amigo?
(WHAT GIVES, PAL?)

...or making pals in Panama

Down Panama way, American ideas of friendliness and good neighborliness are nothing new. Folks there understand and like our love of sports, our humor and our everyday customs. *Have a "Coke",* says the American soldier, and the natives know he is saying *We are friends* . . . the same friendly invitation as when you offer Coca-Cola from your own refrigerator at home. Everywhere Coca-Cola stands for *the pause that refreshes,*—has become the high-sign of kindly-minded people the world over.

*   *   *

In news stories, books and magazines, you read how much our fighting men cherish Coca-Cola whenever they get it. Yes, more than just a delicious and refreshing drink, "Coke" reminds them of happy times at home. Luckily, they find Coca-Cola — bottled on the spot—in over 35 allied and neutral countries 'round the globe.

-the global high-sign

It's natural for popular names to acquire friendly abbreviations. That's why you hear Coca-Cola called "Coke".

COPYRIGHT 1944, THE COCA-COLA COMPANY

FIGURE 3.1   The American way: Making the world safe for Coca-Cola. A representation of the US presence in Latin America, in an advertisement intended for use at home, to US consumers.

Roosevelt decided instead to support a revolution in Panama, which up to this point had been part of Colombia. American ships and soldiers joined in the sudden fight for Panamanian independence, and two weeks later the rebels declared victory. Their new government quickly signed Roosevelt's treaty, receiving no more money than had been offered initially. Despite all appearances, Roosevelt insisted that the United States had acted according to "the highest standards of international morality," intervening only when the Panamanians had asked for help. "It was the action of the American people," he argued, "which alone brought peace. We gave to the people of Panama self-government, and freed them from subjection to alien oppressors."[13] His interpretation was more than a little self-serving; the United States would later (in 1921) agree to pay $25 million to compensate Colombia for its territorial losses.

Immediately after reshaping the borders of southern Central America, Roosevelt in 1904 announced a "Roosevelt Corollary" to the Monroe Doctrine. The United States declared itself henceforth to have the right to police Latin America, particularly in financial matters. As US business boomed—trade and direct investment in Latin America skyrocketed, rising by 750 percent and 1,200 percent, respectively, between 1900 and 1929—American politicians took a hands-on approach to protect this growing investment. In the Nicaraguan civil war of 1909–1912, for instance, the United States brought to power one Adolfo Díaz (who previously had worked for an American mining company). When an uprising threatened his presidency, 2,500 US Marines arrived to put it down. The United States further asserted its hegemony by taking responsibility for delinquent Nicaraguan loans and debts owed to US and European banks. American banks took over local financial networks, and US military officers assumed the role of customs inspectors, holding the power to levy trade taxes and collect tariffs—all of which they then paid directly to creditors, without going through local governments.

This "Dollar Diplomacy," as the US president William Taft called it, undercut the sovereignty of Central American states, as local governments appeared virtually powerless; for years it remained American policy to justify interventions throughout the region. "The proprietary rights of the United States," Calvin Coolidge said in 1927 to explain his decision to invade Nicaragua yet again, "place us in a

---

[13]Theodore Roosevelt, *Theodore Roosevelt: An Autobiography* (New York, 1913), 566–567.

position of peculiar responsibility." "I am sure," he continued, "it is not the desire of the United States to intervene in the internal affairs of Nicaragua or of any other Central American republic. Nevertheless, it must be said that we have a very definite and special interest in the maintenance of order and good government in Nicaragua ... and that the stability, prosperity, and independence of all Central American countries can never be a matter of indifference to us."[14] Coolidge— like Harding, Wilson, Taft, Roosevelt, and McKinley before him, and like any number of lower-ranking officials from both the Republican and Democratic parties—seems (when he thought about it) to have expected Latin Americans to welcome US investment, military presence, and political oversight, and simply to accept the sincerity of the United States' stated good intentions. American leaders allowed little room for local ambivalence, and expressed surprise when Latin Americans seemed not to appreciate them—as when José Martí, the Cuban writer and independence leader who died in battle in 1895, denounced what he called "Yankeemania," or "an excessive love of the North."[15] Such language made no sense to most Americans. Writing from Peru in 1933, one US diplomat noted quizzically that "our excessive loans and the introduction of American capital for legitimate development have had the peculiar result of provoking ill will and resentment."[16] How, he wondered, could this be?

Hindsight makes it easy to criticize such views, and to see them as either self-serving or self-deluding (or both). Yet they do suggest the genuine sincerity felt by at least some US officials, many of whom firmly believed in the rightness of their cause—like many colonial administrators and missionaries in Africa or India. Even as they sought primarily to protect US interests and markets, that is, they also persuaded themselves that US power would help Latin America. US efforts, they thought, shielded the region from predatory Europeans while simultaneously uplifting its poor and helpless people by bringing US-style prosperity, health, and freedom. At the same time, of course, such views show an obliviousness to (or perhaps self-delusion about) the texture of life in neo-colonial Latin America. These American observers seemed either not to know or not to care about the harsh character of everyday life on Caribbean sugar and coffee

[14]Quoted by James Malin, *The United States after the World War* (Boston, 1930), 399.

[15]Robert Holden and Eric Zolov, eds., *Latin America and the United States* (New York, 2000), 62.

[16]Quoted by O'Brien, *The Revolutionary Mission*, 1.

plantations, or the demanding conditions established by American multinational fruit companies in places like Honduras, Costa Rica, Panama, and Guatemala.

The arrival of hundreds of thousands of new laborers from faraway places like China and South Asia had pushed down wage levels. Very few of these immigrants had any hope of owning land (only in Trinidad did some indentured servants receive their own smallholding upon release). Hence they competed with local populations for jobs that paid either salaries or piece-rate wages. Since landlords and companies could explain wage reductions through the "invisible hand" of market forces, it was difficult for local men and women to see whom to blame for low incomes and the glut of workers—and at first they tended to target the new arrivals, rather than the wealthy landowners and state officials who subsidized this population flow.

Poor workers of all origins meanwhile faced grim conditions— with endemic hookworm infection and frequent killer epidemics like cholera—which also made powerful companies and plantations harder to resist. Like the hurricanes that struck at coastal communities nearly every year, fatal diseases found many of their victims among the most weakened parts of the population, where people could not withstand further strain. Cholera hit repeatedly during the nineteenth century, striking first and hardest among the most disadvantaged. In urban areas, it killed blacks disproportionately, mostly because they tended to have poorer water supplies and thus poorer hygiene. In the countryside, it attacked field-workers, who worked long hours in the sun with few breaks, and so gulped large amounts of water when they had the chance—a practice that allowed the virus to overwhelm the body's stomach acids. Colonial and state authorities, especially before 1898, seemed unsure how much to worry. Protestations of support for civilized health and hygiene practices notwithstanding, one investigating commission in British Guiana in 1871 described plantation hospitals as "filthy holes," finding some with no beds—and at least one that had been taken over by supervisors as a personal mansion.[17]

The intensity of economic exploitation only increased in the early twentieth century, as huge fruteras set up shop in Central America and large US sugar mills moved into the Caribbean. (Some economic historians argue that such intervention—and thus economic

---

[17]Quoted phrase is from Hugh Tinker, *A New System of Slavery* (Oxford, 1974), 198.

dependency—was less pronounced on the mainland of continental Latin America.) In both cases they created newly corporate structures for local agriculture. By pursuing land monopolies while simultaneously integrating their industries vertically and horizontally, they developed almost complete control over local societies. Many small farmers, who in the past had grown just enough to feed their own families, lost their land and had to abandon subsistence farming. The new system forced peasants either to exploit marginal lands (with serious environmental consequences if the rains stopped) or take paid jobs—another risky move that often led to poverty. Peasants had to compete with immigrants for wage jobs, but could easily be fired if world market prices dropped for coffee, sugar, or bananas. In the past they had relied on family and neighbors in crises like drought or flood, but many such safety nets now disappeared. Large companies provided few training programs or guarantees, and showed little interest in worker welfare; local governments did not have the resources to pay for social programs or anti-drought measures, even if their elite constituencies had wished them to do so (which few did).

It all led to economic torpor—with Latin America seeming to fall ever farther behind the United States, the powerhouse to the north. Much of this comparative underdevelopment can be ascribed to neo-colonial policies and structures, not explained as the inevitable result of some shortcoming within Latin America (such as its supposedly indolent people, or an alleged lack of natural resources). In the United States, per capita GDP had soared between 1800 and 1913, rising by 600 percent. In Mexico, the figure was 150 percent. In Brazil, on the other hand, productivity per person during this period did not change at all. Why the apparent stagnation? Historians sensitive to neo-colonial patterns of dependency have argued that Britain played a key role: it clung to commercial treaties that grew out of its earlier domination of Portuguese trade. After independence, these treaties preserved a commercial imbalance, and guaranteed permanent Brazilian state poverty. Tariffs on British goods in Brazil were capped at 15 percent while after 1827 Brazil's major exports (such as coffee) faced duties of up to 300 percent. The state had to finance its ongoing deficit with high-interest loans from British banks. These loans in turn could never be repaid—which necessitated more borrowing. It all created an inescapable cycle of indebtedness—alongside a weak, albeit technically still "free," Brazilian government.

RETHINKING THE HIDDEN EMPIRE: COLONIAL
REBELLION AND ITS COSTS

By the 1910s US (and to a lesser degree, European) domination of Latin American economies, politics, and culture appeared overwhelming. The success of a US model, in particular, both in achieving raw power and in setting forward principles of democratic governance and cultural "progress," did appeal to a variety of political and labor leaders, who made the case for "Americanization" in their countries. The nineteenth-century liberal president of Argentina, Domingo Faustino Sarmiento, took such a position. Such reform-minded figures criticized their societies' prior elites, and saw in the United States a model of democratic republicanism and modern industry. In Puerto Rico, the socialist-led labor movement even struck an electoral bargain with the pro-annexation business sector. Puerto Rican workers took this step—after many strikes and violent confrontations—because they believed US law offered better guarantees to workers than they were likely to receive from Puerto Rico's ruling class. Black Puerto Ricans such as José Celso Barbosa (a political leader and physician, who in 1880 had earned a medical degree from the University of Michigan) sided after 1898 with the US colonial government. Barbosa—who even during the Spanish colonial period had chosen to be educated in the United States—favored US annexation of Puerto Rico, and ultimately US statehood, because he saw the island's Spanish-era political establishment as insufficiently committed to racial equality.

Yet as shown in the speech quoted below, by the Argentine writer José Ingenieros, neo-colonial relationships also produced a deep backlash. Voices critical of the US model (and of what its neighbors saw as an annoyingly self-righteous and patronizing attitude) appeared among the region's cultural and political elites almost as soon as the Monroe Doctrine became American policy. As early as 1829, Simón Bolívar described the United States as a country that "seems destined by Providence to plague America with torments in the name of freedom."[18] Decades later, in 1894, the Cuban nationalist writer José Martí declared contemptuously that "the North American character has gone downhill since the winning of independence," finding it "crude, uneven, and decadent."[19] Perhaps most influentially, the

---

[18]Holden and Zolov, eds., *Latin America and the United States*, 18.

[19]José Martí, *Inside the Monster* (New York, 1975), 1:53–54.

Uruguayan writer José Rodó acknowledged in 1900 that while the American contribution to higher cultural and spiritual life had not been "entirely negative," in his view the United States offered little more than a blueprint for material prosperity and a culture that emphasized individual drive. He admired the United States, he insisted, for its stress on action, on efficiency, on practicality. But in an essay that remains widely read throughout Latin America, Rodó concluded that such a culture of overriding utilitarianism had its limits. "North Americans," he said, "openly aspire to pre-eminence in universal culture, to leadership in ideas; they consider themselves the forgers of a type of civilization that will endure forever." From his perspective, though, North American life offered only "insufficiency and emptiness"; it "perfectly describes the vicious circle identified by Pascal: the fervent pursuit of well-being that has no object beyond itself." In calling on his compatriots and neighbors to resist the American model, Rodó declared that while the United States might someday develop further and become worthy of emulation, it currently resembled "a well-laid fire to which no one has set a match."[20]

Although few expressed their views so articulately, many ordinary men and women also resented growing American power. Poor Latin Americans, after all, felt most directly the costs of neo-imperial domination. They fought back as best they could against American businesses (and against the soldiers and politicians who intervened to help US companies), as in the two decades of labor unrest that started in Honduras in 1913. Similar actions spread throughout the region, encompassing Peruvian mines as well as United Fruit fields. Workers seized plants owned by General Electric and took control of American sugar refineries, sometimes going so far as to form **soviets** (the Russian word for "councils"; these grassroots organizations had just succeeded in bringing about a communist revolution in Russia, and thus terrified many capitalist businessmen). Although outcomes varied from place to place, these pent-up grievances and sharp resistance to neo-colonial exploitation did, over time, force local states to change—speaking for more than a small elite, intervening in disputes more often on workers' behalf, regulating foreign companies, and offering at least some protection to ordinary citizens. Perhaps the most dramatic change came in Mexico, where a revolution in the 1910s removed the long-standing conservative president

---

[20]Quoted passages are from José Rodó, *Ariel* (Austin, 1988), 79, 86–87.

(some would say dictator), Porfirio Díaz, before devolving into a complicated civil war.[21] In 1934 a radical president, Lázaro Cárdenas, took office—and broke up and distributed the land of large farms, while confiscating the assets of US oil companies in order to nationalize the country's petroleum wealth.

By the late 1920s American companies and the US government could no longer deny the high costs of repression—and the political threat from radical socialist and communist groups focused the minds of American leaders and suggested the need to revise US policy. Anti-imperialist critics within the United States added their voices to the fray, creating an internal political cost to the maintenance of American hegemony. Almost immediately after the American victory over Spain in 1898 they had started arguing, in pointed language, that the United States was failing to live up to its professed goals and ideals, and that in places like the Philippines it had been motivated by the seamiest of financial and military interests. One such critic, David Starr Jordan, is quoted in a document below. Another, the Christian socialist George Herron, declared roundly in 1899, "There is one sole purpose behind imperialism and expansion, and that ... is commercial speculation. Having destroyed the purchasing power of the people here in America—the power of the people to buy what they produce— the large corporations now seek markets abroad; they seek contract-slavery; they seek an inferior labor-market; they seek not only to take possession of weaker nations for markets, but to ... send the sons of this nation, at the people's expense, to protect them in their exploitation."[22] From such a perspective the United States' high principles of democracy and civilization served only as a smokescreen, and US colonial administrators ranked as little better than those in the Belgian Congo. Such vociferous criticism remained a constant presence in American politics for the next three decades, hammering relentlessly at perceived hypocrisy in US policy. Such internal criticism alone, though, did not bring about change: a succession of presidents continued to invade Latin American countries. It took the perceived mounting costs of colonial rebellions overseas finally to turn the tide.

Largely in response to this violent resistance, soon after his election in 1928 a new US president, the Republican Herbert Hoover,

---

[21]The *Connections* book by Cyrus Veeser, *Great Leaps Forward* (2010), has a chapter dedicated to the career of Porfirio Díaz.

[22]Quoted in Charles Beard and Mary Beard, *The Rise of American Civilization* (New York, 1927), 4:583.

struck a new tone. He declared that the United States should seek to be a "good neighbor" in Latin America, working to build goodwill rather than routinely invading nearby countries. Such rhetoric marked a striking change, although of course Hoover's predecessors had also sometimes spoken empathetically, and it made little immediate difference on the ground. In 1933, though, Hoover's successor, the Democrat Franklin Roosevelt (who had earlier worked on US occupations of Haiti, Veracruz, and the Dominican Republic), codified the new approach by promising that the United States would henceforth follow a "Good Neighbor Policy." The United States abandoned its self-proclaimed right to intervene in Latin America—a decision formalized by treaty and then reiterated in 1936. This shift represented a major change of policy, but by then many US officials welcomed it as a way to escape comparisons with despots like Leopold of Belgium (all the more after 1946, when the Philippine Islands at last gained their independence). The fruteras and other major US companies in Latin America had to do serious work to change their methods and approach. They agreed to pay new taxes and to allow more government oversight; they offered new industrial-welfare protections for their workers, hired more local personnel into white-collar and managerial positions, and declared themselves "partners" with local governments in an effort to develop the region. By 1934, one US diplomat in Chile wrote home in ironic relief, "we are no longer conscious of Chilean mobs howling for the blood of American industrialists."[23]

Certainly, the United States remained the most powerful country in the Americas, and it retained much economic and cultural influence—and the long-term legacy of mistrust, hostility, and intervention did not disappear overnight. In some cases the mistrust simply went underground, with spies and covert agents picking up where the Marines had left off—especially during the Cold War, when the region's leftist politics came to be interpreted in new geopolitical terms. In the 1950s, the CIA toppled another Guatemalan president who favored land reform; three decades later, American operatives worked to fund the "Contra" rebels who sought to overthrow a socialist government in Nicaragua. (Such episodes will be discussed at greater length in a *Connections* volume on the Cold War.) Yet the

---

[23]Quoted by O'Brien, *The Revolutionary Mission*, 198.

American policy shift of the 1930s did mark an important change in the legal framework for hemispheric relations—and it signaled, at least rhetorically, the end of the United States' neo-imperial domination of Latin America. Perhaps it should be seen as the New World's second moment of decolonization—following political independence, which had come a century earlier.

This shift marked a more unheralded and largely unacknowledged decolonization, since after all the United States always denied that its informal empire even existed. Henceforth, American companies and officials had to pursue their goals through legal means, using diplomacy, foreign aid, and personal lobbying—or to hide their tracks if they did not. Sometimes this new approach worked—after several years of effort, US diplomats managed to secure payment for the oil companies whose Mexican assets had been nationalized by President Cárdenas. Sometimes it did not. But as revolutions swept pro-American governments from power in Cuba (1959) and elsewhere, and as Latin American governments successfully nationalized the property of some of its largest corporations, the United States' ability simply to subdue all its southern neighbors encountered serious limits.

Over the decades since 1933 the United States has had to, on the one hand, devise new strategies to preserve its interests and remain a first among equals, yet still to play by—or at least to appear to play by—the rules that govern other states. On the other hand, the United States, even as a "Good Neighbor," has not shown itself averse to continued involvement in Latin America when it judged such intrusion to be necessary. After 1933 the litany of interventions continued, including the Guatemalan coup mentioned above (1954), as well as a US-backed invasion of Cuba at the Bay of Pigs (1961), and direct US invasions of the Dominican Republic (1965), Grenada (1983), and Panama (1989). The United States has continued to use economic pressure to achieve policy goals, most notably through a decades-long commercial embargo of Cuba. In the light of 150 years of prior historical experience, it may thus be understandable that Latin Americans, ranging from leaders such as Fidel Castro (Cuba) to Hugo Chávez (Venezuela) or Evo Morales (Bolivia), through the less prominent women and men working in banana forests, coffee plantations, or oil fields, are still deeply skeptical about, or hostile to, American intentions in the region, and see the "Good Neighbor" as based more on rhetoric than reality.

SOURCES

■ An Empire of Ideals: The United States as a Colonial Power (1899)

Although the United States had already purchased Louisiana (from France) and Alaska (from Russia), and had also incorporated vast Native American and Mexican lands, it only became an overseas colonial power following military victory over Spain in 1898. Thereafter the United States assumed responsibility for several Spanish colonies— chief among them Cuba, Puerto Rico, and the Philippine Islands. These acquisitions presented American officials with various problems and complications, as they tried to design a colonial administration that would safeguard the United States' political, military, and economic interests, yet simultaneously live up to its oft-stated ideals of democracy and freedom. Here Major General Leonard Wood, writing as the military governor of Santiago province, explains the US approach in Cuba.

How does Wood want readers—subscribers to a popular magazine, *The Century*—to see American colonialism? How does he portray Cubans, and what does he present as their primary needs and desires? Does he empathize with them? Is he candid about problems—and if so, what does he see as the shortcomings of American work so far? What is at stake, and what are the risks? Can you read between the lines to gauge how Cubans perceive the policies Wood is defending?

I believe the problem which confronts the United States today in Cuba to be a simple one. The Cuban people, as a class, are anxious to work, and there is not the slightest difficulty in getting all the men necessary to do any work, excepting labor in the mines....In fact, the problem has been rather to find something for them to do, and the money to do it with. For the last ten months I have had … daily applications from the mayors of different towns to have necessary public work in their immediate vicinity begun in order to remedy bad conditions and give employment to those needing and desiring it. They are anxious to have a thorough reorganization of their school system and to have the schools started. Without exception all desire—I might say demand— American teachers. They are anxious to learn English; they are anxious to become Americanized; they are not anxious to continue under the former educational, judicial, and administrative conditions. The simple hoisting of the American flag over Spanish institutions and Spanish laws is not satisfactory to the people of Cuba. So far as I can learn, the discontent we have in the island today arises from the fact that the reforms which they expected under our control have not materialized. We are giving them an honest government so far as it goes, but we are not teaching them those things which they wish to learn, and it is the failure to do this which is causing the present discontent....

I can speak only from my own experience in regard to the condition of affairs in Cuba, but [on that basis] I can state positively that if we give the Cubans an honest, economical, non-political government under military control, and use every means to put the most desirable and competent Cubans in office, liberalize and Americanize their institutions, improve the sanitary and other conditions of their towns, organize and put in effect a suitable school system, get rid of the present intolerable administration of criminal law, and put in operation an equitable system of taxation, we shall find that there is no Cuban question left, and that we are dealing, not with a distrustful, suspicious, and resentful people, but with a people who will appreciate what we are doing for them and will give us their cordial support.... We are [in Cuba] to develop those latent qualities [of an honest and self-respecting people] and to establish a government which shall be creditable to the United States.... The people of the island desire that it shall be as nearly like our own as possible, and I know that we can establish a government which will render life and property safe to all the inhabitants of the island of Cuba, whoever they may be or wherever they may come from. This we must do, or we shall stand in an unenviable position before the world at large. In doing it we can count upon the support and approval of the inhabitants of the island. There are, of course, agitators and dissenters, seekers after notoriety and position by lawful means and otherwise; there are robbers and murderers and all classes of people; but the majority of the people of Cuba want a good government, liberal in form, and they look to us for it. This government must be under military control until it is completely established.

Source: Leonard Wood, "The Present Situation in Cuba," *The Century* 58:4 (August 1899), 639–640.

■ Ideals Against the Empire: The United States Should Not Be a Colonial Power (1898)

This excerpt comes from a speech in 1898 by David Starr Jordan, the first president of Stanford University and a zoologist by training, who worked actively for anti-imperialist causes. (He also served on the board of the Congo Reform Association.) This speech was published several times, including as a pamphlet, from which this version is taken.

What audience does Jordan have in mind? How does his portrait of Cubans, Puerto Ricans, and Filipinos differ from Wood's? What does he see as the main risks of imperial entanglement, and how does he argue against the US pursuit of empire? Does the basis for his critique surprise you? Is it possible to judge how these (or Wood's) views corresponded to wider American sentiment, or to gauge how different audiences within the United States might have responded to either of these pieces?

Colonial expansion is not national growth. By the spirit of our Constitution our Nation can expand only with the growth of freedom....

The territorial expansion now contemplated would not extend our institutions, because the proposed colonies are incapable of civilized self-government. It would not extend our nation, because these regions are already full of alien races, and are not habitable by Anglo-Saxon people. The strength of Anglo-Saxon civilization lies in the mental and physical activity of men and in the growth of the home. Where activity is fatal to life, the Anglo-Saxon decays, mentally, morally, physically. The home cannot endure in the climate of the topics. Mr. Ingersoll[24] once said that if a colony of New England preachers and Yankee schoolma'ams were established in the West Indies, the third generation would be seen riding bareback on Sunday to the cockfights. Civilization is, at it were, suffocated in the tropics....

The Latin Republics fail for reasons inherent in the nature of the people. There is little civic coherence among them; feelings are mistaken for realities, words for deeds and boasting for accomplishment. Hence great words, lofty sentiments, fuss and feathers generally take the place of action....

We shall find in Cuba all the problems that vex Latin America. There are three things inseparable from the life of the Cuban people,— the cigarette, the lottery ticket and the machete. These stand for vice, superstition and revenge....

The people of Cuba prefer the indolence of Spanish rule, however corrupt and brutal, to the bustling, blunt ways of the Anglo-Saxon. They would take their chances at starvation or butchery rather than

---

[24]Col. Robert Ingersoll, a politically active lawyer, Civil War veteran, renowned public speaker, and free-thinking humanist and agnostic, died in 1899.

clean up their towns. To suppress lottery and cock-fight would make life not worth living. The Puritan Sabbath and the self-control it typifies would be worse to them than the flames of Purgatory.[25] ...

We take Cuba, Puerto Rico and Hawaii, not because we want them, but because we have no friends who can manage them well and give us no trouble, and it is possible that in a century or so they may become part of our nation as well as of our territory. American enterprise will flow into Cuba, no doubt, when Cuba is free. It will clean up the cities, stamp out the fevers, build roads where the trails for mule-sleds are, and railroads where the current of traffic goes. Doubtless a great industrial awakening will follow our occupation of Cuba when we have taken away the barrier of our tariffs....

[But] it is the axiom of democracy that "government must derive its just powers from the consent of the governed."[26] ... No such consent justifies our hold on Alaska, Hawaii, Cuba, Puerto Rico, the Ladrones[27] or the Philippines. The people do not want us, our ways, our business, or our government. Only as we displace them or amuse them with cheap shows do we gain their consent. These are slave nations, and their inhabitants cannot be units in government. In our hands ... they will have no voice in their own affairs, but must be subject to the sovereign will of Congress alone. This implies Taxation without Representation, a matter of which something was said in Boston one hundred and thirty years ago. Our Constitution knows no such thing as permanently dependent colonies, else the acquisition of such would have been formally forbidden....

This, according to John Morley,[28] is England's experience in bringing peace to suffering humanity in the tropics: "First, you push on into territories where you have no business to be, and where you had promised not to go; secondly, your intrusion provokes resentment, and, in these wild countries, resentment means resistance; thirdly, you instantly cry out that the people are rebellious and that their act is rebellion (this in spite of your own assurance that you have no intention of setting up a permanent sovereignty over them); fourthly, you send a force to stamp

---

[25]He contrasts the Roman Catholic doctrine of Purgatory—a place where sins are expiated in the afterlife, and a belief that Protestants reject as superstition—with the more austere practices of Reform Protestantism. Nearly all Cubans were, of course, Catholic.

[26]Quoted from the American Declaration of Independence.

[27]The Mariana Islands, most notably Guam.

[28]Starr quotes a speech of September 1897 by John Morley, a British newspaper editor and Liberal Member of Parliament. Morley served as chief secretary for Ireland (1886, 1892–1895) and later became secretary of state for India (1905–1910).

out the rebellion; and fifthly, having spread bloodshed, confusion, and anarchy, you declare, with hands uplifted to the heavens, that moral reasons force you to stay, for if you were to leave, this territory would be left in a condition which no civilized Power could contemplate with equanimity or with composure...." No wonder England now cheers us on. We are following her lead. We are giving to her methods the sanction of our respectability.

Source: David Starr Jordan, "Imperial Democracy" (Boston: n.p., 1898), 3–6, 8–9.

■ Economies of Exploitation: The Rubber Trade in Putumayo (1911)

After a childhood in Ulster (Northern Ireland), Roger Casement joined the British Foreign Service in the early 1880s. He spent twenty years in Africa, rising through the diplomatic corps, and in 1901 became British consul to the Congo Free State. His painstaking report on the Belgian king's abuses of the Congo population came as a bombshell, and helped launch a European movement for Belgian reform. When Casement was posted to Brazil in 1906, he continued to explore colonial labor practices; the excerpt that follows comes from his investigation of the rubber-gathering economy in the Upper Amazon basin, along the Putumayo River. This area, technically in Peru but near its border with Colombia and Brazil, was only nominally subject to any government's authority. Outside traders and rubber companies (especially the Peruvian Amazon Company) participated in a free-for-all, perpetrating enormous abuses in their pursuit of profit. Casement's report chronicled near-universal floggings, long after such punishments had been outlawed; it noted the reliance on forced marches of up to sixty miles to reach the coast, with Indians of all ages carrying huge loads of rubber; and it quoted eyewitnesses to other atrocities. These included the cutting off of arms and legs, the rape and seizure of women, and punitive drownings and the use of kerosene to burn alive men, women, and children—all to terrorize Indians into gathering more rubber. Casement submitted this report in 1911. Its publication earned him even greater renown (and a knighthood). He retired in 1912, but soon became active in yet another colonial struggle—for Irish independence. In 1916, following his efforts to secure German assistance for an Irish rebellion, and perhaps even to organize captured Indian POWs into an anti-British brigade, the British government took away his knighthood and hanged him for treason.

How does Casement describe the people of Putumayo? Do you see any tensions or contradictions in his portrait? How does his sense of "civilization" compare with Jordan's (or other authors')? How does the rubber economy compare with that in Africa? How does Casement characterize company goals? What are the effects of this labor system on local society? Why do some local people cooperate? Are there any reasons to see this account as questionable, or is it a credible and convincing source? How would you expect British politicians and the public to react?

Had any form of administrative authority accompanied the early settlers or searchers for Indians, as they should rightly be termed, their relations with these wild inhabitants of the forest might have been controlled and directed to some mutually useful end. But the *caucheros*[29] came as filibusters,[30] not as civilizers, and were unaccompanied by any executive officers representing a civilized control. The region was practically a no-man's land, lying remote from any restraining authority or civilizing influence, and figuring on maps of South America as claimed by three separate republics.

Those who came in search of rubber had no intention of dwelling longer in the forest than the accumulation of the wealth they hoped to amass necessitated. They wanted to get rich quickly, not to stay and civilize the Indians or make their homes among them. The rubber trees themselves were of no value; it was Indians who could be made or induced to tap them and to bring in the rubber on the white man's terms that all the invading *conquistadores* were in search of.... An Indian would promise anything for a gun, or for some of the other tempting things offered as inducements to him to work rubber. Many Indians submitted to the alluring offer only to find that once in the conquistadores' books they had lost all liberty, and were reduced to unending demands for more rubber and more varied tasks. A *cacique* or "captain" might be bought over to dispose of the labor of all his clan, and as the cacique's influence was very great and the natural docility of the Indian a remarkable characteristic of the Upper Amazon tribes, the work of conquering a primitive people and reducing them to a continual strain of rubber-finding was less difficult than might at first be supposed. Moreover, their arms of defense were puerile weapons to oppose to the rifles of the *blancos* [whites].

---

[29]"Rubber sap gatherers," here meaning those who exploited the Indians who gathered sap.

[30]*Filibusteros,* literally "freebooters"—heavily armed Americans who had no official role, but went to Latin America to fight for adventure, wealth, and power. The most famous filibustero, William Walker, actually took control of Nicaragua in the 1850s.

Lieutenant Maw relates how, as long ago as 1827, the inferior firearms of that day filled the Indians with terror. He says, speaking of the then Portuguese raids up the Japurá:

"So great is the dread of white men among these Indians, who are said to fight desperately if opposed to each other, that if, as is sometimes the case, a hundred or more of them are seen dancing at night round a fire, seven or eight 'brancos' [sic] by taking different stations and firing a few shots may seize as many as they can get hold of, the others thinking only of escape. If the Indians get information of 'brancos' being on any of these hunting expeditions they dig holes in the paths and different parts of the woods, and fix strong poisoned spears in them, after which slight rotten sticks are placed across and covered with leaves, earth, etc., and it requires much caution and some experience to avoid them." ...

The civilizing white men were always, I found, particularly anxious that arms of precision should not fall into the hands of the wild Indians, and if by theft or otherwise Indians became possessed of them continual raids were made until the possessors were caught and the captured arms recovered. The only Indians who were permitted the use of rifles were those young men who were being trained to oppress their countrymen in the interests of the *caucheros*. These *muchachos*[31] were generally young Indians taken from one tribe and used in acts of terrorization in another district over people who were not their immediate kinsmen. No special qualification was needed to be a muchacho. Just as the bulk of the male adult Indians in any district "conquered" by the caucheros were required to bring in fixed quantities of rubber at stated periods, so some of the subdued tribesmen were compelled to come into the white man's dwelling-house and there serve him in this special capacity of muchacho. Some muchachos would grow into the service from being first *cholitos*, or small Indian boys, possibly orphans, growing up around the white man's station and trained to do his bidding. The muchachos would very often be married, many of them with children, and they and their families dwelt in one of the station buildings erected by the forced labor of the surrounding tribes for the white man's use.... The muchachos, generally speaking, were as bad as those they served, and in some cases, by reason of the utter thoughtlessness of the Indian's character and his extreme proneness to obey without question any order given him by a white man, the crimes they committed on their brethren were atrocious in the extreme.

In fairness to the Indian character, however, it must be pointed out that the worst crimes charged against Indian muchachos serving white masters were committed under the direct orders of their white lords. Moreover, the muchacho, no more than the Indian rubber gatherer could refuse to obey the white man. If he did not maltreat his brother

---

[31]Literally, "young men."

Indian at the bidding of the white man who had invaded his country he himself might be murdered. I came across very many muchachos during my journey in the forest, and some of them gave the distinct impression of being thoroughly demoralized, and capable of any crime in the calendar. Others, on the contrary, seemed amiable Indian lads or men who not too willingly fulfilled their odious role of oppressor. To be a muchacho was a species of promotion, of selection on approval; and as it quickly entailed the possession of a rifle and cartridges with which to terrorize the rubber-gathering Indians, it followed that the muchacho was able to indulge his own predatory instincts at the expense of his unarmed and defenseless countrymen....

The payments made to the Indians for the rubber they were compelled by this lawless organization to furnish were as capricious as were the names of the sections. No fixed or recognized scale of payments or of rubber values seem to have anywhere existed....

The Barbados men,[32] who were fairly trustworthy witnesses of the manner of dealing with the Indians, frequently gave me details of how they had seen *fabricos* [large shipments of rubber] paid for. Thus, Evelyn Batson at Santa Catalina had seen an Indian receive a tin bowl as payment for an entire fabrico (which might possibly be put at 80 kg. [176 lbs.]), which he had thrown on the ground and left behind him in disgust. Frederick Bishop declared that he had been present at payments where a single coin—a Peruvian *sole*, or two-shilling piece— had been given to an Indian as reward for 70 or 80 kg. [i.e., between 154 and 176 lbs.] of rubber. I met numbers of Indians who wore these coins strung around their necks as ornaments.

Source: Roger Casement, "Correspondence Respecting British Subjects and Native Indians Employed in Collection of Rubber in Putumayo Districts," House of Commons Sessional Papers 68:9 (14 February 1912–March 1913), 27–28, 31, 48, 50.

■ Cash Colonies: Tracing Finance and Politics in a Neo-colonial World (1922)

The Argentine socialist writer, philosopher, and trained psychiatrist José Ingenieros was born in Palermo, Sicily; his family moved from Italy while he was a child, settling first in Uruguay, and then moving to Argentina. Ingenieros worked as a professor of psychology at the University of Buenos Aires, writing books of intellectual history and

---

[32]Casement's investigation included testimony from thirty black men from Barbados whom the company had hired as overseers since 1903.

philosophy. He delivered this after-dinner speech in October 1922 to an elite audience in Mexico City. Ingenieros, long active in anti-imperialist politics, proposed that the nations of Latin America work together to resist US expansion and hegemony. His audience may have been particularly sensitive on this topic, since at the time the United States was refusing to recognize Mexico's nationalist government. His idea bore fruit in 1925 (the year Ingenieros died), when intellectuals and politicians met in his hometown, Buenos Aires, to form a "Unión Latin Americana," aiming to secure its members' "independence and freedom against the imperialism of foreign capitalist states."

How does Ingenieros perceive US activities, especially economic activities, in Latin America? Why does he call it "capitalist imperialism"? What does American influence mean for local societies and governments? How does Ingenieros understand the idea of national sovereignty? How might US officials such as Wood—or independent activists such as Jordan—respond? Would particular parts of the Latin American public be more or less likely to respond to this call for action?

We are not, we no longer wish to be, we cannot continue to be pan-Americanists. The famous Monroe doctrine, which for a century seemed to us the guarantee of our political independence from the threat of European conquest, has gradually been revealed as a reservation of the North American right to protect us and intervene in our affairs. Our powerful neighbor and intrusive friend has developed to its highest level the capitalist mode of production and has achieved, in the last war, global financial hegemony. With this economic power the voracity of its privileged class has grown as well, pushing policy more and more towards imperialism, to the point of converting the government into an instrument of its corporations, with no principles other than to capture sources of wealth and speculate over the labor of humanity, already enslaved by an immoral financial elite that lacks both nation and morals. At the same time, among the ruling classes of this great State, an urge for expansion and conquest has grown to the point that the classic "America for the Americans" actually means "America—our Latin America—for the North Americans." ….

This is the implication of the recent North American imperialist policy, which has followed an alarming course for all of Latin America. Since the war with Spain it [the United States] took possession of Puerto Rico and, upon Cuban independence, imposed the vexing conditions of the Platt Amendment.[33] It did not take long to amputate the Isthmus of Panama from Colombia, which had joined its coasts to the Atlantic and the Pacific. It later intervened in Nicaragua to secure for itself the possible route of another interoceanic canal. It threatened the sovereignty of Mexico with the unfortunate Veracruz adventure.[34] It took military possession of Haiti, under puerile pretexts.[35] Shortly thereafter it carried out the embarrassing occupation of Santo Domingo, alleging the usual pretext of pacifying the country and restoring its finances.[36] ....

I see on many faces the usual objection: Panama is the natural limit of expansion, and there capitalist imperialism's expansion will be stopped. Many, in fact, believed this until just a few years ago....The most distant nations, Brazil, Uruguay, Argentina and Chile, thought themselves safe from the eagle's claws, trusting that the torrid zone would stop its flight.

Lately, some of us have realized that we were wrong. We now know that voracious tentacles extend across the Pacific and the Atlantic, looking to secure direct or indirect financial control over various nations of the South....We know that some governments—which we will not name to avoid hurt feelings—live under a de facto guardianship, very similar to the ignominy sanctioned by the Platt Amendment. We know that certain recent loans contain clauses that assure American financial control and imply to some extent the right of intervention. And, finally, we know that in the last few years North American influence has been felt with growing intensity in all political, economic, and social activities in South America....

...the danger does not begin with annexation, as in Puerto Rico, nor with intervention, as in Cuba, nor with a military expedition, as in

---

[33]The Platt Amendment (passed by the US Congress in 1901, and included in Cuba's constitution in 1902) asserted the USA's right to intervene on the island—ostensibly to protect Cuban independence. It barred the Cuban government from signing foreign treaties without US permission, forbade it from interfering with US sanitation and hygiene programs, and required Cuba to follow prescribed tax policies. Overall it established a quasi-protectorate status for the island, and justified four US interventions between 1906 and 1920. It ended in 1933, when President Franklin Roosevelt launched a "Good Neighbor" policy toward Latin America.

[34]The US Navy occupied Mexico's port city of Veracruz for six months in 1914, in response to a perceived insult to American sailors during the Mexican revolution.

[35]Following a riot in 1915 that killed the pro-American president and threatened US investment in the country, US Marines invaded and occupied Haiti. The country remained under American military government for nineteen years, until 1934.

[36]A similar intervention in 1916—following years of attempts to influence local politics—established a US military occupation of the Dominican Republic. It lasted until 1924. In this as most of the cases Ingenieros mentions, US troops and their local allies faced ongoing armed rebellions and guerrilla resistance movements.

Mexico, nor with guardianship, as in Nicaragua, nor with territorial secession, as in Colombia, nor with armed occupation, as in Haiti, nor with purchase, as in the Guianas.[37] In its first phase, the danger begins in the progressive mortgaging of national independence through loans destined to grow and be renewed incessantly, under conditions that are progressively more detrimental to the sovereignty of the beneficiaries....

For the peoples of Latin America, the issue is quite simply a case of national defense, although many of their rulers often ignore or hide it. North American capitalism wishes to capture the sources of our national wealth and to secure its control, with the right of intervention to protect its investments and assure returns on them. In the meantime, we are allowed the illusion of increasingly nominal political independence. As long as a foreign State expressly or surreptitiously has the right of intervention, political independence is not effective; as long as it refuses to recognize any government that does not support its policy of privilege and absorption, it threatens national sovereignty; as long as it does not demonstrate with deeds that it renounces such a policy, it cannot be considered a friendly country.

Source: José Ingenieros, "Por la Unión Latino Americana: Discurso pronunciado el 11 de Octubre de 1922 ofreciendo el banquete de los Escritores Argentinos en honor de José Vasconcelos." Buenos Aires: L. J. Rosso, 1922, 6–11. Translated by Sarah Hamilton.

---

[37]Like fruit companies in Honduras, sugar producers dominated the economic landscape in Guiana. Plantations expanded, and ownership was concentrated. In British Guiana the number of sugar estates fell from 136 in 1870, to 50 in 1900, and 19 in 1950. Remarkably, in 1950 just one company—the London-based Booker Brothers McConnell—controlled eighteen of these estates, along with a multitude of retail establishments, transportation services, and manufacturing plants. Guianese joked that country's name should be changed to "Booker's Guiana."

CHAPTER

4

Empires of Freedom:
The Modern Imperial and
Social State in Asia, 1731–1991

It is not hard to find "typical" empires in modern East or Central Asia. New Zealand and Australia developed into settler colonies, to the detriment of Maoris and other aboriginal groups; much of New Guinea was grabbed by Germany, Britain, and the Netherlands; and after 1870 the Dutch greatly expanded their colonial system in Indonesia, based unapologetically on force and direct, intrusive control. As in Africa, new technologies like steamboats, machine guns, and anti-malaria drugs enabled (but did not cause) such conquests, making it easier to crush rebellions in Bali and Aceh. These empires remained globally interconnected: African troops from Senegal, for example, protected French colonies in Indochina. In some cases intervention led to indirect forms of control: China retained at least its nominal sovereignty, but following defeat in two "Opium Wars," the Qing emperor faced economic and military threats as outside powers forced his government to sign a series of unequal treaties. (But ironies abound: China also conquered a western empire of its own in Central Asia.) Other than Japan, only Thailand among these Asian states managed to play Europeans against one another to protect most of its territory and independence.

153

This chapter, however, focuses not on typical empires, but on colonial realms that represented themselves in new, self-consciously modern ways. This raises more questions about imperialism. First, is it necessarily European? Japanese expansion into Taiwan, Korea, and Manchuria, starting in the 1890s and involving considerable brutality and exploitation, suggests otherwise. Tsarist expansion in Central Asia, too, asserted Russia's claim to European identity, an idea many thought open to debate: Russian officials aimed to prove they were advanced enough to bring "civilization" to colonized Turkestan. Second, is there after all such a thing as "colonial liberation"? The USSR, Japan, and the United States all denied that their far-flung domains were, in fact, imperial, in the sense of being administered exploitatively. All styled themselves, in different ways, as "empires of freedom." Japan proclaimed a desire to protect other Asians (and some non-Asians) from rapacious Westerners. The United States claimed it sought to build a new and better life for former Spanish subjects. The USSR maintained an explicitly anti-colonial, liberationist ideology that aimed at a cross-ethnic socialist future. All of these states insisted that they wanted to help local populations, that only they could bring the benefits of modernity, progress, and freedom—and ironically, that other empires should be denounced as unjust and evil. Not all of their efforts may have been strictly "colonial"—public health campaigns also became a priority in imperial capitals like Moscow, Tokyo, and Washington. Yet leaders in those cities saw millions of faraway Uzbeks, Koreans, or Filipinos as populations that remained, in key ways, fundamentally different from their own people (a perception, crucially, that these colonized peoples also shared); and they administered systems that retained practical political, economic, and military power at an imperial core.

In March 1929 the Uzbek poet, playwright, and social reformer Hamza Hakim-zade Niyoziy faced an unruly crowd of his countrymen—one that before his eyes turned rapidly into a mob. Hamza had faced hostile crowds before as he traveled across Uzbekistan and beyond, making the case for Soviet power. Yet this group, in the provincial town of Shohimardon, a small Uzbek enclave on the border with modern-day Kyrgyzstan—a place where Hamza was known and where he had lived, on and off, for several years—seemed especially angry. Why? Local Soviet officials typically gave him a hero's welcome and introduced him with praise wherever he went: he was, after all, doing the hard work of revolution. According to Soviet sources, most recently he had delivered a firm speech telling the people of Shohimardon that they should stop visiting the nearby tomb (*mazar*) of an Islamic saint—according to legend, the tomb of Ali (a cousin, son-in-law, and successor of Muhammad). Stories differ about what precisely happened next, but the gathering turned ugly. At some point shouts broke out; the crowd turned violent; and Hamza bore the brunt. Someone threw a first punch—or threw a first stone—or took out a knife and lunged, depending on the version—and the poet fell. As his protected status melted away, Hamza, one of the leading writers in Uzbekistan, lay bleeding and dying. The Muslim voice of a communist revolution had been silenced.

When Hamza died, Soviet newspapers lionized him as a great writer whose work would live forever—despite the brutish attempt of mobs to silence him. Soviet courts quickly punished those accused of his murder. The village of Shohimardon even took on a new name, "Hamza City" (Hamzaobod), becoming an official shrine to Hamza's memory. Bolshevik officials went so far as to destroy the mazar he had criticized—although local residents (without asking permission) quickly rebuilt it. Following a second effort at demolition, in 1940, Soviet bureaucrats replaced the mazar with a "Museum of Atheism," and then, more than a decade later, a statuesque mausoleum and museum dedicated to Hamza. At this point, they thought, the story had ended. Yet despite all their efforts, and the clear power of a Stalinist state and the Red Army, Muslim pilgrims kept coming—to honor Ali, not Hamza—while Sufi incantations, prayer rituals, and sacrifices continued apace.

Why did Hamza's speech inspire such passion? How had he given offense sufficient to spark a riot? Twelve years earlier the Communist Party had seized control of most of the tsarist Russian Empire, and after fighting and winning a brutal civil war, its power had grown more secure. By the mid-1920s Bolshevik leaders felt confident enough to redraw the map of Central Asia, declaring that liberation and self-determination had come to the tsars' colonial subjects—that Soviet Muslims had gained their freedom.

They divided the tsarist province of "Turkestan" ("Land of the Turks") into smaller, supposedly national republics, such as Uzbekistan—an entity that had never before existed—and put local officials like Hamza in control. A politically sympathetic Uzbek, Faizulla Khodjaev, became the head of government; another, Akmal Ikramov, took over the local Communist Party. Russians filled lower-level positions, ostensibly as assistants. They all set about making local lives better. Supportive Uzbeks, such as Hamza, liked what they did. Activists built schools, treated the sick, and provided jobs and land to the poor. Emboldened Bolshevik officials closed mosques and religious schools, seizing the assets of Muslim endowments (*waqf*). Their explanation was that previous rulers and religious authorities had cared more about wealth than the people's welfare. In 1927 they even launched a campaign to liberate—as they saw it—the women of Turkestan. In Uzbekistan, as discussed in two documents below, this campaign aimed to persuade Muslim women and girls to throw off their veils—heavy horsehair-and-cotton ensembles that reached from head to toe, and which, to Russian eyes, perfectly symbolized their subjugation and second-class status. Soviet power declared itself opposed to such dress, which it intended to eliminate in just six months—in time to celebrate the Revolution's tenth anniversary. It did not happen nearly that quickly, but Soviet activists did not give up. Hamza, in fact, reportedly convened a meeting in Shohimardon on March 8, 1929—the socialist holiday of International Women's Day— at which twenty-three women had "liberated" themselves. Through such emancipation, the USSR declared itself a modern state with a vision of class and anti-colonial liberation that would bring freedom to all former colonies—first in Central Asia, then around the world.

Yet as Hamza learned to his great cost—the attack came a scant ten days after he organized this meeting for women to unveil— Uzbeks did not straightforwardly welcome such policies, nor did they necessarily accept Soviet understandings of liberation. Often they perceived Bolshevik campaigns—whether for land reform, hygiene and literacy, or women's rights—through an imperial lens, evaluating such efforts in the light of decades of Russian colonization. From this perspective Soviet officials represented the latest chapter in an ongoing story of empire—not its end. Not all historians agree that the USSR should be called a colonial empire: like other modern states, it shared a wider impulse for social reform, and unlike the empires that had colonies in Africa or India, it claimed to treat citizens of all nationalities equally. It targeted both Russian peasants *and* non-Russian groups for transformation, and argued that its goal was to overcome the marks of colonial difference through a process of "growing together" (*sblizhenie*), perhaps even ultimately a "merger" (*sliianie*) of Soviet peoples. Yet in key ways the Bolsheviks' Uzbek critics were right. The rhetoric of anti-colonialism overlay a system that remained functionally imperial: in the USSR's economic structures, for instance, or in its firm political oversight (backed up by military occupation) from Moscow. Few in Moscow or the Asian periphery saw the system as anything other than permanent; there was little pretense that inter-ethnic "merger" would happen anytime soon (unless it meant assimilation to Slavic or Russian ways), and no chance at all that a non-Russian republic could leave the system if it wished. Difference, distance, and domination: all three axes of empire still characterized the ostensibly anti-colonial Soviet realm in Central Asia.

PARADOXES OF SOCIALIST COLONIALISM: NEW VISIONS FOR CENTRAL ASIA

This Russian, and later Soviet, story began in the fifteenth century, when the tsarist state (then known as Muscovy) established a string of fortresses along its steppe frontier to protect against nomadic attack. Or perhaps it began in the 1550s, when Ivan IV ("the Terrible") conquered the Muslim khanates of Kazan and Astrakhan, both of which were located in the Volga region north of the Caspian Sea. Yet for centuries attempts to push farther into Central Asia—such as a disastrous expedition to Khiva in 1717—failed (see Map 4.1). Many decades passed before any Central Asian leader sought (or accepted) Russian protection, and then it happened only fitfully. In the northern steppe, in 1731, a Kazakh khan, Abul Khayr, first sought tsarist Russian help against other enemies (the neighboring Kalmyks), thus hoping to solidify his own political position. Other Kazakh clans later followed suit. Abul Khayr swore his people's allegiance to Russia and agreed to pay tribute (*yasak*) to the tsar—a decision that actually exceeded his customary authority (and thus, endangered his rule). This step proved fateful. Abul Khayr may have seen it as a temporary alliance, but the tsars treated his declaration as accepting permanent subordination. Although they never managed to collect the promised tribute payments, Russian authorities forced later Kazakh khans to reiterate the expressions of allegiance: 1731 thus marks the start of Russian control in the heartland of northern Central Asia. Over the next century tsarist soldiers moved southward into the steppe, extending Russian authority (and building fortresses). The last major conquests came in the 1860s and 1870s, following a push southward to the Afghan border.

This timing was no accident. Shortly before, Britain and France, allied with the Ottoman Empire and the kingdom of Sardinia, had easily defeated Russia in a war fought on its own doorstep (the Crimean War, 1853–1856), leading many to question Russia's status as an important state, let alone a "great power." Some even doubted that it counted as European, given that most of its territory lay in Siberia, east of the

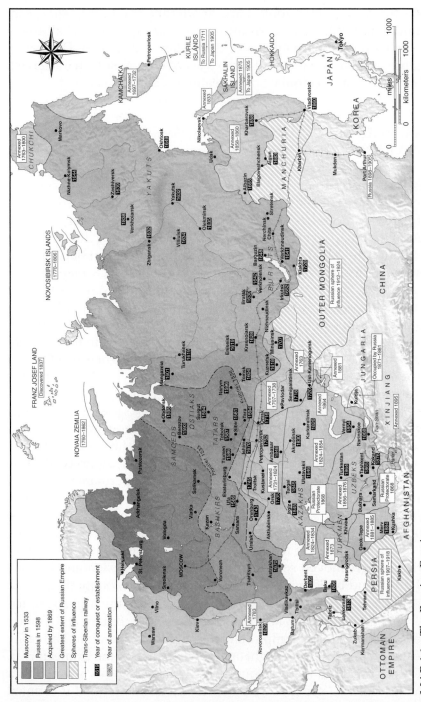

MAP 4.1 The Russian Empire.

Urals, hence in Asia. Russia's conquest of southern Central Asia—a process completed in 1881, with the final defeat (and massacre) of Turkmen armies at Gök Tepe—partly assuaged such worries, showing that it could fight effectively to acquire colonies. Recall how Europeans seized African lands at precisely this time: and in Central Asia, too, colonial competition could be fierce. Britain was pressing north from India at the same moment, creating a client state (Afghanistan) dependent on London for its foreign relations. Qing China, which already controlled Mongolia and exercised indirect authority in Tibet, seized the Muslim lands abutting Russian Turkestan to the east—dubbing this area a "New Frontier" [Xinjiang] and launching a flow of Chinese pioneers to settle its own Wild West. Virtually all of Central Asia was swallowed by outside empires, becoming (like Africa) a token in a new "Great Game," the global geopolitical competition for colonies. By 1895 the borders between the British and Russian empires sat only twenty miles apart in the Pamir mountains—a far cry from the 2,000 miles that had separated them a century earlier.

Turkestan thus provided a key platform to prove the tsarist state's strength. It gave Russia a European-style imperial domain, an arena to demonstrate Russia's power and European character, through what all sides deemed obvious differences between its Slavic/Christian culture and the Turko-Persian/Muslim world of "natives." This contrast provided tsarist officials (and later, their Soviet successors) with a readily apparent "civilizing mission" among supposedly backward Muslims, one that resembled the self-proclaimed tasks of British missionaries in India or French teachers in West Africa. It also laid the groundwork for the anti-Russian, anti-Soviet, and anti-colonial sentiments that ultimately cost Hamza his life.

From a Central Asian point of view, Russian colonization looked very threatening. Its massive settlement first transformed the steppes. By 1917, more than a million Slavic peasants had flooded the grassy steppes of northwestern Central Asia (present-day Kazakhstan), forcing its nomads to make an agonizing choice: give up their way of life altogether, settling in one place; flee with their herds; or die. This Hobbesian choice sparked clashes as nomads fought in desperate resistance and contributed to huge armed rebellions in 1916.

In the sedentary (i.e., agricultural, non-nomadic) areas farther south, the already densely populated river basins could not support large-scale Slavic settler colonialism, and tsarist administrators and soldiers used a model that more closely resembled British India. They established military authority in major cities (e.g., Tashkent, Bukhara,

Samarkand) but otherwise delegated administrative responsibility to indigenous elders and officials, thus washing their hands of local needs and ignoring deep social divisions. Russian support propped up existing elites, as long as they professed allegiance, and tsarist officials mostly turned a blind eye to famine, disease, and corruption. The khan of Khiva and the emir of Bukhara even retained a measure of sovereignty, as their realms became protectorates rather than being formally swallowed into the Russian empire; Russian troops put down a series of rebellions to keep them in power. Until 1917 Turkestan served as a garrison for the Russian army—an important geopolitical asset especially against British India, across the mountains to the south.

Virtually all Russian-funded development—from railways and telegraph lines to efforts to boost cotton production—focused on the security and economic needs of the tsarist metropole. As in Africa or India, infrastructure development first served colonial interests; other priorities ranked much lower, and a "civilizing mission" (with its priority of helping local populations) seemed more prominent in rhetoric than as a guide to practice. In policy terms, the tsarist state seemed to care little about the Muslims of Central Asia, and Russians held themselves apart. One guidebook to the imperial city of Tashkent filled more than 500 pages with descriptions of such attractions as the Orthodox cathedral and the Russian governor's home, mentioning only in passing the fact that Muslims also lived in Turkestan. The thinness of Russian presence outside the capital of Tashkent was striking: in Fergana, a mere fifty-eight Russian officials (with just two translators) ruled two million residents in 1910—a ratio of one to every 33,000 inhabitants.

This corrosive mix of colonial control, imperial self-interest, and near-total ignorance of local needs not surprisingly influenced Central Asian views of tsarist, and later Soviet, initiatives. Imperial conquest spurred Muslim reformist movements—shaping some Central Asians like Hamza, who worked alongside Russian revolutionary socialists. (He joined the Communist Party in 1920.) Yet most indigenous reformers, known as *jadids* (from the Arabic word for "new"), wanted to build a modern but still Muslim society—using European technology and education, and cooperating with Russians (while drawing upon some of their ideas), but not adopting European ways wholesale (which they also perceived to be Christian). Central Asians learned to be suspicious of the supposedly selfless sentiments of colonial administrators. When Bolshevik leaders announced that the tsar had been overthrown—and that their sweeping reforms would help Central

Asians—that suspicion remained. Distinctions among Russians (Communists vs. monarchists) mattered, but less than the basic fact of continuing Russian control. Following decades of colonial rule, the policy changes of the 1920s did not immediately seem self-evidently better to all Central Asians. Experience taught that they likely would amount to more of the same: not freedom or progress in a locally meaningful way, nor necessarily help for the poor and downtrodden, but rather ongoing control by alien, urban, non-Muslim outsiders.

Hence many Central Asians chose to fight back. Men reacted badly to the spectacle of veil burnings, the turning of mosques and shrines into "Museums of Atheism," and children being dragged to Leninist literacy schools. Soviet archives also preserve stories of women's varied reactions to their "liberation": some welcomed it and participated eagerly, but most ignored or fled from party activists. A few even worked against the unveiling campaign—denouncing women who participated as prostitutes or attacking police officers and Communists. In Shohirmardon, Hamza associated himself with all of these "liberation" campaigns, and his actions thus fell afoul of anti-Russian, anti-Soviet, and anti-colonial resistance more than sixty years in the making. For years he had traveled throughout Central Asia to stage plays, make speeches, and recite poems—many with a political message, praising what he saw happening in the USSR, and denouncing what he saw as the old, backward social order that had no choice but to fall away. That was why Soviet publicists had dubbed him the "Singer of the Revolution." His luck ran out when the crowd in Shohirmardon thus judged him a collaborator with the alien, atheistic, and still undeniably imperial Russian Bolsheviks.

Even as politicians renamed towns in Hamza's honor and tore down saints' tombs, local men and women quietly rebuilt their lives—and, with permission or not, their pilgrimage sites. Uzbek men (and more rarely, women) continued to administer local government and party organizations—at least officially—but it became painfully clear that in the Soviet system final political, military, and economic authority remained firmly in Moscow. Central Asian men faced conscription into the Red Army, usually serving in integrated units where they had to speak Russian, eat pork, and drink vodka. In the 1940s hundreds of thousands fought and died for the USSR against Nazi Germany (see Figure 4.1). New cities appeared, full of European-style apartment blocks, and Central Asian languages shifted into the Cyrillic alphabet, as children learned Russian in school. The regional economy still looked colonial, focused on

FIGURE 4.1   World War II memorial, Panfilov Park, Almaty, Kazakhstan. The sculpture commemorates twenty-eight soldiers from Almaty, all members of the ethnically mixed "Panfilov Division," who died defending Moscow—almost 2,000 miles to the northwest—from Nazi attack in 1941. An eternal flame burns in front of this sculpture, and newly married couples still come here to lay flowers on their wedding day.

the export of primary products, above all cotton—with further processing, and most other forms of industrial development, concentrated in Russia and the western Soviet republics.

Yet as previous chapters have shown, power is never absolute. Even in Stalin's Soviet Union, ambiguities remained, and subtle forms of resistance, too. On the surface, Central Asian faces remained visibly front and center in the Communist Party. By the 1960s, however, the region's Soviet leaders—the successors of Hamza, Khojaev, and Ikramov—proved adept at making profuse statements of loyalty to Moscow while mobilizing elaborate patronage networks to work against the center's interests. They mastered the centralized system of economic planning, which on the surface appeared to work against a colonial periphery, but in reality could be turned to the periphery's advantage. Russian critics had long resented the drain of economic assistance funds to develop Central Asia (and other "backward" areas). Then in the 1980s it emerged, in a saga known as the "Great Cotton Scandal," that Uzbekistani authorities had bilked the central Soviet treasury of billions of rubles—by reporting the harvest of millions of tons of cotton that had never existed. In fury, Moscow sent scores of investigators and prosecuted hundreds of officials—but Uzbekistan's Communist Party leader (and later, post-Soviet president) Islam Karimov managed to have the trials transferred back to Central Asia, where the chief culprits received only token penalties.

To many Central Asians, the designers of this ingenious scheme (principally Karimov's predecessor, Sharaf Rashidov) became folk heroes, and the imperial Soviet state had met its comeuppance. That imperial state finally buckled a few years later, in 1991, as the USSR collapsed, one generation after decolonization had swept across Africa and Asia. Uzbekistan and the other Soviet republics became independent, sovereign nations—but the paradoxes of socialist colonialism continued. Under Karimov's leadership, the new country of Uzbekistan built its identity and asserted its standing in the world by seeking national grandeur and asserting a sweeping patriotic heritage. In the middle of Tashkent, Lenin Square became Independence Square, with its massive statue of the Soviet leader swapped for a sculpture of the globe—a globe that (bizarrely) showed only one country on its surface, an oversized outline of Uzbekistan. Meanwhile the main plaza across from the Hotel Uzbekistan, Karl Marx Square,[1] lost its bust of the socialist theorist. It, too, was removed, supplanted by a huge equestrian statue of a new national hero, Amir Tëmur (Tamerlane, r. 1370–1405), who had transformed Samarkand into the capital of a short-lived empire. This violent, would-be world conqueror who invaded, devastated, and subjugated vast areas of West, Central, and South Asia has gone down in history as an imperialist par excellence.

BENEVOLENT ASSIMILATION: AMERICAN COLONIAL POWER ACROSS THE PACIFIC

The previous chapter told the story of an American empire in the Caribbean, growing out of US military victory in the Spanish-American War. That story need not be repeated, but the collapsing Spanish empire had an Asian component, too. Article III of the peace

---

[1]Previously the square had been named for Stalin; before that, the October Revolution; and before that, the first tsarist governor-general of Turkestan, Konstantin von Kauffman.

treaty, signed in Paris in December 1898, ceded the Philippine Islands to the United States, in return for payment of $20 million. (Article II did the same for Guam, without payment.) Five months earlier the US Congress had separately, and unilaterally, annexed the Hawaiian Islands. Taken together, these settlements put the United States in the business of running colonies scattered across the Pacific, a business that lasted nearly half a century—until near-continuous resistance at last secured Filipino independence in 1946 (see Map 4.2).

To justify this expansion, American officials invoked language similar to that heard in Cuba (and to that used by tsarist and Soviet observers in Central Asia). One such speech by Senator Albert Beveridge is excerpted below, combining a potpourri of economic, political, and racial/cultural arguments. Beveridge concluded that Asians needed help to overcome generations of backwardness and exploitation created by a "real" (that is, Spanish) empire. William Howard Taft, the first civilian governor of the Philippines (and later US president), declared that his goal was "to govern the Philippine Islands for the benefit and welfare and uplifting of the people of the islands." His boss, President William McKinley, announced that he too wished to "win the confidence, respect, and affection" of Filipinos as he pursued a policy of "benevolent assimilation." As Daniel Williams, secretary of the Philippine Commission, explained in his journal for 1901, this meant a benign kind of civilizing mission, one based on American models:

> A new government is being created from the ground up, piece being added to piece as the days and weeks go by. It is an interesting phenomenon, this thing of building a modern commonwealth on a foundation of medievalism—the giving to this country at one fell swoop all the innovations and discoveries which have marked centuries of Anglo-Saxon push and energy. I doubt if in the world's history anything similar has been attempted; that is, the transplanting so rapidly of the ideas and improvements of one civilization upon another. The whole fabric is being made over.[2]

This vision required US authorities to start from scratch, and in a logistically complicated situation: they had to devise a system to administer more than 7,000 islands, and seven million people. They

---

[2]Quotations are from Julian Go and Anne Foster, eds., *The American Colonial State in the Philippines* (Durham, NC, 2003), 1, 11; and Vicente Rafael, "White Love," in Amy Kaplan and Donald Pease, eds., *Cultures of United States Imperialism* (Durham, NC, 1993), 185.

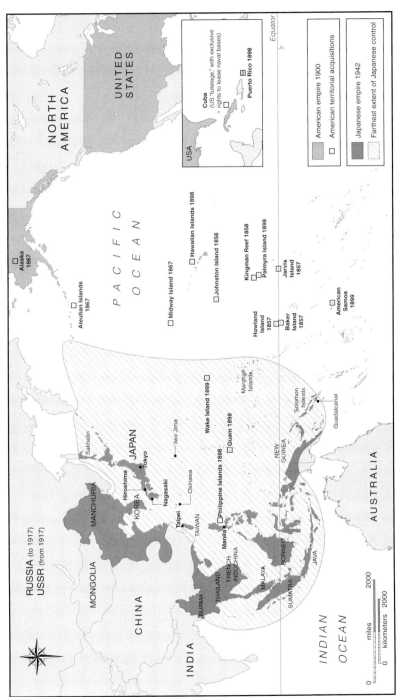

MAP 4.2 Japanese and US empires in Asia and the Pacific.

could not simply adopt the Spanish bureaucracy (since, after all, its failings had justified American presence). Elite universities like Cornell and Chicago stepped in and tried to help, starting programs to train students interested in developing tropical colonies. Such classes drew on recent US experiences establishing Indian reservations in Oklahoma and the West, and also on US Reconstruction, which had rebuilt a new kind of US South after the devastating civil war of the 1860s. They also drew upon colonial practices from other empires to design a wholly new social, legal, economic, and political order for the Philippines—one that would not necessarily be identical to the United States—since virtually everyone also agreed that the islands would not become an American state.

On this single point, at least, Americans and Filipinos agreed. As the Filipino leader (later president) Manuel Quezon, put it, "Differences in race, customs, interests, and the thousands of miles of water which separate both countries, are insurmountable obstacles to Philippine statehood. The idea of assimilating the Filipinos and making Americans out of an Asiatic people should be recognized by any sane person as utterly impossible."[3] Hence Filipino courts were not made part of the US legal system (except that they were ultimately subject to the US Supreme Court); US domestic laws did not apply; and the peso, not the US dollar, remained legal tender. The Philippines remained officially at arm's length; the colony even had to support itself, raising taxes and tariffs sufficient to pay for the benefits supposedly provided by US overseers—the full array of development efforts, government expenses, and security requirements.

A softer side of American power aimed to win hearts and minds—ironically foreshadowing Soviet policies—by redistributing land to the poor and building roads, hospitals, schools, power stations, and communications networks. Public health and urban renewal were prominent—all the more after 1902, when General Leonard Wood, previously governor of Cuba, moved around the world to command US military forces in the Philippines. A self-congratulatory US Senate report of 1904, "What Has Been Done in the Philippines," chronicled a litany of such efforts, listing the dollars invested in trade and development campaigns, and announcing that now "tranquility prevails throughout the islands" more than ever under Spanish authority. Any resistance, it went on, could not possibly be construed

---

[3]Quoted by Maximo Kalaw, *The Case for the Filipinos* (New York, 1916), 178.

as anti-American; since, after all, who would resist such a benevolent government? Any violence that remained had to be seen as random criminal impulses, carried out by antisocial gangs of "highwaymen [and] robbers"—like the gangs that roamed the western United States during the days of Jesse James and Wyatt Earp.[4]

Filipinos tended to see this unrest differently. Although some did work for American authorities—7,500 Filipinos gathered data for the 1903 census—many saw even the most obviously beneficial US policies (such as anti-cholera campaigns, or suppression of the opium trade) as insidious ways for the colonial state to legitimize and expand its presence. Such anti-US interpretations—however "irrational" they appeared to American observers—found support given the wider context of US military occupation during what many Filipinos saw as an ongoing anti-colonial, nationalist revolution. American credibility also declined as US officials, for practical reasons, started relying on local notables for assistance in administration and public works efforts—a decision that only entrenched and enriched some of the people US officials had initially denounced as corrupt "oligarchs." And of course the purely benevolent intent of American power could be hard to see amid the presence of 70,000 US combat troops.

Filipinos told the overall story of US intervention very differently. From their point of view the American military had first encouraged Filipino rebels, such as their top leader Emilio Aguinaldo, to attack Spanish outposts in 1898. Aguinaldo's troops successfully expelled Spanish forces nearly everywhere except Manila; he went so far as to declare Filipino independence unilaterally in June 1898. Once Spain capitulated and agreed to cede the islands, however, the US position on Filipino independence changed completely. The turnabout infuriated nationalists, who denounced what they saw as betrayal and hypocrisy. (They frequently quoted from the United States' own Declaration of Independence.) Aguinaldo, whose view is presented in a document below, thus found himself fighting a new war. Machine guns, which the United States possessed in small numbers, produced carnage similar to that wrought in Africa, helping to crush organized resistance by 1902—although small groups of rebels fought on until 1913. Indeed, despite his medical training, US General Leonard Wood also took command of the fight against Muslim Moro rebels in the south,

---

[4]US Bureau of Insular Affairs (War Department), *What Has Been Done in the Philippines* (58th Congress, 2nd Session, 1904). Both phrases are from p. 7.

carrying out a scorched-earth policy that included massacring entire villages. Filipino casualty counts in this conflict are highly uncertain, but battlefield estimates cluster around 20,000, with a total civilian toll (including deaths from disease) ranging upward of 250,000.

Domestic critics of American empire weighed in again. Mark Twain denounced US intervention, and the Anti-Imperialist League held lectures and published pamphlets. Litanies of statistics also suggested that US occupation had produced widespread damage, far more than McKinley's "benevolent" colonialism could repair. One of the League's pamphlets chronicled wide-ranging collapse in the city of Balayan: from 1896 to 1905, its population had declined from 41,308 to 13,924; the sugar harvest plummeted from 520,000 *picos*[5] to 12,300; and the hen population dropped from 96,000 to 5,000. All twenty-five steam mills closed, as did all but 50 of the 675 iron mills, and all eleven large cargo ships under sail. From this perspective, Filipino skepticism about American sincerity was no surprise. David Starr Jordan went so far as to declare that "The only sensible thing to do would be to pull out some dark night and escape from the great problem of the Orient as suddenly and as dramatically as we got into it."[6] It took two generations, but Filipino resistance ultimately forced the granting of partial autonomy in 1935 (when Quezon won election as president), and—after another occupation, this one Japanese, during World War II—independence in 1946. The complications of America's presence, though, lasted even longer, as witnessed by such struggles as that over a huge US Navy base at Subic Bay, which closed only in 1992, following Philippine refusal to extend its lease.

EMULATING EMPIRE WHILE ASSISTING ASIA: PARADOXES OF JAPANESE IMPERIALISM

In a book largely concerned with modern European empires, it may seem odd to close with a long section on Japan. Yet Japan's birth as a colonial metropole in the late nineteenth century complicates the narrative in important ways. In some ways it echoes the story of the United States, which also achieved its own independence only

---

[5]In Manila one *pico* equalled approximately 140 pounds. (It varied elsewhere in East Asia.)

[6]David Starr Jordan, "Imperial Democracy" (Boston, 1898), 9. (This document is excerpted above, in Chapter 3.)

to assert imperial control over faraway peoples. Between 1895 and 1945, Tokyo built a vast, varied, and complex empire, and one that at its peak exceeded the scope of most European colonial realms. No discussion of modern empires, therefore, can ignore this case. The lateness of its start makes Japan's success all the more remarkable: by 1943, at its brief but greatest extent, the Japanese empire controlled as many as 439 million people. (By comparison, Britain's empire governed by one count 449 million inhabitants, the French empire fifty-six million, and the Dutch sixty-one million.) As shown on the map (again see Map 4.2), Japan's colonial territories covered a wide area across the western Pacific, including a total land area roughly three-quarters the size of that encompassed by Britain's empire (and five to six times the extent of French or Dutch colonies). When war came, moreover, this empire was likewise defended in the name of freedom. As an official declaration asserted in 1943, Japan's effort in World War II aimed "to liberate Greater East Asia from the thrall of the Anglo-American powers"[7] who only exploited Asians for their own benefit—unlike, or so it said, the Japanese.

Military power, economic exploitation, and attempts to impose sociocultural change—and the bitter, creative resistance such efforts provoked—all characterized Japan's imperial dominion, just as they characterized the European and American empires already discussed. Japan's colonial history offers examples of direct imperial control and settler colonialism, cases of indirect power exerted through puppet states, and also some territories left largely alone, administered from afar as sources of raw material. Japan self-consciously emulated the forms and practices of Western empires, yet also developed its own approaches, even developing an academic field of "colonial studies." Japan's colonial doctrines included unusual economic models calling, for example, for industrial development in the periphery, outside the metropole. Yet, as in the USSR or United States, some in Japan only reluctantly called its system an "empire," a word that seemed to contravene what they deemed good (Asian) values.

Japanese imperial ideology mixed these themes. On the one hand, politicians argued that empire demonstrated Japan's greatness, and that Japanese colonies would surely enrich the state. On the other hand, they declared that Japanese expansion meant something good not just for Japan, but for the wider region: it represented a

---

[7]Quoted by Peter Duus, "Introduction," in Duus et al., eds., *The Japanese Wartime Empire, 1931–1945* (Princeton, 1996), xxvii.

defense of East Asia against outsiders, indeed (ironically) a bulwark against Western colonialism. Many saw possessions like Manchukuo (the Japanese-created and -dominated, but nominally independent, state of Manchuria, 1932–1945) as a colonial stage, a place to build a utopian future for all Asia. Colonial societies would thus benefit from Japanese assistance and Japanese culture—its language and educational systems, hygiene, and urban planning—even if, as sometimes happened, such features had not yet reached Japan itself, and even if Koreans, Chinese, and others showed little appreciation for the benefits of superior Japanese civilization.

Arising rapidly in the late nineteenth century—barely a generation after US warships had arrived in Tokyo, forcing the shoguns to grant trade access and to accept unequal treaty obligations similar to those foisted upon China—Japan's imperial success showed that Asians could successfully escape the Western grasp. Moreover, when it fought and won wars, first with China (1894–1895) and then with Russia (1904–1905), it demonstrated that Asian states could compete with (and even directly defeat) European powers in the game of empire—a message warmly applauded by colonized peoples around the world. A number of Muslims, for example, joined the Turkish feminist leader, Halide Edip, in naming their sons "Togo" following Japan's startling defeat of Russia.

After incorporating Hokkaido in 1869 and Okinawa in 1871—the last acquisitions that became integral parts of a Japanese metropole—the new Meiji government carried out breakneck industrial and military development, social and cultural reforms, and political and economic centralization, all to create a powerful, united nation-state. The speed and depth of these reforms aimed to modernize Japan, quickly and completely, in order to protect against Western powers that were subordinating China and seemed intent on conquering all of Asia. Given the wider contexts of global imperial competition, Japanese politicians in the late nineteenth century argued that a top goal should be building a "cordon of interest"—expanding Japanese influence or control preemptively—to prevent Europeans coming near the Japanese mainland. A Prussian advisor to the Meiji government went so far as to declare that Korea represented "a dagger thrust at the heart of Japan," and that China's presence there had to be reduced.[8]

---

[8]Major Meckel, quoted by Mark Peattie, "Introduction," in Ramon Myers and Mark Peattie, eds., *The Japanese Colonial Empire, 1895–1945* (Princeton, 1984), 15.

Once such efforts succeeded, though, and as Japan withdrew from its unequal Western treaties (abrogating the last in 1911), it was only a short step to argue for further territorial expansion. Very quickly, across the political spectrum, Japanese politicians, soldiers, and writers—joined by private citizens in "colonization committees" and "war support associations"—argued that countries proved their greatness only by acquiring an empire. Like European governments, the Meiji—and their successors, the Taisho and Showa—generated support by whipping up patriotic interest in overseas adventure. Few citizens publicly dissented, although one anarchist writer, Kotoku Shusui, did denounce the amorality of empire, decrying all governments' tendency to use militarist expansion to distract people from failings at home—publishing his views in 1901, a year before the British economist John Hobson published his classic critical analysis of imperialism (arguing that empires were driven by ever-larger markets and investments overseas).

Aside from a few radical critics, Japanese commentators agreed that colonies both provided material gains and offered opportunities to bring "civilization" to less fortunate parts of the world. They told a pro-imperial history that started with an attempt in 1876 to "open" Korea—and accelerated after the wars and military conquests at the turn of the century. Japan's empire grew quickly in size and complexity as it took formal control of Taiwan (Formosa) from China in 1895 and Karafuto (southern Sakhalin) from Russia in 1905, and annexed Korea (under the name Chosŏn) in 1910. In 1922 the League of Nations transferred German possessions in the Caroline and Marshall Islands to Japan as a **mandate** (a territory administered by a foreign power, on behalf of its people or an international organization, but without formal possession or sovereignty). Japan then established an informal empire in China, first in Liaodong and later, following the invasion of Manchuria in 1931–1932, in the puppet state it called "Manchukuo." Lastly, beginning in 1941, Japanese soldiers seized Dutch and French possessions in Indochina and Southeast Asia, attacked and conquered the US-held Philippines and various central and south Pacific islands and prised away British colonies in Singapore, Malaya, and Burma.

Once in possession of this variegated empire, Japanese bureaucrats, politicians, soldiers, and businessmen had to figure out what to do with it. Taiwan served as a crucial early laboratory. Inazo Nitobé, Tokyo University's first professor of "colonial policy studies," explains its main lessons in one of the documents below—lessons later applied to Korea, and expanded to Manchuria and Southeast Asia. Nitobé, who studied at Johns Hopkins (in the United States) and Halle (in Germany), explicitly placed Japanese efforts into a global-imperial context, looking for the most effective techniques, policy, and institutional models, along with cautionary lessons from the European and American experiences. In the 1910s he reportedly started every university lecture by writing on the blackboard, "Colonization is the spread of civilization."[9] He designed his students' training—in law, diplomatic history, economics, and specialized languages such as Russian, Chinese, Korean, and English—to help them build a new and better imperial world. Thousands graduated from these courses in Tokyo and elsewhere, including a new Takushoku University (literally, "Colonial Development University"), and went to the colonies. For Nitobé, Japan's seizure of an empire amounted to its national coming-of-age.

Japanese specialists in "colonial studies" agreed that good empires required both firm control and personal examples of administrative efficiency and superior culture. Control came from an assiduous investment of military resources and the widespread use of violence—whatever it took to expand Japan's empire. Nearly half a million Japanese soldiers died fighting Russia in 1904–1905, and another quarter million battled Red Army forces in Siberia from 1918 to 1920. In Korea, the first Japanese governor-general, Terauchi Masatake, supposedly greeted his subjects by threatening to whip them with scorpions—and then established ten years of brutal military rule. The Meiji constitution did not apply in Korea, so Masatake built a highly centralized, authoritarian system that put down all opposition—most notoriously, crushing a large rebellion in 1919. Laws banned Koreans (but not Japanese) from trafficking women or children, a disparity that enabled the infamous program of *ianfu*—which transformed more than 100,000 Korean women into sexual servitors ("comfort women") for Japanese troops. In China, too, Japan used very harsh tactics: the 1937 occupation of Nanking (Nanjing) still stands out for its shocking brutality. By one horrifying count, from 1931 to 1945 China lost 3.8 million soldiers (killed), with fully eighteen million civilians dead and wounded. The scale of such losses is nearly impossible to comprehend.

Such widespread, systemic violence had long-lasting consequences in China and Korea, and made it difficult or impossible to

---

[9] Alexis Dudden, *Japan's Colonization of Korea* (Honolulu, 2005), 135.

persuade colonized populations that Japanese rule could have any benefits. In the short term, though, it also served imperial interests by enabling classic forms of colonial exploitation. By 1930 colonies provided four-fifths of Japan's rice imports, and roughly two-thirds of its sugar. Even before it invaded Manchuria, Japan had surpassed Britain as the largest source of foreign investment in China—and by 1941 it invested another six billion yen, building networks for imperial communication and the export of raw materials. The South Manchurian Railway (Mantetsu), using conscripted labor under near-starvation conditions (as depicted in a later Chinese memorial, see photograph, p. ix), by 1945 had built 5,300 km of rail lines, enabling Japan to reach and build mines, settlements, and ports. This rail system stretched toward China proper and interlinked with Korean and Russian networks. In its pursuit of metals and textiles, Japan also acted like European empires in the 1940s as it extracted resources from a newly expanded outer ring of colonies in Southeast Asia.

Like colonialists elsewhere, Japanese scholars, soldiers, and politicians did not seem to realize the impossibility of winning hearts and minds while carrying out brutal campaigns of occupation and exploitation. Some appeared not to care; but others stressed the softer side of Japanese power, depicting coercion as a necessary but short-lived component of imperial growth. They optimistically anticipated that once political and military authority had been established, the simple power of example—the experience of personally observing "civilized" Japanese men and women—would persuade Koreans, Chinese, and others to abandon their opposition. Personal examples came first from colonial administrators, and secondly—crucially—from thousands of ordinary Japanese settlers who followed. This launch of large-scale settler colonialism marked a dramatic departure for a country (unlike China) that had had to this point no large diaspora and, indeed, few expatriate citizens anywhere. Yet during the colonial era—even before the occupation of Manchuria, and prior to the huge military expansion of World War II—Japanese settler colonies bloomed throughout the Pacific and beyond, in Japanese-occupied lands as well as more distant non-colonized territories, such as the United States (see Figure 4.2).[10]

---

[10]The bar graph of Figure 4.2 shows substantial Japanese migration to Hawai'i and the mainland United States by 1920. The US Immigration Act of 1924, however, barred any further Japanese settlement. Hence all *Issei* (first-generation Japanese) living in Hawai'i or the United States at the outbreak of war in 1941 had arrived before 1924.

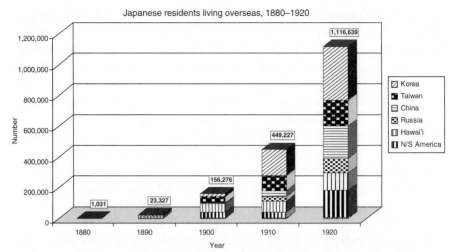

FIGURE 4.2   Japanese Residents Living Overseas, 1880–1920.

Years	Other	N/S America	Hawai'i	Russia	China	Taiwan	Korea	Total
1880	7	23	0	0	166	0	835	1,031
1890	92	2,077	12,675	374	864	0	7,245	23,327
1900	3,296	35,847	57,486	2,621	3,243	37,954	15,829	156,276
1910	3,061	38,641	70,764	30,641	36,529	98,048	171,543	449,227
1920	5,261	177,706	112,221	94,329	212,651	166,621	347,850	1,116,639

Note: North America includes mainland US and Canada. South America includes only Peru and Brazil. China includes mainland China, Kwantung, and Manchuria. Russia includes Karafuto (Sakhalin) and Vladivostok. Overall figures also include Australia.

Source: Peter Duus, *The Abacus and the Sword* (Berkeley, 1995), 290.

The Meiji government particularly encouraged settlement in occupied areas, announcing in 1905 that settlers to South Sakhalin would receive low-interest loans, tax benefits, even free land, houses, and supplies like tools and seed. In Korea the amount of land owned by Japanese citizens, just 2.7 percent in 1910 (albeit concentrated in fertile districts), tripled in five years. Nitobé argued that the very word "colony" (*shokumin*)—which first appeared in Japanese dictionaries in 1862—should be translated not as "increasing people," a phonetic equivalent, but "planting people."[11] Settlement became a key goal, especially in the colonies acquired before 1940, as (in the face of Korean and other rebellions) a large Japanese presence also seemed the best way to ensure long-term political stability.

By 1930 official records already reported 233,749 Japanese civilians living in Manchuria. This influx accelerated further over the

---

[11]Dudden, *Japan's Colonization of Korea*, 137.

next decade, with roughly 800,000 more civilians arriving after the invasion. Some Japanese villages sent half their population to build a "new heaven on earth (*shintenchi*)."[12] Imperial authorities announced plans to resettle five million farmers in Manchuria—seeking to create a new group of "continental Japanese." This state-sponsored migration aimed to create a large Japanese minority, comprising 10 percent of the Manchurian population; it hoped to produce a situation like the one in Algeria, with powerful local interests deeply invested in continued imperial power. The export of its poor tenant farmers to China helped the Japanese government in other ways too, removing a fractious and rebellious group and thus, exporting social discontent.

Notably, the vision that induced settlers to move to Manchuria included very few Chinese people—most Japanese commentators imagined Manchukuo as a vast empty space. The South Manchurian Railway declared that these pioneers had launched a "covered wagon movement" on the Manchurian prairie, like the one that carried American settlers across the Great Plains.[13] Yet the rhetoric of Japanese officials—like Soviet activists in Uzbekistan, or American engineers in the Philippines—also stressed the benefits colonial power would bring local populations. Pointing to the alleged backwardness of Korean and Chinese villages before Japan's arrival, propagandists spoke effusively of the Meiji desire to transform and renew decaying Asian civilizations, to pull them into the modern era. Such pronouncements underlay the Okuma doctrine (1897), for example, in which the Japanese prime minister declared that Japan had a duty to help China, stressing efforts such as building hospitals and health clinics; hygiene and vaccination campaigns; even the creation of new banks and trade institutions—all for China's own good.

This view of empire as bearing a Western-style civilizing mission (*kyoka*)—a "yellow man's burden"—applied most urgently to the "inner empire" of Taiwan, Korea, and China. It applied less to the more distant and short-lived "outer empire" of Southeast Asia, where any civilizing mission moved with agonizing slowness. In "inner" areas, though—those with stronger historical ties and perceived cultural links to Japan—imperial authorities declared that they wanted to help Asians stand up for themselves. (Okuma explained that Japan

---

[12]Louise Young, *Japan's Total Empire* (Berkeley, 1998), 5.

[13]Yoshihisa Tak Matsusaka, *The Making of Japanese Manchuria, 1904–1932* (Cambridge, MA, 2001), 390.

owed China its support, as Japan itself earlier benefitted from Chinese civilization.)

Such views rested on the idea of *dobun-doshu* ("common culture, common race"). This created, proponents said, a special relationship with China, Korea, and Taiwan. "Common" does not mean "identical," and the Meiji did not see these areas as indistinguishable from Japan. Far from it: a crucial territorial distinction remained between ostensibly non-colonial Hokkaido and Okinawa, on the one hand, and colonial Taiwan or Manchuria, on the other. As already discussed, Korean, Taiwanese, and Chinese civilians never received anything close to equal treatment under Japanese rule. (Although "native" groups in Japan, such as the Ryukyuan-speaking Okinawans, or the Ainu on Hokkaido, faced discrimination too, receiving treatment similar to that meted out to Native Americans in the United States.) Yet the ideological framework of dobun-doshu represents an important complication, a departure from the tendency of European empires to stress the depth and permanence of differences between colonizing and colonized populations.

The idea of dobun-doshu, by cutting across the axis of colonial difference, implied the possibility of integrating the "inner" colonies into a less exploitative kind of imperial system, in ways that most European empires (other than the USSR) refused to accept. Once enunciated, it suggested the importance of racial/cultural affinity and the centrality of an "Asian" frame of reference. As a justification for empire it thus implied a relatively privileged position, at least in the long term, for Chinese, Korean, and Taiwanese subjects. Certainly this could not happen while Koreans continued to rebel; but perhaps for this reason Manchukuo remained nominally sovereign and separate from Japan, in a strange (and expensive) arrangement as a puppet state.[14]

Such oddities help explain another curious feature of the Japanese empire, its economic structure. As already noted, Japan exploited colonies for their resources, as other empires around the world also did. Following its division into "outer" and "inner" zones, though, Japan created institutional arrangements that privileged its closer Asian "cousins." A "Greater East Asia Co-Prosperity Sphere" called for heavy industry not just in the metropole, but throughout the core areas of the inner empire—Korea, Taiwan, Manchukuo, and northern China, as well as mainland Japan. Manchuria, for instance,

---

[14]Manchukuo's supposed sovereignty was exercised under the "rule" of Puyi, China's last Qing emperor (r. 1908–1912 and 1917), whom the Japanese established as a puppet in 1934.

saw new factories built to produce iron and steel, automobiles, and advanced chemicals. In the words of Foreign Minister Arita Hachiro, geography and economy should join culture and race: "The countries of East Asia and the regions of the South Seas are geographically close, [and] historically, racially, and economically very closely related to each other. They are destined to cooperate and minister to one another's needs for their common well-being and prosperity, and to promote peace and progress in their regions."[15]

Japanese power thus presented itself as helping Asia—portraying military growth as a benevolent expansion that would assist its neighbors in resisting *other* marauding invaders, namely from the West (see Figure 4.3). Leftist and reform-minded bureaucrats

FIGURE 4.3   An imperial society? Wearing historic uniforms to mark the 2,957th anniversary of the foundation of the Japanese Empire, young boys march through the streets of Tokyo in 1937. Ideas of imperial vigor and military assertiveness, as shown by these schoolchildren, seemed to suffuse Japanese society even at home—far from any colony—by the late 1930s. Yet this parade also suggests the complexities of this imperial self-conception. Although they led a brand-new world power, Japanese authorities nevertheless emphasized the historical depth of Japan's culture and military presence.

---

[15]Quoted by Duus, "Introduction," in Duus, *The Japanese Wartime Empire, 1931–1945,* xxii.

went still farther, seeing Manchuria and other colonial possessions (despite Manchuria's theoretically sovereign status) as a platform to modernize Japan itself. Often stymied at home by conservative opponents, these progressive officials used the empire as a template for the metropole, spending huge sums to show what modern social reforms could look like in practice. From health care and public hygiene to urban renewal and planning, they built a new world in the colonies. Perhaps counterintuitively, then, alongside the brutal and systemic violence that defined occupation policy, the colonies also received practical social benefits—sometimes before citizens in Japan.

Starting in the 1890s with Taipei, Japan's first colonial capital, planners, architects, and engineers launched a wholesale urban rebuilding campaign. Directed by the colonial administrator Goto Shinpei, who like Leonard Wood had been trained as a physician, urban reformers used the latest technologies to solve practical problems of city living. Gleaming sewage systems, water supply pipes, and open-air parks showed Japanese know-how; Goto pointed to lowered mortality rates in Taiwan to show the practical benefits of Japanese rule. He then moved to Korea, where he directed similar campaigns in Seoul, and later to Manchukuo, where he took over the South Manchurian Railway. Such efforts proved Japan's bona fides as a modernizing state, one capable of bringing civilization to backward, benighted peoples. Its work in the empire always had to be best and latest—under Goto the Manchurian railway developed an elite "Asian Express," with refrigeration and air-conditioning, that traveled across the plains of North China at the remarkable speed of 110 kilometers per hour (about 68 mph).

Manchuria in particular became a central showcase for Japanese colonial architecture and ideas of contemporary urban design. Its capital, Changchun, saw more than hundred public structures built after 1931, along with about 10,000 other residences, offices, and stores. Renamed Xinjing (New Capital), everything about it aimed to be modern. Wide, straight, tree-lined streets ended in parks, plazas, or public sites, such as war memorials or cemeteries. New construction codes required the latest techniques and best materials—for example, mandating indoor plumbing and water closets in private residences. (It took another thirty years before toilets reached most homes in Japan itself.) Similar efforts took place in Harbin and Fengtian, Manchurian entrepôts with wildly diverse populations that also came under Japanese control. Dozens of smaller towns received new city plans, too. Not all of these could be as extravagant, but they nevertheless received the essentials: public utilities, parks, hospitals, and new roads and rail connections (and, of course, a Japanese military base).

The Japanese colonial administrators who carried out such campaigns proved competent and exceedingly efficient. Many showed a real desire to learn as much as they could about the colonies, speaking local languages and tromping through villages (in ways that few American officials in Manila, or Russian Bolsheviks in Tashkent, matched). Yet after the workday ended, Japanese experts—and even more, Japanese settlers—kept physically separate from the people around them, living wherever they could manage it in newly constructed enclaves, where they found familiar tastes, sounds, and smells. "Japantowns" sprouted in every treaty port and in most colonial and puppet-state cities: Shanghai's massive "Little Tokyo" district, for example, offered pickled radishes to eat, street signs in Japanese, and Shinto shrines by Japanese cemeteries. As one sympathetic observer, Isabella Bird Bishop, wrote of Seoul's Japanese district: "There, in acute contrast to everything Korean, are to be seen streets of shops and houses where cleanliness, daintiness, and thrift reign supreme, and unveiled women, and men in girdled dressing gowns and clogs, move about as freely as in Japan." The rest of the city, she noted with distaste, had garbage strewn in streets and "a whirl of unpleasant filth."[16]

Demonstrating the superiority of Japanese culture obviously implied that Chinese or Korean culture had to change—thus undercutting the potentially unifying message of dobun-doshu, and sparking continued resistance to Japanese rule. As in other empires, local customs came under attack as inferior, lazy, squalid, barbaric, or uncivilized. Despite the perceived cultural links, Japanese commentators infantilized and patronized Chinese and Koreans at every turn. One compared Koreans with Africans, Eskimos, and aborigines. "Like most barbarians," he declared, "they cannot understand precise arithmetic." Another called Koreans "monkeys who stand and walk upright." Even Nitobé wrote that Koreans lacked a work ethic, and were backward, lazy, and slothful. (See his views of Chinese and Taiwanese culture in the document below.) At the most extreme, one particularly hostile Japanese traveler, Okita Kinjo, wrote a supposed exposé (*Korea Behind the Mask*) that focused on the omnipresence of dung, both human and animal, concluding that the "seven

---

[16]Quoted in Peter Duus, *The Abacus and the Sword* (Berkeley, 1995), 325.

major products of Korea" were a mix of the exotic and repulsive—
"shit, tobacco, lice, *kaesang* [courtesans], tigers, pigs, and flies."[17]

The vehemence of such denigration, of course, says more about
Japanese insecurity than Korean or Chinese culture. Like Russia and
the United States, Japan remained a latecomer to the global competition for empire—and itself only narrowly escaped being swallowed
along with its neighbors. Even some Japanese observers saw their
country as something of a semi-colony, subject to Western treaties
until 1911; many saw it still as a victim (even as it started dominating
other countries). For such Japanese, the empire allowed them to see
themselves as superior to others in Asia, while equal to Europeans
and Americans. Yet Japan remained heavily reliant on Western
models as well as Western technologies—so from the perspective
of Asian critics, even if Japan had excellent gunboats, why would
this fact serve as evidence of Japanese superiority? From a Chinese
or Korean point of view, they had been borrowed from others—
and from a (defensive) Chinese perspective, Japan itself had only a
derivative culture, one drawn heavily from China's imperial past.

Such persistent attitudes, alongside the backlash produced
by Japan's brutal occupation in Korea and China, made it difficult
to persuade colonial subjects to abandon their culture and adopt
supposedly superior Japanese ways. Imperial administrators tried
to teach colonial children how to act by stressing allegedly shared
imperial values and lifestyles—learning Japanese language, customs,
and dress, and aiming at an ultimate goal of *doka* (assimilation). In some
places this work made headway, especially Taiwan, where fluency
in Japanese increased dramatically—at least according to official
figures—but even there one finds little evidence that Taiwanese people
thought of themselves as "Japanese." In other areas doka made little
visible progress, leading to a policy shift in the 1930s toward a harder-
edged approach of *kominka* (imperialization), which stressed subjects'
duty to the emperor more than the rights they shared with Japanese
citizens. This shift backfired, as very few colonized groups welcomed
such a duty. (In Indonesia, some nationalists did cooperate—as they
did in Burma, where kominka targeted the previous colonial language,
English, for elimination.) But in most places the policy meant an attack
on indigenous languages, religions, even names, using coercion to make
Chinese and Koreans "true Japanese." Korean Christians faced arrest,

---

[17]*Ibid.*, 397, 401, 406.

and Buddhist temples faced demolition, many replaced with Shinto shrines. Public events in Korea (although not Taiwan) had to open with a loyalty oath: "We are the subjects of the imperial nation; we will repay His Majesty as well as the country with loyalty and sincerity."[18]

Especially in Korea, this frontal attack on indigenous culture, alongside ongoing military occupation, political domination, and economic exploitation, yielded a massive backlash and widespread resistance to virtually every Japanese initiative. Not only did kominka fail to inculcate a sense of loyalty to Japan, but its focus on crushing Korean language usage meant parents en masse spurned Japanese schools. Other colonial reforms (land redistribution to poor farmers, reducing elite social privileges, expanding and improving public health) genuinely helped ordinary Koreans. Yet just as the USSR discovered in Central Asia, and the United States learned in the Philippines, acceptance could be far harder to achieve when reforms— even welcome and potentially helpful reforms—are imposed forcibly, and when they bear an association with hated occupiers. Armed resistance thus remained a near-constant phenomenon in Korea (it started even before annexation), forcing Japan to keep large numbers of troops to put down rebellions, such as the one in 1919.

Open resistance confronted Japanese authorities nearly everywhere—even in Taiwan, where as Nitobé concedes in the document below, aboriginal rebels launched attacks for decades. In frustration, some Japanese observers suggested selling the island to France. Guerrillas also fought Japanese troops in Indochina, Malaya, and Burma. When Japan seized the Philippines, ironically, local nationalists developed new sympathy for their previously detested American colonial rulers; at a Greater East Asia conference in Japan, the Filipino president refused even to give a speech, justifying himself on the flimsy grounds that he had not had sufficient time to write anything down.

As the president's excuse shows, resistance can take many forms. And as the preceding case studies have shown, empires produce complicated patterns on the ground. Some of the outcomes in Korea struck Japanese imperial observers as frankly irrational (and thus, justified their views of Korean backwardness). Japanese settlers arrived alongside utility networks in Korean cities, for example, so natural gas and electricity service came to be associated with Japanese

---

[18]Quoted by Wan-yao Chou, "The Kominka Movement in Taiwan and Korea," in Duus et al., *The Japanese Wartime Empire*, 42.

power. Korean schoolchildren reportedly started throwing rocks at homes of Korean "collaborators"—so identified because they lived in houses with electric lights.

In the face of overwhelming Japanese military power, as against Maxim guns in Africa or against the Stalinist secret police, armed rebellion could be very dangerous. But as elsewhere around the world, colonial groups here too devised creative ways to resist—often hiding their actions from colonial authorities, or publicly minimizing their political significance, but nevertheless expressing them in ways that could be seen clearly by family, friends, and neighbors. To mention just one more example, Japanese imperial policy reached its peak of intrusiveness in the early 1940s, when it launched a remarkable campaign to change the very names of many of its colonial subjects— rendering them in Japanese forms to show the supposed cultural connections that bound the empire together.

This effort quickly encountered problems. In Taiwan it remained optional, perhaps because coercion did not seem necessary—Japanese schooling and literacy, after all, had not been widely resisted in Taiwan. One might suppose the naming campaign, likewise, would proceed without problems. Yet Taiwanese men and women made the most of this "optional" status: by the end of 1943 only 2 percent had selected new Japanese names. In Korea, by contrast, authorities announced that the campaign would be mandatory. In practical terms this made sense: in the face of constant Korean rebellion, there was little hope of voluntary effort making headway. Officially, Koreans had to choose a surname—not "change" a surname—because they all lacked one. In Japan's view, Koreans remained too backward even to *have* surnames (since only 250 surnames existed for twenty million people, colonial authorities announced that these were merely clan, not family names). The Korean campaign started in February 1940; like Soviet efforts to unveil Muslim women, it allowed only six months. Schools sent students home, not to return until they selected new names; employers fired, demoted, and discriminated against those who refused to comply. Some Koreans registered names while wearing black armbands to mourn—then visited cemeteries to atone to their ancestors. A few even committed suicide. In the end, most acceded: by August, officials reported that 75 percent had chosen new names.

Even here, however, the details suggest a less than total victory for Japanese ideals. Most Koreans changed their names as little as possible. Many selected words linked to local geographic or ancestral origins; a few alluded to other messages, such as blasphemy toward the emperor. Others picked names that masked religious or cultural meanings. One Korean man wrote in his memoir that his father chose their new name as Iwamoto ("foundation of rock"), which the Japanese authorities allowed because they lived near a large mountain. His Presbyterian father, however, had selected it to recall Jesus' words to Peter ("on this rock I will build my church") and thus to lodge a hidden protest against Japanese antireligious campaigns.[19]

Most historians agree that despite the efforts in building new schools, hospitals, and factories, Japan's imperial presence left little behind in most of its former colonies. In Southeast Asia, this legacy amounted to little more than a few high-level individuals who attended Japanese schools or otherwise worked alongside Japanese forces (a few, such as Sukarno, remained prominent after 1945). This quick disappearance may have resulted in part from the brief duration of Japan's empire, especially in the "outer" areas, which left Japanese control in 1945. Such brevity gave Japanese ideals little time to sink in. Or perhaps, as other historians have suggested, Japan's pronounced selflessness was simply too transparently self-serving for Koreans, Chinese, and others to accept. At the same time, though, from a contemporary perspective the Japanese empire in some ways does live on. Scholars have noted that words like "liberty," "democracy," and "nation" (not to mention "proletariat") reached the Chinese language through Japanese teachers, books, and translations—which could have an impact in shaping their meanings and associations in China. Most obviously, the historical legacies of Japan's military conquest—the brutality of Nanking, the conquest of the China Sea, or the subjection of Korean "comfort women"—continue to rankle and shape relations between states in East Asia today.

SOURCES

■ Anti-Colonial Empire: Liberating Women in Soviet Central Asia (1927)

Family reform—especially efforts to improve the position of indigenous women—justified many colonial regimes. When imperial Russian troops occupied Muslim Turkestan, tsarist colonial officials

---

[19]*Ibid.*, 61.

pointed to the harems maintained by khans (and the multiple wives of other wealthy men), and to the veils worn by urban women, as easy ways to show the backwardness of local society—but did little to change such customs. After the revolutions of 1917, Soviet officials denounced tsarist oppression of colonized populations. Acting in the name of anti-colonial liberation (but ironically using their inherited imperial authority to do so), Soviet activists targeted such gender practices for change. Like their British counterparts who tried to abolish sati (widow immolation) in India and clitoridectomy (female infibulation) in Africa, Communist activists decided to "unveil" women in Muslim Central Asia. After debating how best to do so, on International Women's Day (March 8th) in 1927 they invited local women to throw off their heavy horsehair veils—and, with a theatrical flourish, to light them on fire. The first excerpt below, taken from a speech in Moscow by a prominent Soviet women's activist, Serafima Liubimova, explains why an avowedly anti-colonial (but functionally imperial) government decided to focus on women's rights by launching a *hujum* (assault) against the old ways. She and her comrades, however, soon discovered that "liberation" depends partly on perspective. The second excerpt, a threatening letter sent to local officials, illustrates how many men (and even some women) saw this Soviet campaign in different terms, and bluntly refused to cooperate.

In the first extract, what is Liubimova's attitude toward Central Asians? How does this speech compare with previous documents, especially those from different empires in which speakers discuss the need to "civilize" other groups? How far do Soviet customs appear to have taken root in Central Asian society? Why does Bolshevik policy focus on the veil? Does this campaign appear "colonial"? Can we tell what Soviet power means to Muslim men and women? How does Liubimova's perspective compare with that expressed in the second letter? Why do its authors not agree that Communist activists are "liberating" local women? Can you judge how far this letter represents wider opinion?

And now, a few words about what has been called the "*hujum*"—that is, the assault, the attack, which is now underway in Central Asia. It is clear that without the necessary preconditions (which are already in place) it would be impossible to carry out this "hujum." It would be impossible to carry it out without having already implemented a land reform,[20] without having taken economic measures, without having sufficiently strengthened the soviets,[21] without having expelled from these soviets all kinds of hangers-on and old bureaucrats,[22] without having created cadres of sufficient strength from the local nationalities.[23] Only after all this, did the party and soviets in Central Asia find that the time had come for a more decisive blow against outdated customs with regard to women. The party and soviets in the first instance entered into a battle against brideprice,[24] seclusion, and other [customs] in the lives of key party and soviet workers. The "hujum"—the attack against old ways of life—began with the casting off of the *paranji* [veil]. Many of you saw a paranji at the Congress' exhibition hall.

This attire is not a simple dress like the ones we all wear, being changed into another; it is not a simple trading of one dress for another.

It is a way of dressing which is connected to centuries-old religious statutes and institutions, a way of dressing about which mullahs[25] say that every Muslim man must ensure that his wife and sisters walk about wearing. And here, notwithstanding that religious statutes are connected with this mode of dress, notwithstanding that among us many are still allies of the old ways of life (such as mullahs, landlords, and all forms of kulaks[26]), ninety thousand Uzbek women have taken this paranji, connected with centuries-old institutions, and cast it off.[27]

To throw off the paranji means to break with the old ways of life. It means quarrelling with mullahs, quarrelling with all kinds of old-style people in the family and neighborhood, it means standing in defiance of all that is old. And it is not strange that when on March 8th many Uzbek

---

[20]In 1925–1926 Soviet authorities tried to take away the land and water (irrigation) rights of large landowners, and to redistribute these resources to poor and landless peasants (including women).

[21]Local councils.

[22]Officials and administrators from the old (pre-revolutionary) government.

[23]Soviet policy in the 1920s sought to "indigenize" Bolshevik power by selecting and training thousands of locals to fill positions of political authority and economic clout.

[24]A payment (of money, livestock, or goods) from the groom's family to the bride's family. As noted previously, such practices had complicated meanings, and involved the long-term creation of connections between families. Outsiders often did not see such local outcomes, or chose to dismiss them—denouncing brideprice as no more than the buying and selling of women. A forthcoming *Connections* series book on slavery in world history discusses how this tradition has been viewed and condemned by some as a form of slavery.

[25]Muslim religious authorities.

[26]Prosperous, land-owning peasants, deemed by Soviet authorities to be "class exploiters" (because they hired less well-off peasants to help in the fields) and counter-revolutionaries.

[27]Taking population figures into account, if 90,000 Uzbek women had indeed unveiled by October 1927, this represents roughly 5 percent of such women living in the Uzbekistan Soviet Socialist Republic.

women decided to take off this paranji, that when this became known to the populace, the mullahs instigated the most furious campaign [of opposition]. They said that the end of the world had come, that believing Muslims were being seduced by unbelievers, that it [would be] impossible to live as a true-believing Muslim, that if women unveiled earthquakes would follow. In a word, mullahs unfurled this rabid campaign, and not only in words: they went further, intimidating the population, saying in the mosques that if you unveil your wife, we will not bury you according to the accepted religious customs, we will expel you from the mosque, etc. Mullahs went so far as to organize the murder of women. In the spring months 14 Uzbek women who had unveiled were murdered.

But notwithstanding all this, the unveiling grew into such a large movement that now it cannot be stopped. Who supported this movement, who came to meet it along the way and lend their help? The peasant poor, of course, came, as did the workers. The peasant poor came from many villages to party committees and soviets and asked, "Give us someone who will explain how to carry out this process of unveiling our women."...There were cases where paranjis were burned on the squares, surrounded by mosques, on the squares where mullahs croaked and cawed about doomsday.

The unveiling of ninety thousand Uzbek women says clearly above all that the old ways of life are finished, that the main steps in this direction have been taken. These steps have been difficult for the Eastern woman, but they have been taken by the women of Uzbekistan. The women of the other republics and regions must travel their path....

At the eleventh anniversary of [the] October [Revolution] we must show even greater intolerance for old-style customs which continue to exist in the East, we must take an even harder line in the struggle with them, organizing in this struggle not tens and hundreds, as at the tenth anniversary, but millions of Eastern women....

Source: Report by Serafima Liubimova, October 12, 1927. Published in *The All-Union Congress of Female Workers and Peasants* (Moscow: n.p., 1927), 38–41. (Original translation.)

To the authorities in Auchi, Kalacha, and Sheikhan:[28]

You have greatly offended the local population [by saying] that men and women should be together [in everyday social life]. There is [therefore] nothing extraordinary [about it] if we come to you before [the holiday of] Hayit Ramadan[29] [to say that] you, the women, and the teachers await punishment....

---

[28]Three villages located in the province of Farghona (Fergana).

[29]The first day of a three-day festival celebrating the end of Ramadan, the month of fasting. Hayit Ramadan is a national holiday in independent (post-Soviet) Uzbekistan.

As punishment we will bury alive in the earth, cut off the hands, cut out the tongues and throw into the river all the [Soviet] officials of the three villages, the teachers and those studying in their schools. We are 80 people [strong]. God gives [us the authority to do this] and we will come. What we say to everyone, from small to great, is: you must be upright. If these words are not brought to life, then you [must] prepare yourself for death.

Source: Letter to Soviet village administrators in Uzbekistan, April 1928. From the Russian State Archive of Socio-Political History (RGASPI), f. 62, op. 2, d. 1694, l. 50. (Original translation.)

■ The Case for Colonizing the Philippines (1900)

Following a quick military victory over Spain in 1898 (and after paying $20 million in compensation), the United States claimed sovereignty over the Philippine Islands. Some Americans, such as Albert Beveridge, a US Senator from Indiana, thought this expansion presented a golden opportunity. In the Senate speech quoted below, delivered in 1900, Beveridge argued that the moment must not be squandered.

What justifications does Beveridge offer for US expansion into the western Pacific and East Asia? How does he explain American empire, and how does he think it will work? What economic, political, and cultural worldview underpins his approach, and how does it compare with other writers, such as Wood (whose views on US colonialism in Cuba appeared in the previous chapter)? How does Beveridge portray Filipinos? Would his rhetoric be familiar to colonial officials from Britain, France, or the Netherlands? How does he explain current problems, and how does he understand rebellions against US power—like the major one, led by Emiliano Aguinaldo, that was underway as he spoke? Is there evidence in this speech to suggest how popular Beveridge's views may have been?

Mr. President,[30] the times call for candor. The Philippines are ours forever, "territory belonging to the United States," as the Constitution calls them. And just beyond the Philippines are China's illimitable markets. We will not retreat from either. We will not repudiate our duty in the archipelago. We will not abandon our opportunity in the Orient.

[30]Here Beveridge addresses the presiding officer of the Senate, not the US president.

We will not renounce our part in the mission of our race, trustee, under God, of the civilization of the world. And we will move forward to our work, not howling out regrets like slaves whipped to their burdens but with gratitude for a task worthy of our strength and thanksgiving to Almighty God that He has marked us as His chosen people, henceforth to lead in the regeneration of the world.

This island empire is the last land left in all the oceans. If it should prove a mistake to abandon it, the blunder once made would be irretrievable. If it proves a mistake to hold it, the error can be corrected when we will. Every other progressive nation stands ready to relieve us.

But to hold it will be no mistake. Our largest trade henceforth must be with Asia. The Pacific is our ocean. More and more Europe will manufacture the most it needs, secure from its colonies the most it consumes. Where shall we turn for consumers of our surplus? Geography answers the question. China is our natural customer. She is nearer to us than to England, Germany, or Russia, the commercial powers of the present and the future. They have moved nearer to China by securing permanent bases on her borders. The Philippines give us a base at the door of all the East.

Lines of navigation from our ports to the Orient and Australia, from the Isthmian Canal[31] to Asia, from all Oriental ports to Australia converge at and separate from the Philippines. They are a self-supporting, dividend-paying fleet, permanently anchored at a spot selected by the strategy of Providence, commanding the Pacific. And the Pacific is the ocean of the commerce of the future. Most future wars will be conflicts for commerce. The power that rules the Pacific, therefore, is the power that rules the world. And, with the Philippines, that power is and will forever be the American Republic....

But if they did not command China, India, the Orient, the whole Pacific for purposes of offense, defense, and trade, the Philippines are so valuable in themselves that we should hold them. I have cruised more than 2,000 miles through the archipelago, every moment a surprise at its loveliness and wealth. I have ridden hundreds of miles on the islands, every foot of the way a revelation of vegetable and mineral riches....

Reluctantly and only from a sense of duty am I forced to say that American opposition to the war has been the chief factor in prolonging it. Had Aguinaldo not understood that in America, even in the American Congress, even here in the Senate, he and his cause were supported; had he not known that it was proclaimed on the stump and in the press of a faction in the United States that every shot his misguided followers fired into the breasts of American soldiers was like the volleys fired by

---

[31]The Panama Canal.

Washington's men against the soldiers of King George, his insurrection would have dissolved before it entirely crystallized. . . .

But, senators, it would be better to abandon this combined garden and Gibraltar of the Pacific, and count our blood and treasure already spent a profitable loss than to apply any academic arrangement of self-government to these children. They are not capable of self-government. How could they be? They are not of a self-governing race. They are Orientals, Malays, instructed by Spaniards in the latter's worst estate.

They know nothing of practical government except as they have witnessed the weak, corrupt, cruel, and capricious rule of Spain. What magic will anyone employ to dissolve in their minds and characters those impressions of governors and governed which three centuries of misrule has created? What alchemy will change the Oriental quality of their blood and set the self-governing currents of the American pouring through their Malay veins? How shall they, in the twinkling of an eye, be exalted to the heights of self-governing peoples which required a thousand years for us to reach, Anglo-Saxon though we are? . . .

And so our government must be simple and strong. Simple and strong! The meaning of those two words must be written in every line of Philippine legislation, realized in every act of Philippine administration. . . .

Mr. President, this question is deeper than any question of party politics; deeper than any question of the isolated policy of our country even; deeper even than any question of constitutional power. It is elemental. It is racial. God has not been preparing the English-speaking and Teutonic peoples for a thousand years for nothing but vain and idle self-contemplation and self-admiration. No! He has made us the master organizers of the world to establish system where chaos reigns. He has given us the spirit of progress to overwhelm the forces of reaction throughout the earth. He has made us adepts in government that we may administer government among savage and senile peoples. Were it not for such a force as this the world would relapse into barbarism and night. And of all our race He has marked the American people as His chosen nation to finally lead in the regeneration of the world. This is the divine mission of America, and it holds for us all the profit, all the glory, all the happiness possible to man. We are trustees of the world's progress, guardians of its righteous peace. The judgment of the Master is up to us: "Ye have been faithful over a few things; I will make you ruler over many things."

Source: Senator Albert J. Beveridge, "In Support of an American Empire," *Record,* 56th Congress, 1st Session, 704–712.

■ The Case against Philippine Colonization (1899)

Not everyone agreed with Senator Beveridge: especially not in the Philippines, since as already noted, Beveridge's speech was delivered amidst a major rebellion against US authority. In 1898, under the leadership of Emiliano Aguinaldo, a soldier and politician who fought for Filipino independence from Spain, local fighters had temporarily joined forces with US troops. American assurances had persuaded Aguinaldo to return from exile in Hong Kong to take up the battle. Tensions grew, however, when, after the Spanish surrender, American authorities occupied the islands rather than bringing about Filipino independence. An anonymous Filipino diplomat (possibly Aguinaldo himself) wrote the essay that appears below, in an attempt to explain the indigenous point of view. It appeared in the same popular journal quoted earlier, the *North American Review*.

What does US power look like from a Filipino point of view? Does this author agree with Beveridge in any way? How does this essay explain the outcome of war against Spain, and how does it portray the roots of anti-Americanism? How does it portray Filipinos? How does it use *American* history and ideals to advance its cause, and how does this rhetoric compare with Beveridge's invocation of the American past? What response would you expect from various segments of the US public? Is there any way to tell whether either author represents wider public opinion?

We Filipinos have all along believed that if the American nation at large knew exactly, as we do, what is daily happening in the Philippine Islands, they would rise *en masse*, and demand that this barbaric war should stop....

You have been deceived all along the line. You have been greatly deceived in the personality of my countrymen. You went to the Philippines under the impression that their inhabitants were ignorant savages, whom Spain had kept in subjection at the bayonet's point.... We have been represented by your popular press as if we were Africans or Mohawk Indians. We smile, and deplore the lack of ethnological knowledge on the part of our literary friends. We are none of these. We are simply Filipinos....

I will not deny that there are savages in the Philippine Islands, if you designate by that name those who lead a nomad life, who do not pay tribute or acknowledge sovereignty to any one save their chief. For, let it be remembered, Spain held these islands for three hundred years, but never conquered more than one-quarter of them, and that only superficially and chiefly by means of priest-craft. The Spaniards never professed to derive their just powers from the consent of those whom they attempted to govern. What they took by force, they lost by force at our hands; and you deceived yourselves when you bought a revolution for twenty million dollars, and entangled yourselves in international politics.... You imagined you had bought the Philippines and the Filipinos for this mess of pottage. Your imperialism led you, blindfold, to purchase "sovereignty" from a third party who had no title to give you....

In the struggle for liberty which we have ever waged, the education of the masses has been slow; but we are not, on that account, an uneducated people, as our records show.... It is the fittest and the best of our race who have survived the vile oppression of the Spanish Government, on the one hand, and of their priests on the other; and, had it not been for their tyrannous "sovereignty" and their execrable colonial methods, we would have been, ere this time, a power in the East, as our neighbors, the Japanese, have become by their industry and their modern educational methods.

You repeat constantly the dictum that we cannot govern ourselves. Macaulay[32] long ago exposed the fallacy of this statement as regards colonies in general. With equal reason, you might have said the same thing some fifty or sixty years ago of Japan; and, little over a hundred years ago, it was extremely questionable, when you, also, were rebels against the English Government, if you could govern yourselves. You obtained the opportunity, thanks to political combinations and generous assistance at the critical moment. You passed with credit through the trying period when you had to make a beginning of governing yourselves....

Now, the moral of all this obviously is: Give us the chance; treat us exactly as you demanded to be treated at the hands of England, when you rebelled against her autocratic methods....

Now, here is a unique spectacle—the Filipinos fighting for liberty, the American people fighting to give them liberty. The two peoples are fighting on parallel lines for the same object. We know that parallel lines never meet. Let us look back to discover the point at which the lines separated...

You went to Manila under a distinct understanding with us, fully recognized by Admiral Dewey,[33] that your object and ours was a common one. We were your accepted allies; we assisted you at all points. We besieged Manila, and we prevented the Spaniards from

---

[32]Thomas Babington Macaulay (1800–1859), an English politician, historian, and essayist (and author of a document in chapter 1).

[33]Admiral George Dewey (1837–1917), victor at the Battle of Manila Bay (May 1898).

leaving the fortified town. We captured all the provinces of Luzon. We received arms from you. Our chiefs were in constant touch with your naval authorities. Your consuls vied with each other in their efforts to arrange matters according to the promise made to us by your officials. We hailed you as the long-prayed-for Messiah.

Joy abounded in every heart, and all went well, with Admiral George Dewey as our guide and friend, until the arrival of General Merritt.[34] Either on his own responsibility, or by orders from the Government at Washington, this general substituted his policy for that of Admiral Dewey, commencing by ignoring all promises that had been made and ending by ignoring the Philippine people, their personality and rights, and treating them as a common enemy.

Never has a greater mistake been made in the entire history of the nations. Here you had a people who placed themselves at your feet, who welcomed you as their savior, who wished you to govern them and protect them. In combination with the genius of our countrymen and their local knowledge, you would have transformed the Philippine Islands from a land of despotism, of vicious governmental methods and priestcraft, into an enlightened republic, with America as its guide—a happy and contented people—and that in the short space of a few months, without the sacrifice of a single American life. The means were there, and it required only the magic of a master-hand to guide them, as your ships were guided into Manila Bay....

The rest is a matter of history....

Your officials and generals have broken their promises with our countrymen over and over again. Your atrocious cruelties are equalled only by those of Spain....

In the face of the world you emblazon Humanity and Liberty upon your standard, while you cast your political constitution to the winds and attempt to trample down and exterminate a brave people whose only crime is that they are fighting for their liberty. You ask my countrymen to believe in you, to trust you, and you assure them that, if they do so, all will be well. But your action is on a plane with the trick which the vulgar charlatan at a country fair plays upon the unwary with three cards and an empty box.

You will never conquer the Philippine Islands by force alone. How many soldiers in excess of the regular army do you mean to leave in every town, in every province? How many will the climate claim as its victims, apart from those who may fall in actual warfare? What do the American people, who have thousands of acres yet untilled, want with the Philippines? Have you figured up the cost?

---

[34]Major General Wesley Merritt served briefly as military governor in 1898.

The conclusion of the matter is this: You were duped at the very beginning. You took a wrong step, and you had not sufficient moral courage to retrace it. You must begin by conquering the hearts of the Philippine people. Be absolutely just, and you can lead them with a silken cord where chains of steel will not drag them. We excuse your want of knowledge in the past, for you have had no experience in treating with our people; but retrieve your mistake now, while there is time.

Source: A Filipino, "Aguinaldo's Case Against the United States," *North American Review,* 169:514 (September 1899), 425–431.

■ Japan as Colonizer: Imperial Power in Taiwan (1912)

Japan's military victory over Russia in 1905 came as a deep shock to European and American observers. Suddenly an Asian state had defeated a European power, a development that seethed with unsettling political, economic, and racial implications. For Japan, the victory made it possible to emulate Europeans in another way— proving its national greatness by building a colonial empire. How (if at all) would an Asian empire differ from a European one? In the excerpt below Nitobé Inazo, a leading specialist in "colonial policy studies," explains Japan's approach. In a lecture tour of American universities in 1911–1912, Nitobé discussed Japan's experience in Formosa (Taiwan), its first major colonial possession. Since 1895, Nitobé said, Formosa had "educated us in the art of colonization," and as such was a precedent for Japanese policy in other territories, such as Sakhalin (acquired in 1905) or Korea (1910).

How does Nitobé argue for the success of seventeen years of Japanese rule, and, according to him, how has it overcome the difficulties that hindered previous rulers? What challenges remain? How does he present Japan's priorities and goals, and how firm is its control? Does Nitobé's language and attitude resemble or differ from that of Western colonizers? What connections existed with other imperial systems, and what cross-imperial comparisons does he make? Why did Nitobé *want* to explain what Japan was doing, and how would his American audience react? From this source is it possible to gauge how Asian populations (at least on Taiwan) were responding to Japanese rule?

When Japan proposed [in 1895] that China should cede the island [of Formosa/Taiwan], we were not at all sure that the suggestion would be regarded with favor. But the Chinese plenipotentiary, Li Hung-Chang [Li Hongzhang],[35] took up the proposition, as though it were wise on the part of his country to be freed from an encumbrance, and he even commiserated Japan for acquiring it. He pointed out that the island was not amenable to good government: (1) that brigandage could never be exterminated; (2) that the practice of smoking opium was too deep-rooted and wide-spread among the people to eradicate; (3) that the climate was not salubrious; and (4) that the presence of head-hunting tribes was a constant menace to economic development. The island, somewhat like Sicily, had, in the course of its history, been subject to the flags of various nations. Holland, Spain, and China ruled it at different times; a Hungarian nobleman once dominated it; and at one time Japanese pirates had practically usurped supreme power over it. In 1884, the French under the celebrated Admiral Courbet planted the tricolor on its shores, where it waved for eight months. Such instability in government is enough to demoralize any people; but among the inhabitants themselves there were elements which put law and order to naught.

If these were the main causes of chronic misrule or absence of any rule in Formosa, let us see what Japan has done.

[Ed.: When Japanese troops arrived in 1895, some Chinese soldiers resisted, establishing a "republic."] The republic of Formosa lasted only three weeks, during which mobocracy and deviltry in all its forms reigned supreme... At this time the professional brigands took advantage of the general disturbance to ply their trade. Peaceful citizens suffered more from the hands of their own countrymen—that is, from Chinese troops and brigands—than they did from us. Evidence of this lies in the fact that, as our army approached the different towns, it was everywhere received with open arms as a deliverer from robbery and slaughter....

Though the island was pacified, no one knew what would happen next. We did not understand the character of the people. Very few Japanese could speak Formosan, and fewer Formosans could speak Japanese. There was naturally mutual distrust and suspicion. The bandits abounded everywhere. Under these conditions military rule was the only form of government that could be adopted until better assurance could be obtained of the disposition of the people....

[Ed.: Military rule was suspended in 1898, or made subordinate to civilian authority, with the arrival of Viscount Kodama as governor-general, and Baron Goto as his deputy.] Kodama and Goto, to whom English colonial service was an inspiring example, surprised the official world by a summary discharge of over one thousand public

---

[35]China's most eminent statesman and diplomat during the second half of nineteenth century, he died in 1901.

servants of high and low degree. They collected about them men known and tried for their knowledge and integrity [especially among the police].... Twelve years ago the brigands were so powerful that the capital of Formosa, Taihoku (Taipei), was assaulted by them; but in the last ten years we have scarcely heard of them. I went to Taihoku ten years ago, and, whenever I went a few miles out of the city, half-a-dozen policemen armed with rifles used to accompany me for my protection. For the last five or six years a young girl could travel unmolested from one end of the island to the other—of course, outside of savage or aboriginal districts, of which I shall speak later....

Then, another great evil in the island, to which Li Hung-Chang [Li Hongzhang] alluded, was the smoking of opium. When the island was taken over, this subject was much discussed by our people. Some said opium-smoking must be summarily and unconditionally abolished by law. Others said: "No, no, let it alone; it is something from which the Chinese cannot free themselves; let them smoke and smoke themselves to death." What took Baron Goto for the first time to Formosa was the mission of studying this question from a medical standpoint, and the plan he drew up was for the gradual suppression of the evil. The modus operandi was the control of the production by the Government; because, if the Government monopolizes the production and manufacture of opium, it can restrict the quantity as well as improve the quality so as to make it less harmful. Smuggling was watched and punished. A long list of all those who were addicted to this habit was compiled, and only those who were confirmed smokers were given permission to buy the drug... and strict surveillance was instituted by the police.... The annual returns... show a distinct and gradual decrease. In 1900 those addicted to the habit numbered in round figures 170,000, or 6.3 per cent of the population. As the older smokers die off, younger ones do not come to take their place; so there is a constant diminution. In five years the number decreased to 130,000 or 3.5 per cent of the population. It may interest you, perhaps, to know that American commissioners from the Philippine Islands came to study our system, and that they expressed much satisfaction with its results....

But there are [also] formidable natural enemies which confront the sound economic development of the island. I mean its sanitary disadvantages, especially some prevalent forms of disease—above all, malaria and bubonic plague and tropical dysentery.

What money and the spirit of enterprise have undertaken has so often been largely nullified by a small mosquito. There are no less than eight kinds of Anopheles,[36] responsible yearly for at least twenty per cent of all cases of sickness, many of which end in death.

---

[36] A genus of mosquito, many species of which transmit parasites and disease.

Chiefly owing, directly or indirectly, to malaria, the population of Formosa has never been very great. It appears that in pre-Japanese days, the population of the island was recruited by immigrants from China. Only lately is the birth-rate slowly showing a net increase over and above the death-rate. The mortality from malaria has been roughly estimated at three-and-a-half per thousand of population. Among the Japanese, this rate is diminishing, but not among the Chinese. The fact that newcomers from Japan are so easily attacked, is the greatest drawback to colonizing the island. Sugar mills, for want of sufficient labor, have imported Japanese; but usually one-third of them cannot be depended upon—that is to say, the efficiency of labor may be said to be diminished by one-third on account of malaria. When I went to Panama last winter, nothing commanded my respect for the American work conducted there more than Colonel Goethals's[37] system of sanitation. As I meditated upon the careful detail of medical supervision in the Canal Zone, I naturally compared the results with the situation in Formosa, and thought if we could afford to spend as much money as the Canal Commission does, if Taiwan were smaller in size, if it could be brought under military administration, and if there were no rice fields—then we might succeed better in our crusade against the insect. Even under present conditions every effort is made to drive out malaria; and in the meantime an army of scientists is advancing against the Anopheles in biological, physiological, and chemical columns, with clearly visible results. In the barracks outside of Taihoku, there is little malaria. In the town itself, the improved drainage—a sewerage system having been constructed of the stones of which, in Chinese days, the city walls were built—has evidently contributed toward the same end. So, also, has the good water supply, which has taken the place of wells and cisterns. Then, too, new building regulations enforce better ventilation and access to sunlight. In the principal cities, large portions of the town have been entirely rebuilt. I have heard it said by medical men that if the Japanese coming to Taiwan make their domicile in the capital (Taihoku) and remain there, they are quite free from malaria. Other cities...are making sanitary improvements, so that they will probably show a similar immunity within a few years. As for the island at large, owing to the fact that irrigation is the very life of rice-culture, there are necessarily unlimited breeding places for mosquitoes. Consequently, general hygienic progress, such as Dr. Boyce[38] describes with just pride in writing of the West Indies, will not be so easy to accomplish in Formosa....

---

[37]George Washington Goethals (1858–1928) supervised construction of the Panama Canal.

[38]Sir Rubert Boyce (1863–1911) was renowned for his study of yellow fever.

Thus the third great impediment which Li Hung-Chang [Li Hongzhang] thought would prohibit progress in Taiwan is being steadily overcome, and now I reach the fourth and last obstruction—namely the presence of head-hunting tribes....These Malay people[39] are the oldest known inhabitants of the island....At present they number about 115,000. They are in a very primitive state of social life....They have scarcely any clothing; a few tribes wear none....Scrupulously clean in their personal habits, bathing frequently, they keep their huts very neat. In character, they are brave and fierce when roused to ire; otherwise, friendly and childlike....

What concerns us...in their manner of life, is their much venerated custom of consecrating any auspicious occasion by obtaining a human head. If there is a wedding in prospect, the young man cannot marry unless he brings in a head....A funeral cannot be observed without a head. Indeed all celebrations of any importance must be graced with it. Where a bouquet would be used by you, a grim human head, freshly cut, is the essential decoration at their banquet....

The district where they roam is marked off by outposts....Like the "Forbidden Territory" or *boma* in British East Africa, no one is allowed to enter the "Savage Boundary" without permit from the authorities. The importance of this decree will be obvious if I state that its area covers more than half of the island, and when the savages want a head, they steal down, hide themselves among the underbrush or among the branches of trees, and shoot the first unlucky man who passes by....With such people it is practically impossible to do anything. We have made repeated attempts to subjugate them; but so far we have not succeeded in doing as much damage to them as they have done to us.

During Chinese ascendancy the Government built a line of military posts, somewhat like the *trocha*,[40] of which one still sees remains in Cuba. But after we had tried different methods, we came at last to the use of electrically charged wire fences. At a safe distance from savage assaults, generally along the ridge of mountain ranges, posts about five feet high are planted at intervals of six or seven feet, and on them are strung four strong wires. On each side of the fence a space of some thirty feet or so is cleared of brush, so that any one approaching may be detected at once. All along the fence are block-houses, perhaps three, four or five in a mile, guarded by armed sentinels (usually Chinese trained as police), who are semi-volunteers. The most important feature of the fence is that the lowest wire has a strong electric current

---

[39]The indigenous (aboriginal) peoples of Formosa, of Malay origin, spoke various Malayo-Polynesian languages.

[40]A strategic line of defenses.

running through it. Such a wire fence stretches a distance of some three hundred miles. It costs thousands of dollars to keep it in order; yet every year we extend some miles farther into the savage district, so that their dominion is being more and more restricted to the tops of the mountains. When they are practically caged, we make overtures to them. We say, "If you come down and don't indulge in head-hunting, we will welcome you as brothers,"—because they are brothers. These Malay tribes resemble the Japanese more than they do the Chinese, and they themselves say of the Japanese that we are their kin and that the Chinese are their enemies. Because the Chinese wear queues,[41] they think that their heads are especially made to be hunted. And now every year...we are getting better control over them by constantly advancing the fence, and owing to the fact that they are in want of salt, cut off as they are from the sea. Then we say, "We will give you salt if you will come down and give up your weapons." Thus tribe after tribe has recognized our power through the instrumentality of salt, and has submitted itself to Japanese rule.... When they submit themselves, we build them houses, give them agricultural tools and implements, give them land, and let them continue their means of livelihood in peace....

As far as the Japanese are concerned, they do not trouble themselves about [questions of assimilation] any more than do the English in their colonies. I think assimilation will be found easier in Korea, for the reason that the Korean race is very much allied to our own. In Formosa, assimilation will be out of the question for long years to come, and we shall not try to force it. We put no pressure upon the people to effect assimilation or Japanization. Our idea is to provide a Japanese *milieu*, so to speak, and if the Formosans adapt themselves to our ways of their own accord, well and good. Social usages must not be laid upon an unwilling people. An ancient saying has it: "He who flees must not be pursued, but he who comes must not be repulsed." If the Formosans or the Koreans approach us in customs and manners, we will not repulse them. We will receive them with open arms and we will hold them as brothers; but if they do not desire to adopt our way of living, we will not pursue them. We leave their customs and manners just as they are disposed to have them, as long as they are law-abiding. Our principle is firmness in government and freedom in society. Firmness in government is something which they did not have before, and that is what we offer to them.... At the same time, Japan must know that the secret of colonial success is justice seasoned with mercy.

Source: Inazo Nitobé, "Japan as Colonizer," in his *The Japanese Nation: Its Land, Its People, and Its Life* (New York: G. P. Putnam, 1912), 236–257.

---

[41]The Manchu long plait of hair, hanging down the back, imposed on all Chinese men.

Epilogue: Making Connections
An Imperial World, Then and Now

With several case studies of empire now complete, it is time to ask in conclusion: Do we still live in "An Imperial World"? What have we learned by looking at imperial and colonial histories from various perspectives (military, social, economic, political, cultural, and ecological)? Did these imperial politics and colonial connections change the globe? Do empires have lasting consequences, even where they no longer exist? How have groups and individuals around the world responded to, and resisted, apparently overwhelming imperial powers—and how have those lessons been taken up and developed by those who confront strong governments today? What legacies did empires and colonial systems produce for global environments, for national economies and states, and for individuals and families? What similarities and differences characterize colonial and post-colonial experiences around the world—and how do such experiences interconnect? All of these questions suggest avenues for further reading, thought, and discussion.

This book started with a suggestion: the idea that the "footprints of empire" are all around us. If one knows how to look, these footprints are clearly visible—from the popularity of curry in London (the consequence of direct imperial rule) to bananas in US supermarkets (the outgrowth of indirect economic influence). The anthropologist Ann Stoler calls such variegated phenomena "imperial debris," and she thinks it can be found everywhere, even in quiet corners of the globe that appear to have nothing to do with colonialism. Some of these imperial residues, she suggests, may be "ignored as innocuous leftovers, others petrify, [while] some become toxic debris."[1] Their omnipresence, though, makes sense in the light of the previous chapters. Two world wars were fought in the twentieth century to a substantial degree over imperial resources and the control of colonies, and drawing on troops and matériel from around the globe. By the early 1920s, indeed, fully 84 percent of the globe (not counting its oceans) stood covered by colonies or former colonies.

On every continent, empires created new social units and identities. An Italian royal decree of 1929, to take one example, declared that Libyan "tribes" (and thus "chiefs") henceforth would be defined not by their members, but by the imperial governor. Many such colonial categorizations, and the imperial connections that brought them into being, persist today. Consider the continuing existence of a British Commonwealth (now called the "Commonwealth of Nations"), or the *Organisation Internationale de la Francophonie*, the *Comunidade dos Paises de Lingua Portugesa*, the *Comunidad Iberoamericana de Naciones*, the *Neederlandse Taalunie*, or even the *Sodruzhestvo Nezavisimykh Gosudarstv* (Commonwealth of Independent States). These organizations' presence suggests lasting cultural, linguistic, and political connections among the former colonies of, respectively, the British, French, Portuguese, Spanish, Dutch, and Russian/Soviet Empires (see Maps 5.1A–F). Other empires, such as the Japanese, Ottoman, German, Belgian, and Italian, may not have such visible institutional legacies, but it is still possible to find linguistic, legal, or social practices held in common among their former colonies, and appeals sometimes made to a shared history. In Suriname, for example, a small country on the northern edge of South America, Dutch is now the *only* official language, and is spoken as a "native" tongue by nearly two-thirds of the population. This situation makes no sense unless one is aware of Suriname's colonial past.

---

[1]Ann Laura Stoler, "Considerations on Imperial Comparisons," in Ilya Gerasimov et al., eds., *Empire Speaks Out* (Leiden, 2009), 51, 53.

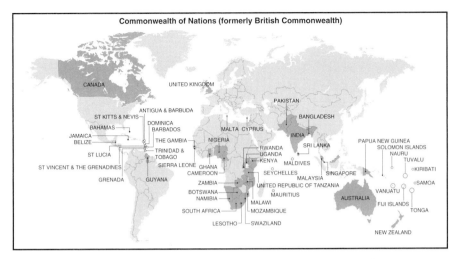

MAPS 5.1A and 5.1B Imperial legacies, and post-colonial connections around the world. (See also Maps 5.1C, 5.1D, 5.1E, and 5.1F, below.)

These imperial systems helped draw the "national" borders that today define many of the world's countries, nearly always by cutting across previous economic, political, or cultural boundaries. National identities in Africa, Asia, and elsewhere arose partly from new interactions structured by these boundaries. In colonial Nigeria, for instance, British imperial structures abruptly placed the previously separate groups of Hausa, Yoruba, and Igbo into one country. Such changes, and the interactions they produced, created the potential for border disputes and irredentist demands, and occasionally

MAPS 5.1C and 5.1D   Imperial legacies and post-colonial connections (continued).

murderous internal divisions—all of which continue to complicate post-colonial life around the globe.[2]

Yet modern national identities also arose from the fierce anti-colonial struggles chronicled in this book, struggles that created other layers of new connections—with rebels near and far, and thus simultaneously tied together potentially hostile groups. Empires—and the encounters and communications they enabled—produced

---

[2]A forthcoming *Connections* series book on twentieth-century genocide describes how Belgian imperial policies in Rwanda contributed to a subsequent genocidal conflict in that nation.

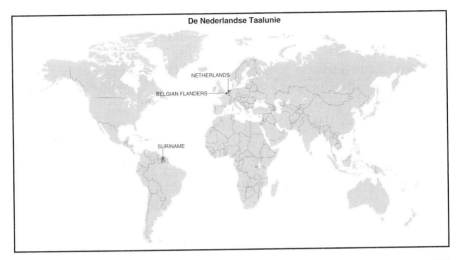

MAPS 5.1E and 5.1F   Imperial legacies and post-colonial connections (continued).

some of the leaders that brought them to an end. Ho Chi Minh
was born in 1890 in French Indochina: he traveled widely (in the
United States, England, France, China, and the USSR), meeting with
activists from Korea, Ireland, China, and India as his radical anti-
imperial and communist political views developed. He then returned
to Vietnam to lead a national, anti-colonial struggle against France
and the United States. Likewise the anti-racist and anti-colonial leader
Frantz Fanon, born in 1925 in Martinique (a French colony in the
eastern Caribbean), trained as a psychiatrist in France before taking up
a medical appointment in another French colony, Algeria, where his

intellectual leadership played a key role in North African struggles against the French state during the 1950s and 1960s.

Through such stories, modern world and imperial history is also now framed by the history of *decolonization*, a global story that unfolded rapidly after 1945, and which—in the usual telling—is said to have concluded by sometime around 1970. If empires collapsed after World War II, though, does that imply an end to this book's imperial story? Ho Chi Minh's and Frantz Fanon's stories suggest that the answer is "no": Empires are still very much embedded in places like post-colonial Vietnam and Algeria, countries where colonial legacies have by no means disappeared.

This book has focused on the development, internal dynamics, and inter-regional connections of major colonial systems since 1750, concentrating on the period before global decolonization. During these centuries, as in the deeper past, many states sought to build empires. Usually they did so openly. Generally, those that succeeded were not shy about it, and their leaders proudly proclaimed such triumphs. In today's world, by contrast, the status of "empire" is more often shunned and denied, and activists use the label to criticize and attack. The category has been taken up (and its applicability contested) in many places since 1945: Kashmir, East Timor, French Polynesia, Puerto Rico, to name but a few. Having already explored the earlier period, a brief final case study will illustrate the complexities of empire (and its denials) in this post-1945 world. The following two extracts are provided without a full statement of context or the substantial background material given in previous chapters. This relative absence of contextual information is intentional. Use the concepts, methods, and background you already have to make sense of these documents. As you read, what questions arise? What conclusions can you reach? How, if at all, do these texts fit into the wider portrait sketched in this book?

Both of these documents come from the northwestern part of the present-day People's Republic of China (PRC) (see Map 5.2). Depending on whom one asks, this area is called either "Xinjiang" or "East Turkistan." Depending again on whom one asks, it may be depicted as a long-standing and integral part of China, a place where Chinese sovereignty dates back at least as far as the Han dynasty (202 BCE–220 CE). For those who hold this view, there have been times when barbarians seized it or separatists broke away, but China never ceded its claim to the area, or gave up its underlying primacy. Others disagree, depicting the region as only recently and forcibly colonized by China. Historically, they say, it has been inhabited primarily by

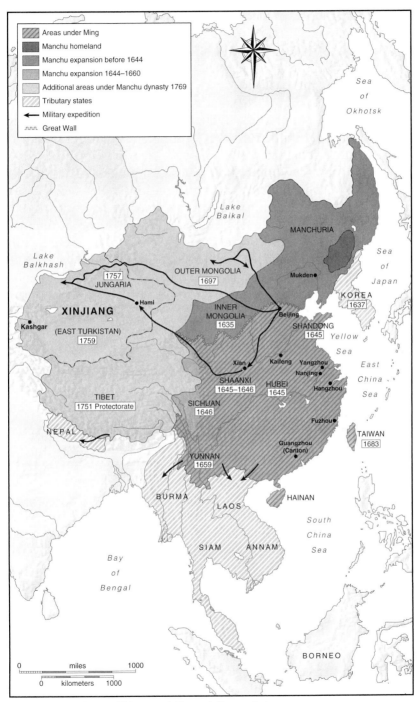

MAP 5.2 Xinjiang, China, and Central/Inner Asia.

non-Chinese people, especially Turkic-speaking Muslims (including a group known as "Uyghurs," specified today in the region's official name, the "Xinjiang Uyghur Autonomous Region"). In this telling, ancient Chinese dynasties played a minimal role and then disappeared—being basically absent for 1,000 years after a rebellion that lasted from 755 to 763 against China's Tang dynasty. This situation changed only in the 1750s, when the Chinese Qing Empire marched west to conquer its "New Frontier" (Xinjiang) in Inner Asia (and reasserted its claim with renewed invasions in the 1820s and 1870s). From this viewpoint, the Chinese Communist state (the PRC) only retained Qing China's Muslim colonies in 1949, when it asserted Beijing's control by terminating the existence of a short-lived but independent "East Turkistan Republic." Since 1949, continuing unrest and periodic violence in Xinjiang has been directed against Chinese police, government officials, and/or Han Chinese settlers, who have arrived in large numbers and may now hold a demographic majority. Such unrest, along with recent discoveries of substantial oil reserves, uranium deposits, and other natural resources, motivates PRC authorities to maintain a strong military presence and firm control in the province.

SOURCES

■ One for All, All for One: Xinjiang as an Inalienable Part of China (2003)

This document expresses the Chinese state's official view of Xinjiang's history and current status, and characterizes its overall trajectory since 1949. On what grounds does the PRC government disagree with Uyghur activists? How does it depict the legacy of Qing expansion in the 1750s and later? Is Xinjiang presented as part of an imperial system? How is Beijing's presence portrayed as helping the people living there? What developments do the report's authors highlight? What connections now link Xinjiang with China and a wider world? How might these ties change life in Xinjiang? How does the language of this document resemble—and how does it differ from—self-depictions by imperial powers in the other case studies, including by states that insisted they were *not* empires? Can we glean anything about the audience for which this document was intended, or how it may have been received? Do you read it differently as an official (government) document, not one written by an individual?

Origin of the "East Turkistan Issue"   In the early 20th century and later, a small number of separatists and religious extremists in Xinjiang, influenced by the international trend of religious extremism and national chauvinism, politicized the unstandardized geographical term "East Turkistan," and fabricated an "ideological and theoretical system" on the so-called "independence of East Turkistan" on the basis of the allegation cooked up by the old colonialists. They claimed that "East Turkistan" had been an independent state since ancient times, its people with its history of almost 10,000 years being "the finest nation in human history." They incited all ethnic groups speaking Turki and believing in Islam to join hands to create a theocratic state. They denied the history of the great motherland jointly built by all the ethnic groups of China. They clamored for "opposition to all ethnic groups other than Turks" and for the "annihilation of pagans," asserting that China had been "the enemy of the 'East Turkistan' nation for 3,000 years." After the "East Turkistan" theory came into being, separatists of all shades raised the banner of "East Turkistan" to carry out activities aimed at materializing their vain wish of establishing an "East Turkistan state."...

Since the peaceful liberation of Xinjiang, the "East Turkistan" forces have never resigned themselves to defeat. The tiny group of separatists who had fled abroad from Xinjiang collaborated with those at home, and looked for opportunities to carry out splittist and sabotage activities with the support of international anti-China forces. Especially in the 1990s, influenced by religious extremism, separatism and international terrorism, part of the "East Turkistan" forces both inside and outside China turned to splittist and sabotage activities with terrorist violence as their chief means. Some "East Turkistan" organizations openly stated that they would use terrorist and violent means to achieve their purpose of separation. The "East Turkistan" forces in China's Xinjiang and relevant countries plotted and organized a number of bloody incidents of terror and violence, including explosions, assassinations, arsons, poisonings and assaults, seriously jeopardizing the lives, property and security of the Chinese people of various ethnic groups, and social stability in Xinjiang....

The Economic Development of Xinjiang After the Founding of New China   Before the founding of the People's Republic of China, the economy of Xiniang was a natural economy, with farming and livestock breeding as the mainstay. Industry was underdeveloped, and there were no railways or up-to-the-mark factories or mines. Famines were frequent in some areas, and people were impoverished. In the past half century, Xiniang's economy and social undertakings have advanced by leaps and bounds:

- **fast growth of the economy**. The GDP of Xinjiang was 148.548 billion yuan in 2001.[3] Taking price rises into account, this was 42.9 times that of 1952, and an annual growth rate of 8.0 percent. The per-capital GDP rose from 166 yuan in 1952 to 7,913 yuan in 2001....

- **swift expansion of communications and transportation**. ...In 1949, Xinjiang had only several crudely built highways, with a total length of a mere 3,361 km, but by 2001, the region's highways had been extended to 80,900 km, including 428 km of express-ways, 230 km of Grade 1 highways and 5,558 km of Grade 2 high-ways. The highway running through the Taklimakan Desert is a long-distance graded highway, the first one in the world built on shifting sands. Now, a highway network covers the whole region, with Urumqi as the center and seven national highways as the backbone linking the region with Gansu and Qinghai provinces to the east, the adjoining countries in Central and West Asia to the west and Tibet to the south....

- **boom in tourism**. With wonderful and rare natural scenery and colorful ethnic customs, Xinjiang has greatly expanded its tourism sector. In 2001, the region hosted 273,000 international tourists, and earned US$98.6 million in foreign exchange. It also hosted 8,393,000 domestic tourists, and earned 7.2 billion yuan.... The tourist trade has become a new economic growth point...

Source: "History and Development of Xinjiang," PRC State Council Information Office (May 2003), www.china.org.cn/e-white/20030526/index.htm.

■ The Emperor Has No Clothes: East Turkistan as an Exploited Domain (2007)

In 2007 Rebiya Kadeer, an exiled Uyghur activist living in the United States, published her autobiography in German and then English translation. Kadeer had lived most of her life in Xinjiang, where she pursued a successful business career before being selected for a seat in China's National Congress. After witnessing a violent confrontation

[3]In 2001 the yuan, or RMB, was set at 8.28 RMB to the US dollar.

in the city of Guldja in 1997, she became steadily more critical of PRC policies in Xinjiang. Finally jailed and then expelled from China—the PRC government now denounces her as a terrorist and has arrested members of her family—today she represents Uyghur nationalist groups.

How does she write about China and its government? Does she offer an anti-colonial critique (explicitly or implicitly), a nationalist critique, or both? Does she see herself as "Chinese"? How does she represent the aims of Chinese policy? How do they compare with, or differ from, the imperial systems in previous case studies? How does Kadeer portray the ethnically Uyghur officials who work on behalf of China—and how does she present herself, and explain her own past? Is she a plausible representative of Uyghur society, or of particular groups within it? Whom does she see as her audience? How is her book marketed? Does it matter that she writes this autobiography in the diaspora, not while living in Xinjiang? Can her book be used to understand the views of Uyghurs living in China? Why or why not?

Finally, take a moment to consider more broadly the issue of present-day nations, large or small, that reject the appellation of "empire" but which might be seen by others as practicing a form of imperial colonization. Are there such states? If so, where are they found, and by what criteria can they be identified? How do they resemble—and how do they differ from—the historical cases presented in this book?

In the National People's Congress Until then my sphere of responsibility was limited to Xinjiang, but in 1992 the leadership chose me to be in the National People's Congress for all of China....Suddenly I had become a woman who sat at the same table with the Chinese premier Li Peng...and debated about the current state of affairs.....Officially it was our duty...to legislate new laws for the nation. In this ostensible parliament, however, there were no discussions. In reality, the party leaders simply dictated to us their programs....

[One day she learned that the premier wished to see her privately. She met with Li Peng and his top aides.] Apparently I was invited there because they intended to appoint me to an even higher position. They wanted to test me first, though....

Without hesitation I gave an account of the corruption, the unfair tax burdens, and the extensive unemployment. In contrast to our people, the Chinese residents found employment without any problem, whereas Uyghurs with equal qualifications had no chance.

I broadened my scope. "You yourselves have said that there should be basic education for all. Then please do not demand such a high school fee from the parents. They cannot afford it." I made a transition from one subject to another. "The Chinese settlers are ruining our land. They log the forests, and our rivers and fields are drying up. Please re-examine your settlement policies. Do not send so many Chinese to us. Furthermore, the impoverished farmers should be treated free in the hospital."

With an encouraging look, Li Peng obliged me to continue.

"You also take so much oil and gas from our land, and you speak of our immeasurable resource as a 'second Arabia.' But in our villages and cities there isn't even running water. It is known that you use the wealth domestically. I implore you to educate at least a thousand Uyghurs from the income of the mineral resources and send them abroad."...

Li Peng let me feel that he was very sympathetic to my ideas... "The improvement of the standard of living of the Uyghurs is one of our most pressing issues. You can count on our being engaged with the problems you've described. Our policy of reform has only just begun. You can already notice that in comparison to previous times very much has improved."...

...[Later she met with the ethnically Uyghur chairman of the Xinjiang Autonomous Region, Ablait Abdureshit.] Ablait and I knew each other well, and privately I often associated with him and his wife. "Ah, come in, come ...how good to see you," he greeted me. "How are you? How are your children and husband?" The two chaperones who had accompanied me were paying careful attention to every word.

Finally he approached the unpleasant topic that had called me to him to talk about. "You and I, the two of us, should not bring trouble onto ourselves because of a few details. It was right that you addressed certain problems while you were in Beijing. Those responsible there are constantly concerned about our people. But we must remember that the standard of living of the population is higher than it previously was."

I looked deeply at Ablait Abdureshit. He asked, concerned, "Why are you looking at me like that?"

"I was just thinking that you have forgotten your past, your childhood. Do you remember how the villages you grew up in looked? Do you still remember the times when we had plenty to eat and were happy? When we celebrated together?" The Uyghur governor came from the North, like I did, from Ili.

"In those times," I continued, "it was rare to find someone who had lied to someone else. Can you explain to me why this same people have become so quarrelsome and false? Don't keep repeating, 'Good, everything is good.' Talk also about the bad side of our lives. If someone always conveys something false, he will eventually become ill." Pained, Ablait Abdureshit grabbed the knot of his tie, as if he wanted to cut off his air supply. "Please stop! Please, let's talk about something else…"

Ablait Abdureshit was considered very weak as a politician. He could not approve of much of the discrimination he was informed of, and it was scarcely tolerable to him the way [the Chinese administrator] dealt with our people. But in his capacity as governor he never complained. Only at home did he express how disparaged he felt by that man at his side.

On the other hand, Ablait Abdureshit had become accustomed to his prosperity. The government had even made it possible for his wife to travel to Germany. She gushed about the freedom of that democratic nation. She couldn't stop talking about it, she was so euphoric.

Source: Rebiya Kadeer (with Alexandra Cavelius), *Stormer of the Sky: China's Public Enemy Number One Tells Her Story* (Munich: Wilhelm Heyne Verlag, 2007).[4]

****

Is China an empire? Is Xinjiang a colony? Answers plainly differ to these deceptively simple questions. For Kadeer as for Li Peng, the categories of "empire" and "colony" are politically fraught. Given all that is at stake, clashes within Xinjiang are represented in fundamentally different ways. From Beijing's perspective, and for many non-Uyghur citizens of the PRC, China is a *nation*, worthy of support and patriotic loyalty, not an empire—which would be illegitimate, exploitative, and/or doomed to fail. To pro-PRC observers, life in Xinjiang is self-evidently better than it used to be, for Uyghurs and all other Chinese citizens who live there. Economic development has expanded trade, standards of living have improved, and growth has spawned skyscrapers, roads, trains, and hospitals. This expansion does sometimes come at the expense of ancient landmarks, such as Kashgar's famous Old City, much of which is now being razed in the name of modernity (and seismic safety). But from this perspective, only the patently irrational (or wantonly violent) could oppose such progress. In skeptical Uyghur eyes (like Kadeer's), by contrast, it is equally self-evident that empires *do* live in today's

[4]Later published in English as *Dragon Fighter: One Woman's Epic Struggle for Peace with China* (Carlsbad, CA: Kales Press, 2009). This excerpt comes from the original publisher's sample English translation, prepared to accompany the German edition (www.randomhouse.de/content/edition/excerpts/14114.pdf), 10–12, 14–16.

FIGURE 5.1   Xinjiang in Uyghur eyes, July 2009. Following protests and riots in the city of Urumqi, *The New York Times* published this Reuters photograph of the unrest. Here an elderly woman (using a crutch) faces down Chinese police and armored vehicles—evocative of a famous image from Tiananmen Square, 1989.

world—notwithstanding a global story of "decolonization"—and many of them would contend that Beijing is an imperial center (see Figure 5.1). The benefits of development in Xinjiang, from their viewpoint, not only come at the cost of priceless sites of Uyghur heritage, but redound disproportionately to the benefit of an imperial Chinese state and its colonial settlers, who dominate the echelons of economic, political, and social power—and whom these Uyghurs see not as sympathetic co-nationals and fellow citizens of China, but rather as fundamentally *different*, geographically and socially *distant*, and politically *dominant*.

Difference, distance, and domination: these concepts under-pinned this book's definition of "empire," key tests to determine whether a particular case fit under the heading of colonialism. If they apply in Xinjiang, then the political, economic, and cultural relation-ships sketched in these excerpts, along with the recurring violence that frequently racks the area, are legitimately part of the global patterns and processes traced in this book. If not, then the confronta-tion between Kadeer and Li Peng should be studied under a different heading. Is China an oppressive empire, in which harsh crackdowns motivate Uyghurs to become freedom fighters? Or is China fighting a good fight against Uyghur separatists, who in the post–September 11 world should be seen as Islamist terrorists, part of global networks of violence?

Outsiders may not think of China as an empire, but Uyghur leaders like Kadeer (joined by Tibetans and others[5]) hope they can be persuaded to do so. Such hopes arise partly from what such activists see as the clear moral connotations of "empire." This apparent clarity arises from their view of imperial history, shaped by decades of anti-colonial critique. Readers of this book are now qualified to stop and consider. Do the last 250 years of world history suggest that there has been a basically common set of colonial and imperial experiences? Despite their obvious differences, did colonies in (for example) South Asia, Africa, the Caribbean, the Pacific, and East, Southeast, or Central Asia have fundamental characteristics in common? How were these societies internally structured and divided, how did they develop and change during the colonial period, and how did they interact with (and influence) other regions? In the end, can we make sense of both the similarities and differences, of underlying continuities along with undeniable changes?

After considering such questions (and none of them is easy), we can probe the moral implications of the argument between Kadeer and the PRC. If world historians discuss "empire" as a phenomenon that transcends individual places or chronological periods—as opposed to a category that is always open to dispute, and can be brought into being or denied depending on context or purpose—is it necessarily dangerous, a political formation always to be opposed and denounced? Or is empire potentially benefi-cial, an avenue that brings widely separated peoples into helpful connection, delivering modern technologies (of health, education, communication) to the betterment of all? Can it be both? Does it depend on circumstances and/or contexts—and if so, how should we judge? What is at stake in telling the story in either way, or in any other? Where does either conclusion leave us—as historians, and as citizens of the world?

---

[5]Tenzin Gyatso, who as the 14th Dalai Lama is the globally visible face of Tibetan Buddhism— and who has lived most of his life in exile in India—wrote the preface to the English-language version of Kadeer's book.

There are obvious dangers in distilling a vastly complex story—encompassing several centuries and hundreds of millions of people—to simple conclusions. As two historians of colonialism in Africa have written, we should avoid

> what might be called the 'scenic railway' approach to writing history, in which the visitor is taken along a preordained route which never varies. The tourist on the pro-colonial track goes past hospitals and housing schemes, schools, cattle dips and wells, and massive government buildings. Sitting in his compartment, he talks to former colonial administrators; he reads statistics about rising population figures and percentile production increases; he returns from his journey as an enthusiastic advocate of empire in retrospect. The rival train takes him on a very different trip. He travels past city slums, slag heaps, and refuse dumps; the train continues through eroded reserves. On the way, the traveler talks to pessimistic economists and angry 'prison graduates'; he reads statistics about social evils, property, and crimes; he may return a convinced opponent of... colonialism in all its forms.[6]

This book gives readers seats on each of these trains—and others too—to show how certain views on these questions cluster in specific social locations, and how the "facts" that support each view are preserved in particular kinds of sources. All historians, of course, need to choose materials through which to research and document their stories. They face limits of space and time: any author can select certain sources but not others, and is unavoidably able only to ask a few of the infinite possible questions. Perfection is impossible. Yet every authorial choice—some visible, some less so—also shapes what the reader will see, how it is presented, and what kind of conclusions can be reached. Readers should therefore always make it a point of stopping to identify the train they are being asked to ride.

It is of course better to go beyond a simple dichotomy (two trains, one pro-empire and the other anti-empire). *An Imperial World* has sought—even in this short space—to suggest some of the paradoxes, ironies, and complicated nuances of imperial and colonial histories around the world. Many other nooks and crannies could

---

[6]Lewis Gann and Peter Duignan, *The Burden of Empire* (Stanford, 1971), 373–374, quoted by Ramon Myers and Mark Peattie, eds., *The Japanese Colonial Empire, 1895–1945* (Princeton, 1984), 44–45.

also have been explored. To be sure, the second train, emphasizing a critical perspective, plays a prominent role in each of this book's case studies. Partly this is because it captures crucial elements of modern imperialism. It is also because modern colonial subjects did not—after all—*invite* these imperial authorities and colonial systems. This underlying fact of coercive power makes the conquerors (whether defined as individuals, groups, institutions, networks, or systems), in my view, answerable for the problems that arose. Readers may disagree; if so, drawing on the documents included here, or by locating new ones, they may develop new conclusions, extending or disagreeing with those I offer. This book succeeds precisely when students do *not* accept all of its conclusions—when they go on to find their own connections, and generate their own interpretations and sustain their own arguments, based on careful historical methods and rigorous approaches to evidence.

When this happens, and if a wider public also takes up such historically informed discussion, then perhaps contemporary political invocations of empire will mean something substantive. Audiences that have never heard of "Uyghurs," for instance, may already assume they know something important about them if told that Uyghurs have a "colonial" story. The impressive successes of anti-imperial rebels since 1945, and the widespread sense today that "empires" are now either gone or doomed, carries a clear implication in contemporary debates about who will ultimately win such struggles. That is why Kadeer and Li Peng would argue over the basic question of whether Xinjiang should be part of this book. Empires and colonies are very much in play all around us—both directly, as the historically identifiable forces that produced the ongoing everyday conditions experienced by billions of people, and rhetorically, as the subject of ongoing politics as suggested by this final case study. The global historical realities of the last 300 years created the depth, power, and political meanings of such concepts today. The footsteps of empire are indeed still all around, and will surely continue to shape this imperial world.

Bibliography
Suggestions for Further Reading

EMPIRES AND COLONIES

The literature on empires and colonies is vast. Much of it deals with specific cases, but general surveys and theoretical analyses are also widely available. Readers wishing to keep up with the latest scholarship may consult issues of the *Journal of Colonialism and Colonial History*, *Itinerario*, or the *Journal of Imperial and Post-Colonial Studies*. There are also scholarly journals that concentrate on regional colonial issues. Two examples are *Ab Imperio*, which is based in Kazan (the capital of Tatarstan, part of the Russian Federation) and focuses on the Russian/Soviet empire, and the *Journal of Imperial and Commonwealth History*, which concentrates on the British imperial past. Scholars working on these issues also communicate on a daily basis through H-Empire, an e-mail network that is open to all (www.h-net.org/~empire).

"Empire"—as a category and a historical phenomenon—may be generally applicable, but in practice is often defined through a particular, usually European or Euro-American, set of historical experiences. David Fieldhouse's survey, *The Colonial Empires* (New York, 1967), like Patrick Wolf's more recent review, "History and Imperialism," *American Historical Review* 102:2 (1997), sets out to provide a general discussion—yet never mentions Japan. Michael Doyle, *Empires* (Ithaca, 1986), goes back to Athens and Rome, but in studying the modern period concentrates on the "Scramble for Africa." The need to escape unstated European frames of reference animates in Ann Stoler et al., eds., *Imperial Formations* (Santa Fe, NM, 2007), and Trevor Getz and Heather Streets-Salter's global narrative history, *Modern Imperialism and Colonialism* (Upper Saddle River, NJ, 2011). An excellent discussion of empire from a global perspective is Frederick Cooper and Jane Burbank, *Empires in World History* (Princeton, 2010). Antoinette Burton, ed., *After the Imperial Turn* (Durham, NC, 2003), offers sophisticated essays on the relationship of imperial and national histories. Two short overviews are Stephen Howe, *Empire* (Oxford, 2002), and Jürgen Osterhammel, *Colonialism* (Princeton, 2005).

For those interested in tracing such theoretical questions backward in time, two classic texts that emphasize the economic rationale for imperial expansion are J. A. Hobson, *Imperialism* (1902), and Vladimir Lenin, *Imperialism: The Highest Stage of Capitalism* (1917). Adam Smith's *The Wealth of Nations* (1776) also offers a critical view, suggesting that colonies often provide greater economic benefits to countries other than their own metropoles. For more documents, see Louis Snyder, *Imperialism Reader* (Princeton, 1962), or the imperialism collection in Paul Halsall's online "Internet Modern History Sourcebook," www.fordham.edu/halsall/mod/modsbook34.html.

Some recent synthetic books that cover empires in the modern period include: Jonathan Hart, *Empires and Colonies* (Cambridge, MA, 2008), which offers a unified chronological narrative since 1415; Gregory Blue et al., eds., *Colonialism and the Modern World* (Armonk, NY, 2002), which includes thematic essays by multiple authors; David Abernethy, *The Dynamics of Global Dominance* (New Haven, 2000), which stresses resistance to imperial powers; and John Darwin's *After Tamerlane* (London, 2007), which is also the subject of an important review essay by Michael Adas, on the pros and cons of comparing empires, in the *Journal of Global History* 4:1 (2009).

Each of the themes explored in *An Imperial World* (politics, economics, gender, etc.) is the subject of its own specialized literature. Many key essays are reprinted in Stephen Howe, ed., *The New Imperial Histories Reader* (London, 2009). To learn more about cultural issues in colonial situations, for example, and particularly gender and sexuality, start with Ann Stoler, *Carnal Knowledge and Imperial Power* (Berkeley, 2002). Stoler has written widely on colonial questions, including an essay reflecting on the costs and benefits of looking across different empires ("Considerations on Imperial Comparisons," in Ilya Gerasimov et al., eds., *Empire Speaks Out* [Leiden, 2009]). Health and medicine are covered in Roy MacLeod and Milton Lewis, eds., *Disease, Medicine, and Empire* (London, 1988). A wide-ranging collection on military matters is David Killingray and David Omissi, eds., *Guardians of Empire* (Manchester, 1999). On economic issues, the classic study by Eric Wolf, *Europe and the People without History* (Berkeley, 1982), is not concerned with empire per se, but addresses the incorporation of colonized peoples into a global capitalist system. On environmental issues, see David Arnold, *The Problem of Nature* (Oxford, 1996). For a global analysis of modern empire's political economy, with particular emphasis on ecological factors, read Mike Davis, *Late Victorian Holocausts* (London, 2001).

You have just read a book that concentrates on empires and colonies since 1750. Clearly there are a huge number of cases, all around the world, that could be explored long before that date. To give just three suggestions to start such a reading list: Susan Alcock et al., eds., *Empires* (New York, 2001), concentrates on the ancient world, showing how archaeology and history can work together to help us understand the distant past; Wendy Kasinec and Michael Polushin, eds., *Expanding Empires* (Wilmington, DE, 2002), moves from ancient Assyria (second millennium BCE) to the sixteenth-century Andes; and David Ringrose, *Expansion and Global Interaction, 1200–1700* (New York, 2001), offers a world-spanning analysis of the five centuries immediately before 1750.

For issues discussed in the epilogue, stretching past 1945, readers should consult Prasenjit Duara, ed., *Decolonization* (London, 2004), or the literary resources available online at www. postcolonialweb.org. William Easterly has argued that older views of "beneficent empire" have been transmuted into developmental economics—and associated views on foreign aid—in *The White Man's Burden* (New York, 2006), especially Chapter 8, "From Colonialism to Postmodern Imperialism."

INDIA AND SOUTH ASIA

An excellent short introduction to modern South Asia is by two leading historians of the region, Barbara Metcalf and Thomas Metcalf, *Concise History of India* (Cambridge, 2002). Readers will also benefit from the prolific work of C. A. Bayly, such as his *Indian Society and the Making of the British*

Empire (Cambridge, 1987), or his study of colonial communication and intelligence gathering, *Empire and Information* (Cambridge, 1996). A good general history of British expansion is Philippa Levine, *The British Empire* (New York, 2007). On the British East India Company, see H. V. Bowen, *The Business of Empire* (Cambridge, 2006); for its Dutch competitor—not in South Asia proper, but dispersed across the Indian Ocean—see Kerry Ward, *Networks of Empire* (New York, 2009).

Bernard Cohn has shaped historians' (and anthropologists') understanding of empire in works about India such as *Colonialism and its Forms of Knowledge* (Princeton, 1996), or "Representing Authority in Victorian India," in Eric Hobsbawm and Terence Ranger, eds., *The Invention of Tradition* (Cambridge, 1983). Scholars have shown how empire shaped India in many arenas: such as Nicholas Dirks, *Castes of Mind* (Princeton, 2001), or David Arnold, *Colonizing the Body* (Berkeley, 1993). But they have also shown that empire shaped Britain, too, in fundamental ways: see Catherine Hall, *Civilising Subjects* (Chicago, 2002); Nicholas Dirks, *The Scandal of Empire* (Cambridge, MA, 2006); or Catherine Hall and Sonya Rose, eds., *At Home with the Empire* (Cambridge, 2006).

South Asian colonial history has inspired original historical methods, most visibly the "Subaltern School" that tries to read between the lines of imperial documents to tell the stories of people who otherwise would be (or have been) forgotten. For a sample, see Ranajit Guha and Gayatri Spivak, eds., *Selected Subaltern Studies* (New York, 1988). The history of Indian indentured laborers is told by Hugh Tinker, *A New System of Slavery* (Oxford, 1974). On the controversy over sati, the place to start is Lata Mani, *Contentious Traditions* (Berkeley, 1998). For a collection of documents from India's colonial past, see Barbara Harlow and Mia Carter, eds., *Archives of Empire* (Durham, NC, 2003), or the texts at www.thescotties.pwp.blueyonder.co.uk/primary-4a.htm. Maps and images are online at www.britishempire.co.uk.

AFRICA

For an introduction to modern Africa, stressing the interaction between demographics and ecology, consult John Iliffe, *Africans* (Cambridge, 2005), or Robert Collins and James Burns, *A History of Sub-Saharan Africa* (Cambridge, 2007). A survey of Africa in global context is Erik Gilbert and Jonathan Reynolds, *Africa in World History* (Upper Saddle River, NJ, 2008). On the colonial period, and for a self-consciously African viewpoint, see A. Adu Boahen, *African Perspectives on Colonialism* (Baltimore, 1987), or his edited volume, *Africa Under Colonial Domination 1880–1935* (Berkeley, 1985). Crawford Young places this period into wider context in *The African Colonial State in Comparative Perspective* (New Haven, 1994). On the recent past, the best overviews are Frederick Cooper, *Africa Since 1940* (Cambridge, 2002), which focuses on struggles over decolonization and the end of empire, and Mahmood Mamdani's *Citizen and Subject* (Princeton, 1996), which considers imperial legacies in Africa.

Scholars of Africa have shaped wider literatures of empire and colonialism. Frederick Cooper and Ann Stoler, eds., *Tensions of Empire* (Berkeley, 1997), is especially strong on Africa. Two anthropologists, John Comaroff and Jean Comaroff, have written an influential history of missionary work, illuminating complex reciprocal interactions on the imperial frontier of South Africa: *Of Revelation and Revolution* (Chicago, two vols., 1991 and 1997). Studies emphasizing the violence and coercion of colonial projects include Caroline Elkins' Pulitzer Prize-winning history of British repression in Kenya, *Imperial Reckoning* (New York, 2005), Adam Hochschild's gripping narrative of horrors in the Belgian Congo, *Leopold's Ghost* (Boston, 1998), and Horst Drechsler's study of the Herero struggle against Germany, *Let Us Die Fighting* (London, 1980).

On earlier (non-European) empires, specifically the subordination of Batwa peoples by the Bantu as late as 1900, see the methodologically innovative work by Kairn Klieman, *The Pygmies Were Our Compass* (Portsmouth, NH, 2003); on the French colonial realm of West Africa, particularly the *Négritude* movement, Gary Wilder, *The French Imperial Nation-State* (Chicago, 2005); on British East Africa, Robert Tignor, *The Colonial Transformation of Kenya* (Princeton, 1976); on anti-imperial movements farther south, Robert Rotberg, *The Rise of Nationalism in Central Africa* (Cambridge, MA, 1965). A local history in global context—including imperial legacies—is Donald

Wright, *The World and a Very Small Place in Africa* (Armonk, NY, 2004). Several decades ago Walter Rodney published a classic economic analysis (partly about empire), *How Europe Underdeveloped Africa* (London, 1972). On technologies of conquest, see Daniel Headrick, *The Tools of Empire* (New York, 1981). The latest word on (West) African armies is Gregory Mann, *Native Sons* (Durham, NC, 2006). Those seeking primary documents may consult in John Hargreaves, ed., *France and West Africa* (London, 1969), or William Worger et al., eds., *Africa and the West* (Oxford, 2010).

THE AMERICAS

General histories of Latin America include John Chasteen, *Born in Blood and Fire* (New York, 2006); Thomas Skidmore and Peter Smith, *Modern Latin America* (New York, 2005); and (on the earlier period) Mark Burkholder and Lyman Johnson, *Colonial Latin America* (Oxford, 2012). Histories of the United States are sufficiently numerous to overwhelm (or at least imbalance) a brief bibliography. Suffice it to say that historians recently have integrated the United States more fully into wider contexts, framing US history comparatively (e.g., as a settler society or imperial metropole), or as part of wider global systems. For such perspectives, see Thomas Bender, ed., *Rethinking American History in a Global Age* (Berkeley, 2002); Carl Guarneri, *America in the World* (Boston, 2007); Ian Tyrrell, *Transnational Nation* (Basingstoke, 2007); and Michael Adas, "From Settler Colony to Global Hegemon," *American Historical Review* 106:5 (Dec. 2001). An original effort to locate "empire" in North America prior to the United States is Pekka Hämäläinen, *The Comanche Empire* (New Haven, 2008).

On US colonialism in general, see Amy Kaplan and Donald Pease, eds., *Cultures of United States Imperialism* (Durham, NC, 1993). On the Pacific, see Julian Go and Anne Foster, eds., *The American Colonial State in the Philippines* (Durham, NC, 2003); Alfred McCoy, *Policing America's Empire* (Madison, 2009); or Sally Merry, *Colonizing Hawai'i* (Princeton, 2000). On Native Americans, see Frederick Hoxie, *A Final Promise* (Lincoln, NE, 2001). On imperial capitalism in North America, see William Robbins, *Colony and Empire* (Lawrence, KA, 1994). On US influence in another area altogether, Europe, see Victoria DeGrazia, *Irresistible Empire* (Cambridge, MA, 2006). Many have argued about whether the United States is an empire—perhaps one in decline. See Charles Maier, *Among Empires* (Cambridge, MA, 2007); Andrew Bacevich, ed., *The Imperial Tense* (Chicago, 2003); and the debate with contributions by, among others, Niall Ferguson, Robin Blackburn, and Anthony Pagden, in *Daedalus* (Spring, 2005).

Many scholars have studied US influence in Latin America. An excellent introduction is Gilbert Joseph et al., eds., *Close Encounters of Empire* (Durham, NC, 1998). Thomas O'Brien, *The Revolutionary Mission* (New York, 1996), concentrates on American business in the early twentieth century, while Richard Tucker, *Insatiable Appetite* (Berkeley, 2000), explores the ecological impact of US enterprises. Steve Striffler and Mark Moberg, eds., *Banana Wars* (Durham, NC, 2003), write about the fruteras, and Walter LaFeber, *Inevitable Revolutions* (New York, 1993), offers a chronicle of political/military intervention—one continued by Greg Grandin, *Empire's Workshop* (New York, 2006). On imperialism in Puerto Rico, especially in the realm of sexuality and gender, see Laura Briggs, *Reproducing Empire* (Berkeley, 2002); for Cuba, see Louis Perez, *Cuba in the American Imagination* (Chapel Hill, 2008), and *On Becoming Cuban* (Chapel Hill, 2008). Aims McGuinness, *Path of Empire* (Ithaca, 2007), traces the transnational impact of US intervention in Panama. For debates over "dependency" in Latin America, see Peter F. Klaren and Thomas J. Bossert, eds., *Promise of Development* (Boulder, 1986), and Robert A. Packenham, *The Dependency Movement* (Cambridge, MA, 1992).

As in other empires, scholars have traced influences of colonial (and neo-colonial) systems back to the US metropole. Examples are Amy Kaplan, *The Anarchy of Empire in the Making of US Culture* (Cambridge, MA, 2005); Alfred McCoy and Francisco Scarano, *Colonial Crucible* (Madison, 2009); and Philip Deloria, *Playing Indian* (New Haven, 1999). Eric Love, *Race over Empire* (Chapel Hill, 2004), argues that racial thinking, perhaps counterintuitively, could serve as an obstacle to imperial growth, since many anti-imperialists had a strong desire to keep the

United States "pure." For primary sources on all of these questions, consult Robert Holden and Eric Zolov, eds., *Latin America and the United States* (New York, 2000), or John Charles Chasteen and James A. Wood, eds., *Problems in Modern Latin American History* (Wilmington, DE, 2004).

EAST ASIA AND CENTRAL ASIA

Sources on the United States' Pacific colonies are listed above. For a general background in Japanese history, consult Marius Jansen, *The Making of Modern Japan* (Cambridge, MA, 2002), or Andrew Gordon, *A Modern History of Japan* (Oxford, 2008). Few overviews of Central Asian history are available in English; the latest one, but focused on earlier history, is Peter Golden, *Central Asia in World History* (Oxford, 2011). David Christian also covers the early period in *A History of Russia, Central Asia, and Mongolia* (Malden, MA, 1998). A thematic approach to the modern Russian/Soviet zone (with documentary extracts) is available at onlinehistories.ssrc.org/centralasia/. The only synthetic history of Xinjiang is James Millward's excellent *Eurasian Crossroads* (New York, 2007).

The best overviews of Japan's imperial system are provided by Ramon Myers and Mark Peattie, eds., *The Japanese Colonial Empire* (Princeton, 1984), Peter Duus et al., eds., *The Japanese Wartime Empire, 1931–1945* (Princeton, 1996), and William Beasley, *Japanese Imperialism* (New York, 1991). Also see Sharon Minichiello, ed., *Japan's Competing Modernities* (Honolulu, 1998). Selçuk Esenbel has analyzed Japanese efforts to speak on behalf of oppressed peoples in Asia (and beyond), in "Japan's Global Claim to Asia and the World of Islam," *American Historical Review* 109:4 (Oct. 2004). Each colonized area has received attention, for example, in Leo Ching's history of Taiwan, *Becoming Japanese* (Berkeley, 2001). On colonial Korea, see Gi-Wook Shin and Michael Robinson, eds., *Colonial Modernity in Korea* (Cambridge, MA, 2000); Mark Caprio, *Japanese Assimilation Policies in Colonial Korea, 1910–1945* (Seattle, 2009); Peter Duus, *The Abacus and the Sword* (Berkeley, 1995); and Peter Dudden, *Japan's Colonization of Korea* (Honolulu, 2005). On Manchukuo, see Yoshihisa Matsusaka, *The Making of Japanese Manchuria, 1904–1932* (Cambridge, MA, 2001); Shin'ichi Yamamuro, *Manchuria Under Japanese Domination* (Philadelphia, 2006); Prasenjit Duara, *Sovereignty and Authenticity* (Lanham, MD, 2003); Mariko Tamanoi, ed., *Crossed Histories* (Honolulu, 2005); and Louise Young, *Japan's Total Empire* (Berkeley, 1998). Hildi Kang has published interviews from Korea in *Under the Black Umbrella* (Ithaca, 2005); for documents from the wartime colony of Sarawak, in Borneo, see Ooi Keat Gin, ed., *Japanese Empire in the Tropics* (Athens, OH, 1998).

On the tsarist colonial system, see Daniel Brower and Edward Lazzerini, eds., *Russia's Orient* (Bloomington, 1997); Michael Khodarkovsky, *Russia's Steppe Frontier* (Bloomington, 2002); Willard Sunderland, *Taming the Wild Field* (Ithaca, 2004); and Brian Boeck, *Imperial Boundaries* (Cambridge, 2009). On imperial Central Asia before 1917, see Virginia Martin, *Law and Custom in the Steppe* (Richmond, Surrey, 2001); Robert Crews, *For Prophet and Tsar* (Cambridge, MA, 2006); Jeff Sahadeo, *Russian Colonial Society in Tashkent* (Bloomington, 2007); and Adeeb Khalid, *The Politics of Muslim Cultural Reform* (Berkeley, 1998). Khalid has argued that the USSR (as opposed to tsarist Russia) ceased to be an empire; Yuri Slezkine shares some of his skepticism in "Imperialism as the Highest Form of Socialism," *Russian Review* 59:2 (2000). For histories that see Soviet colonialism after 1917 as distinctive, yet still analogous (in different ways) to other imperial systems, see Terry Martin, *The Affirmative Action Empire* (Ithaca, 2001); Paula Michaels, *Curative Powers* (Pittsburgh, 2003); Francine Hirsch, *Empire of Nations* (Ithaca, 2005); and Douglas Northrop, *Veiled Empire* (Ithaca, 2004). For documents on Soviet history, including many on these issues, see Ronald Suny, ed., *The Structure of Soviet History* (Oxford, 2003), and also soviethistory.org.

For background on the Qing conquest of Xinjiang, see Peter Perdue, *China Marches West* (Cambridge, MA, 2005). On the Chinese system since 1949, see Justin Rudelson, *Oasis Identities* (New York, 1997); Frederick Starr, ed., *Xinjiang* (Armonk, NY, 2004); and Gardner Bovingdon, *The Uyghurs* (New York, 2010). Unfortunately no collections of documents from this part of China's Inner Asian empire are available in English—perhaps a student now reading this book will make this gap in colonial history her mission, and will enrich our understanding by doing so.

Index

Note: Locators in **bold** refer to illustrations in the text.